ACT®
English and Reading Workbook

ACT®

English and Reading Workbook

By The Staff of Kaplan Test Prep and Admissions

PUBLISHING

New York

© 2009 Kaplan, Inc.

Published by Kaplan Publishing, a division of Kaplan, Inc.
1 Liberty Plaza, 24th Floor
New York, NY 10006

Printed in the United States of America

10 9 8 7 6 5 4 3 2

ISBN-13: 978-1-4277-9769-8

Kaplan Publishing books are available at special quantity discounts to use for sales promotions, employee premiums, or educational purposes. Please email our Special Sales Department to order or for more information at kaplanpublishing@kaplan.com, or write to Kaplan Publishing, 1 Liberty Plaza, 24th Floor, New York, NY 10006.

Table of Contents

KAPLAN

AVAILABLE ONLINE

FOR ANY TEST CHANGES OR LATE-BREAKING DEVELOPMENTS

kaptest.com/publishing

The material in this book is up-to-date at the time of publication. However, ACT, Inc. may have instituted changes in the tests or test registration process after this book was published. Be sure to carefully read the materials you receive when you register for the test.

If there are any important late-breaking developments, or corrections to the Kaplan test preparation materials in this book, we will post that information online at kaptest.com/publishing.

FEEDBACK AND COMMENTS

kaplansurveys.com/books

What did you think of this book? We'd love to hear your comments and suggestions. We invite you to fill out our online survey form at kaplansurveys.com/books. Your feedback is extremely helpful as we continue to develop high-quality resources to meet your needs.

Chapter One: **Understanding the ACT**

Congratulations! By picking up this workbook, you're making a commitment to yourself to learn about the ACT and how you can do your very best on the English, Reading, and optional Writing sections of the test. This chapter tells you what you need to know about the writing and scoring of the ACT. You'll know what to expect on Test Day, so you can walk into your test center feeling confident and prepared. Going into the ACT with that positive attitude is crucial! Familiarizing yourself with the test structure and working through practice problems are a huge part of creating the mind-set per websters that will help you ace the ACT. Let's get started.

ACT STRUCTURE

The ACT is divided into five sections: English, Math, Reading, Science, and Writing. You can elect to take the ACT with only the first four sections. These sections make up the multiple-choice portion of the ACT. The fifth section, in which you produce an essay, is an optional section.

Predictability

No matter where or when you take the ACT, the order of the sections and the time allotted for each is always the same. This consistency works in your favor: The more you know about what to expect on Test Day, the more confident you'll feel. You may know that one section of the test, let's say, Reading, usually seems more challenging for you, but at least you know that Reading will always be section 3. The ACT won't surprise you by making the Reading section the first thing you see when you open your test booklet. Knowing the structure of the ACT will help you feel in control of your test-taking experience.

The following table summarizes the predictable structure of the ACT

Section	Time Allotted	Number and Type of Questions
1: English	45 minutes	75 multiple choice
2: Mathematics	60 minutes	60 multiple choice
3: Reading	35 minutes	40 multiple choice
4: Science	35 minutes	40 multiple choice
5: Writing	30 minutes	1 essay prompt

What Is a Standardized Test?

Here's your first ACT practice question:

> One of the most important ways to succeed on a standardized test is to
>
> (A)   do nothing but practice problems in your spare time the week before the test.
>
> (B)   talk to anyone who will listen about how nervous you are.
>
> (C)   choose option C for any multiple-choice question you're unsure about.
>
> (D)   understand what a standardized test is and why taking it doesn't have to be a demoralizing experience.

Which answer did you choose? Although some of the choices may have made you groan or grimace if you recognized they weren't true, we hope you spotted that option D is the best answer.

As you use this book and apply the Kaplan strategies to work through practice problems, you'll come to see that the test experience need not be demoralizing at all. Right now, however, you may be apprehensive for a variety of reasons. Your own teachers didn't write the test. You've heard the test maker includes trick answers. You feel weak in one of the content areas and don't know how you can possibly improve enough to do well on that test section. Thousands of students will be taking the test. All of these things can seem very intimidating.

Let's look carefully at that last reason. The simple fact that thousands of students from different places take the ACT is actually a good thing. It means that the test is necessarily constructed in a deliberate and predictable way. Because it's a standardized test, the ACT must include very specific content and skills that are consistent from one test date to another. The need for standardization makes it predictable, not intimidating. It's predictable not only in the layout of the test sections in the booklet, but also in the topics that are tested and even *in the way those topics are tested.* Working the practice problems in this book will help you understand not only how each topic is tested but also how to approach the various question types.

If you feel anxious about the predominance of multiple-choice questions on the ACT, think about this fact: For multiple-choice questions, there has to be *only one right answer*, and it's *right there in front of you* in the test booklet. A question that could be interpreted differently by students from different schools, even different parts of the country, who've had different teachers and different high school courses, would never make it onto the ACT. Each question on the ACT is designed to test a specific skill. Either the question or the passage it's associated with (for English, Reading, and Science) *must* include information that allows all students to determine the correct answer.

There can be no ambiguity about which answer is best for a multiple-choice question on a standardized test. This workbook will give you proven Kaplan strategies for finding that answer. The Kaplan strategies, along with your understanding about the structure and writing of the test, will put *you* in control of your ACT Test Day experience.

ACT SCORING

Scoring for the Multiple-Choice Sections: Raw Score, Scaled Score, and Percentile Ranking

Let's look at how your ACT composite score is calculated. For each multiple-choice section of the test (English, Mathematics, Reading, and Science), the number of questions you answer correctly is totaled. There is no point deduction for wrong answers. The total of correct answers for each section is called the *raw* score for that section. Thus, the highest possible raw score for a section is the total number of questions in that section.

Because each version of the ACT is different (more in the wording of the questions than in the types of questions or skills needed to answer them), a conversion from the raw score to a *scaled* score is necessary. For each version of the ACT that is written, the test maker generates a conversion chart that indicates what scaled score each raw score is equivalent to. The conversion from raw score to scaled score is what allows for accurate comparison of test scores even though there are slight variations in each version of the test. The scaled score ranges from a low of 1 to a high of 36 for each of the four multiple-choice sections. Scaled scores have the same meaning for all different versions of the ACT offered on different test dates.

The score for the first three sections of the ACT is broken down further into subscores, which range from 1 to 18. The subscores for a particular section do *not* necessarily add up to the overall score for the section. The following table lists the subscores that are reported for each section.

Test Section	Subscore Ranges
English (75 questions)	Usage/Mechanics (40 questions) Rhetorical Skills (35 questions)
Mathematics (60 questions)	Pre-Algebra/Elementary Algebra (24 questions) Intermediate Algebra/Coordinate Geometry (18 questions) Plane Geometry/Trigonometry (18 questions)
Reading (40 questions)	Social Studies/Sciences (20 questions) Arts/Literature (20 questions)
Science (40 questions)	[no subscores for this section]

What most people think of as the ACT score is the composite score. Your composite score, between 1 and 36, is the average of the four scaled scores on the English, Mathematics, Reading, and Science sections of the test. If, for some reason, you leave any one of these four sections blank, a composite score cannot be calculated.

In addition to the raw score, scaled score, and section subscores, your ACT score report also includes a *percentile ranking*. This is not a score that indicates what percentage of questions you answered correctly on the test. Rather, your percentile ranking provides a comparison between your performance and that of other recent ACT test takers. Your percentile ranking indicates the percentage of ACT test takers who scored the same as or lower than you. In other words, if your percentile ranking is 80, that means that you scored the same as or higher than 80 percent of the students who took the test.

A raw-to-scaled score conversion chart is necessary to take into account slight variations in the difficulty levels of different versions of the test. In other words, it's not possible to say that for every ACT test date if you answer, for example, 55 of the 75 English questions correctly, your scaled score will be always be 24. However, you should know that the variations in each test version, and therefore in the raw-to-scaled score conversion chart, are very slight and should not concern you. The following table gives some *approximate* raw score ranges for each section, the associated scaled score, and the likely percentile ranking.

	Raw Score and Scale Score Approximate Equivalences				
Scaled Score	English Questions Correct (Total = 75)	Mathematics Questions Correct (Total = 60)	Reading Questions Correct (Total = 40)	Science Questions Correct (Total = 40)	Percentile Ranking
32	70	55–56	34–35	35–36	99
27	61–63	45–47	27–28	30–32	90
24	53–56	36–39	22–25	26–28	75
20	42–46	31–32	18–20	20–21	50

Don't get bogged down by the numbers in this table. We've put it here to help you relax! The big-picture message of the chart is that you can get a good ACT score even if you don't answer every question correctly. In terms of how many questions you need to get right, reaching your ACT score goal is probably not as difficult as you might think.

Scoring for the Writing Section

The ACT essay score ranges from 1 to 12 points, with 12 being the highest. To determine the essay score, two trained graders read your essay and assign it a score between 1 and 6. If, as is usually the case, the two graders' scores do not differ by more than one point, then your essay score is the sum of the scores assigned by the two graders. For example, if one grader gives your essay a 5 and the other scores it a 6, your essay score is 11. In the rare instance that the two graders' scores differ by more than a single point, a third grader reads the essay to resolve the difference.

Because the Writing section of the ACT is optional, not every student takes it, and therefore the Writing score has no effect on the composite score. However, if you opt to take the Writing section of the ACT, you will receive two scores in addition to your composite score. First, you will see your essay score, between 1 and 12. Second, you will see a combined English and Writing score, on a scale of 1 to 36. This score is determined by combining your English section score with your Writing section score. It ranges from 1 to 36. If you choose not to do the Writing section, you will not receive an essay score or a combined English and Writing score.

ACT REGISTRATION

All of the information that you need about ACT registration is available on the test maker's website at www.actstudent.org. There are two ways to register for the ACT. You can do so online, or you can use a registration packet and send your forms in by mail. If you need a registration packet, you should be able to get one from your school counselor, or you can request one directly via the test maker's website.

Because each testing location can accommodate a limited number of students, you should plan ahead to register for the ACT. In general, the registration deadline is approximately five weeks before the test date. If space is available at a testing location, you are allowed to register after the deadline, but you must pay a late registration fee in addition to the regular test fee.

If you think that registering for the ACT on time is simply a matter of logistics and fees, with no relation to your performance on the test, think again. Individual testing centers have limited space. When you know that you're interested in a particular test date at a particular location, it is worthwhile to register as soon as possible. The earlier you register, the more likely it is that you'll be able to test at your preferred location. Many students prefer to test at their own high schools, in a familiar setting. The morning of Test Day will go much more smoothly if you don't have to worry about directions to get to an unfamiliar location. Planning ahead for ACT registration can help you avoid such unnecessary distractions.

When you register, you should read all the information the test maker provides. Learn specifically about what to bring with you, including forms of ID, pencils, acceptable calculators, and snacks for the breaks. You should also pay attention to what behaviors are and are not acceptable during the test. The more you know ahead of time about what to expect on Test Day, the more relaxed and confident you'll be going into the test. When you put that confidence together with the Kaplan strategies and practice you'll get from this book, you can look forward to higher scores on your ACT!

Chapter Two: **ACT Strategies**

Taking a strategic approach to the ACT will help you earn the highest score possible. This chapter presents several kinds of strategies. Some are general test-taking strategies, and some are specific to a particular section of the test. Pay special attention to the Kaplan methods for the English, Reading, and Writing sections. You should practice these methods as you work through the test questions in this workbook. The Kaplan methods, building on the general strategies, give you a firm foundation on which to base your plan of attack for each ACT question you'll see on Test Day. Taking a strategic approach means you'll know *how to think about* each question.

GENERAL TEST-TAKING STRATEGIES

1. **Make sure you get the easy questions right!** It's important to understand how the ACT is scored. Each question in a section is worth the same number of points: You don't get more points for correctly answering a tough question than you do for answering an easy question. Work carefully to avoid making careless mistakes on easier questions.

2. **Don't spend too much time on any one question.** You must be constantly aware of the need to pace yourself well. No single question will make or break your ACT score, so no question deserves a disproportionate amount of your time and attention. Don't let yourself get bogged down. If you're stuck on a question, circle the number in your test booklet and come back to it at the end of the section if you have time.

3. **For the multiple-choice sections, circle the letter of your answer choice in the test booklet, and enter your answers onto the answer grid in a logical way, not one question at a time.** You don't get any credit for any marks you make in the test booklet, only for answers you place on your answer sheet. Still, the habit of circling answers in the booklet and transferring them onto your answer sheet in a logical unit, either by page or by passage, will save you time, allow you to focus more easily on answering questions, and reduce the likelihood that you'll make errors filling in the wrong answer bubbles. For the English and Reading sections, it makes sense to work on one passage at a time. When you come to the end of a passage, with answers circled in your test booklet, carefully fill in each answer on the grid. You'll get a mini-break from thinking about test content, and you can concentrate on filling in the grid accurately. As you fill in each bubble on the answer grid, silently voice the question number and answer choice letter to yourself: "Number 1 is B. Number 2 is H…" Especially if you're leaving some questions blank so that you can return to them if you have time left at the end of the section, this

strategy of marking a passage worth of questions all at the same time helps you avoid making mistakes on the answer grid.

4. **Be aware of the ending time for the section you're working on, and make sure you grid in an answer—even if it's only a blind guess—for each question.** You don't lose any points for incorrect answers on the ACT, so it's to your advantage to answer every question. If you're nearing the end of the section and you have questions left unanswered, either ones that you've skipped or ones that you haven't tried yet, fill in answers for those questions on your grid.

5. **If you have time, guess strategically on questions you're not sure about.** Strategic guessing, in which you can rule out one or more answers, is preferable to blind guessing. Still, on the ACT English and Reading sections, for which only four answer choices are offered, even with a blind guess, you have a one-in-four chance of choosing the correct answer. Pay attention to the clock and make sure you grid in an answer for every question, even if it's a strategic or a blind guess.

6. **Get in the habit of using your pencil to help you work through test questions.** This strategy, which we call "thinking with your pencil," is invaluable. While you don't get points for anything you write in your test booklet, there's no rule saying that you have to turn in a clean, blank booklet at the end of the test. Many people who wouldn't dream of working on the Math section without using their pencils to do some scratch work to arrive at the answer never make a single mark in the Verbal sections of the test booklet. This is a mistake! In any multiple-choice section, you can use your pencil to cross out the letters for answer choices you've ruled out. In the English section, it's helpful to circle nonunderlined words in the passage that help you determine what the best answer is. For English questions that have a question stem, you can underline key words in the question. In the Reading section, you should jot down brief notes as you read the passage. (You'll learn more about this in the Reading Overview section.) You can also underline key words if that helps you. For the Writing section, try taking notes before you start the actual essay. You should keep your pencil in your hand throughout the test, not just when you're filling in your answers on the grid.

7. **For multiple-choice questions that are presented with a question stem (all Reading questions and some English questions), read the question stem carefully.** It may seem too obvious to say, but if you don't know what a question is asking, you're not likely to find the correct answer! Specific advice in the English and Reading Overview sections will help you make sure you understand the stem before you try to answer the question.

As you work through the practice questions in this workbook and refine your strategic approach, remember that your goal in practicing is not simply to arrive at correct answers. You should also develop an awareness of the best way to approach each question. On Test Day, you won't see the same questions that are in this workbook. However, because the ACT is a standardized test and covers a specific and limited set of skills, you know that you'll see very similar questions. The more comfort you develop with strategic thinking as you practice, the more confident you'll be that you can work through the questions you'll see in your ACT booklet on Test Day!

Let's take a moment to think about what it means to take a strategic approach. When you use a strategy, you don't approach a problem blindly. Instead, you have a plan for the best way to attack it. Taking a strategic approach and knowing what skills and content each test section covers go hand in hand. The Kaplan methods for English and Reading are designed to help you focus on determining what each question is asking you to do. For each question, it helps to ask: What knowledge or skill is this question testing? When you combine the strategic approach with an understanding of the content covered by each test section, you'll be confident going into Test Day.

STRATEGIES FOR THE ENGLISH SECTION

The Kaplan Method for ACT English

You'll use this three-step method for every question that includes an underlined part of the passage and for most questions that appear with a question stem:

1. READ until you have enough information to identify the issue.
2. ELIMINATE answer choices that do not address the issue.
3. PLUG in the remaining choices to select the most correct, concise, and relevant choice.

Recall the timing for the English section: You have to get through five passages, including a total of 75 questions, in 45 minutes. You need to work efficiently to get through all the questions, and the first step of the Kaplan method addresses the efficiency challenge. Step 1 of the method provides an alternative to the approach that's recommended in the directions for the ACT English section. Those directions include the words, "Read each passage through once before you begin to answer the questions that accompany it."

Our advice, on the other hand, is to answer each question as soon as you've read far enough in the passage to do so. Let's look in detail at step 1 of the Kaplan method. It says, "Read until you have enough information to identify the issue." What do you think "the issue" means here? You might be tempted to say, "the error," but remember that for some English questions "NO CHANGE" will be the best answer. Not every ACT English question includes an underlined part of the passage, and, even for a question that does, the underlined portion is not necessarily wrong. Therefore, instead of reading the passage and looking for an error, think about what issue the question is testing. In other words, "the issue" is the reason that the test maker included the question.

Right now, you may feel as though you have no idea what issues are likely to be tested in the English section. The ACT is a standardized test, so it covers predictable issues. With practice, you *can* know what to expect. The information in the English Overview chapter includes rules and guidelines that are tested on the ACT. To succeed on the ACT English section, you don't need to know every rule in the grammar book. You only need to know what issues are tested and how to recognize them as they appear on the ACT.

Now that you know what "the issue" refers to in step 1 of the Kaplan method for ACT English, let's look at how you know when you've read far enough in the passage to identify the issue. Consider the following excerpt from an ACT English passage, in the standard form. Question 1 asks you to identify which of the four options would fit best in the sentence. Question 2 asks you to identify the sentence that would fit best in the rest of the paragraph. Read until you have enough information to identify the issue (step 1), and then skip down to the explanation.

Mice are <u>small, they are</u> easy to maintain. They breed readily, producing litters of up
(1)
to 8 or 10 young at a time. Because of their small size and short lifespan, mice do not require a large financial investment. Perhaps most important, however, particularly in certain areas of medical research, is that the mouse has a genetic make-up that is similar to the human's genetic characteristics. ②

1. (A) NO CHANGE
   (B) small, being that they are
   (C) small, most are
   (D) small and

2. Which of the following is the most effective first sentence for this paragraph?

   (F) Mice are among the smallest of the mammals.
   (G) Mice are considered by most people to be vermin.
   (H) Mice are used frequently in scientific experiments for several reasons.
   (J) Scientists have found that many antibiotics that are effective in mice are also effective in humans.

If you stopped reading at the end of the first sentence, terrific! The underlined part comes in the middle of the sentence. It should be pretty easy to determine that reading through to the end of the sentence is enough here. Can you tell what the issue is? On the ACT, an underlined comma in the middle of a sentence is often a clue that sentence structure is the issue. Indeed, that is the case here; the sentence as written is a run-on.

Now that you've identified the issue, move on to step 2 of the Kaplan method for ACT English. Step 2 is to eliminate answer choices that don't address the issue. Can you spot any other answer choices that, like choice A, create a run-on sentence? Option C also forms a run-on. You can eliminate this choice because it doesn't address the issue you identified in step 1. Having eliminated two choices, you can now plug each remaining choice into the sentence.

Step 3 of the Kaplan method for ACT English gives you three criteria on which to judge the results of plugging each answer choice in: The best answer uses wording that is correct, concise, and relevant. "Plugging in" means simply reading the answer choice in the sentence in place of the underlined portion. Here, when you plug in choice B, you get, *Mice are small, being that they are easy to maintain.* How does that sound to you? Plug in choice D and decide which sounds better. With choice D, the sentence reads, *Mice are small and easy to maintain.* For question 1, it may be obvious to you that choice D provides the correct answer. If you're not sure, though, consider the criteria of conciseness. Even if you didn't immediately recognize that choice D is correct, you should have noticed that it is considerably shorter than choice B. Because conciseness is one of the issues that's tested on the ACT, a good guideline is *if in doubt, choose the shorter answer.* The shortest answer choice won't always be correct, but it often is.

Now, refer back to question 2 in the passage. The numeral 2 appears in a box at the end of a paragraph. This question is presented not as an underlined portion of the passage, but instead with a question stem. For any question with a question stem, it's important to know what the question is asking. Reading the question carefully will help you identify the issue. For question 2, because the question stem asks you to choose the best first sentence for the paragraph, you can determine that relevance—more so than correctness or conciseness—is likely to be the issue. To address the issue, think about what the first sentence of a paragraph should do: It must introduce the topic of the paragraph. How much of the passage do you think you need to read to determine the best answer? You should consider the whole paragraph, but nothing beyond it.

Ask yourself what the purpose of the paragraph is. Certain words in the paragraph, especially *because* and *most important,* indicate that the paragraph is listing reasons. Choice H uses the word *reasons,* and it is the best answer for this question. In this case, the best answer choice hinges on relevance rather than correctness or conciseness.

Timing Strategies for the English Section

Knowing how the ACT is written will help you manage your time in each section. Recall that the English section contains five passages. The passages are all very similar in length, and each passage has 15 associated questions. Given that you have 45 minutes, you have roughly nine minutes per passage. That's a little less than half a minute per question.

On Test Day, as you pace yourself on the English section, be aware of the time you spend on each passage. Some English questions can be answered more quickly than others can. Often, questions that are presented with a question stem take a little longer to answer than those made up of an underlined segment with various revisions. As you practice in this book, stay focused on step 1 of the Kaplan method for English: Always be thinking about how much of the passage you need to read to identify the issue for a particular question. Identifying the tested issue is the key factor in learning to manage your time efficiently in the ACT English section.

STRATEGIES FOR THE READING SECTION

The Kaplan Method for ACT Reading

Follow this method for each passage in the Reading section. Step 1 addresses what to do on your first read-through of the passage. Steps 2 and 3 provide a plan of attack you take for each individual question. Here's the method:

1. READ the passage, taking notes as you go.
2. EXAMINE the question stem, looking for clues.
3. SELECT the answer choice that best matches your prediction.

Let's consider each step in detail. Why should you take notes as you read the passage? You may think that taking notes will take too much time. However, the notes you take on an ACT Reading passage will be different from note-taking you do in school. Your ACT passage notes should be brief. They should summarize main ideas only, *not* supporting details. The purpose of your notes is to provide a passage map. Think of your notes as signposts guiding you to where in the passage you'll find the answer to a particular question.

One important thing to know about the Reading section is that the questions don't appear in any particular order. For example, the first question for a passage won't necessarily ask about something from the first part of the passage; it may ask about something from the end. Therefore, because the ordering of ACT Reading questions doesn't give you any clues about where in the passage you'll find the answer, you need to create your own passage map to help you find the information you need quickly. Your notes will provide this guidance.

The best way to work through each ACT Reading passage is to read actively. Reading actively simply means asking yourself questions as you read and jotting down a brief note after you read each paragraph. Read a paragraph quickly; then pause to identify briefly the purpose of the paragraph. Ask yourself: Why did the author write this paragraph? How does it contribute to her purpose in the passage as a whole? Working with these questions will help you generate brief, appropriate notes to help you remember what information is located where in the passage. The specific details aren't important for your notes. A short description, often only a word or two that labels the information in the paragraph, rather than a long note that restates the information, is what you want here.

We suggest that you actually jot your notes for each paragraph in a nearby margin. You may be wondering, wouldn't it be quicker simply to underline a few words in the passage? Underlining is possibly a little quicker, but there's a danger involved. If you read through a paragraph thinking you'll underline what's important, you may find yourself underlining too many details. On the other hand, when you read each paragraph with the goal of determining the author's purpose for that paragraph, there's a certain discipline involved. The mental processing required to decide on a note to jot down in the margin is more likely to help you develop a good overall understanding of the passage. Writing a quick note in your own words in the margin is a more active approach than simply underlining words in the passage.

Though you must guard against the dangers of too much underlining, there is a limited use for underlining in step 1. While you shouldn't use underlining to take the place of your own hand-written notes in the margin, it can be helpful to underline an occasional word or phrase on your first read-through. Good words to underline are those that indicate an opinion, such as *fortunately* and *regrettably*. Other words to underline are phrases that direct the logical flow of the passage. These include words that show contrast, such as *however* and *on the other hand,* and words that show cause and effect, such as *as a result of* and *because.* You can also underline names and dates if you feel that's helpful. It may not be necessary, however, because it's usually easy to skim for names and dates if you need to find them to answer a question.

Perhaps the biggest trap that unprepared students fall into with underlining is trying to anticipate on a first reading what specific questions may be for this passage. This is a waste of your time. Your goal in reading through the passage is to get a big-picture understanding. Remember the key questions to guide your active reading: What is the author's purpose here, and how is this information organized? Rely primarily on your passage map notes, and use underlining sparingly. If you practice in this way on all the Reading passages in this workbook, then by Test Day, active reading will have become a habit.

Step 1 of the Kaplan method for ACT Reading guides you through your first reading of the passage. Once that's done, apply steps 2 and 3 of the method for each question. Step 2 is to examine the question stem, looking for clues. The question stem is the part of an ACT question that appears before the answer choices. The stem of an ACT Reading question can contain two kinds of clues. First, the test maker uses certain phrases repeatedly in question stems. You'll frequently see phrases such as, *As stated in the passage* and *The author suggests.* These phrases, along with others that you'll learn about in the Reading Overview, help recognize exactly what a question is asking you to do. This is important because to answer a question correctly, you need to know what it's asking.

Another kind of clue that the question may provide is an indication of where to look back to in the passage to locate the answer. Occasionally, an ACT Reading question stem provides a line reference. If present, a line reference can be a great clue about where to research the passage for the answer. What if the question stem doesn't give you a line reference? In that case, the passage map you created in step 1 is invaluable. If a question stem includes the phrase, *Marc Brown's early education,* and you've made a note in the margin saying, *Brown's childhood,* your note guides you to the right spot in the passage to find information about Brown's early education. Thus, important words in the question stem give clues that work with your passage map notes to help you find *where* in the passage you need to read to find the correct answer.

While step 2 helps you understand what a question is asking and where you need to read to answer it, step 3 helps you avoid the temptation of wrong answers that the test maker includes among the choices. In step 3, you predict (that is, state in your own words) what you think the best answer to the question will be. It's important to make your prediction *before you read any of the multiple-choice answers.* This helps because when you go through the process of predicting in your own words, you do so by focusing your attention on the words in the passage. The correct answer is always based on the passage itself. Predicting will help you avoid thinking too much and falling for a wrong answer that introduces material that isn't in the passage. Predicting also helps you avoid an answer choice that includes a detail from the passage that doesn't answer this particular question.

For nine out of ten questions, an effective prediction will help you easily spot the right answer quickly when you read through the four answer choices. Think of it this way: The process of predicting does take some time, but if you predict, you're certain to spend less time reading and thinking about each answer choice. In the long run, predicting is the best way to work efficiently through the ACT Reading questions.

As you do the practice problems in this workbook, you might want to note your prediction before you even read through the answer choices. You shouldn't write out your prediction on Test Day, because doing so uses valuable time. However, jotting down your prediction in practice will help you develop the skill of predicting. Another strategy, which you can use on Test Day, is to get into the habit of covering the answer choices with your hand until you've verbalized your prediction.

Timing Strategies for the Reading Section

Again, the most important things are to know the test and to be aware of the clock as you work through a section. The ACT Reading section always includes four passages. All four are roughly the same length, and each has exactly ten questions. With four passages to get through in 35 minutes, you should spend less than 9 minutes per passage.

Aim to spend no more than three minutes on your first read-through of the passage, including the time you spend jotting down your notes. This breakdown allows you more than five minutes to spend attacking the questions. You'll have half a minute per question. If you practice all three steps of the Kaplan method, you'll gain a lot in efficiency. Some questions won't take you even half a minute to answer. The time you save is time that you can spend on a more difficult question that may take you a little longer to answer.

Here's another point to consider in managing your time for the Reading section: You don't necessarily have to work through the Reading passages in the order they appear in your test booklet if you feel another order would work better for you. When you consider timing issues for any multiple-choice section of the ACT, it's crucial to make sure that you *get the easiest questions right!* In the Reading section, practice and experience may tell you that one passage type is generally harder for you than the others. If this is true for you, skip over that passage when you come to it, and go back to it when you've finished the other three.

Some people don't find any particular passage type in general to be more challenging than any other, but many people find one particular passage on a given ACT to be harder. It can be useful to take a very *quick* glance at each of the four passages in the Reading section and determine if one seems as if it will be more difficult. If so, it makes sense to leave that passage for last. This can help prevent you from getting bogged down and spending too much time on a particularly tough passage early on. Manage your time wisely, and make sure you answer the questions that are likely to be easiest for you first!

STRATEGIES FOR THE WRITING SECTION

The Kaplan Method for ACT Writing

You can think of the steps of the Kaplan method for essay writing as the four *P*'s: prompt, plan, produce, and proofread. Here's what each step involves:

1. Read the **prompt,** underlining key words that you can use in your essay to maintain your focus on the topic.

2. Jot down a short **plan** in the test booklet that lists your major pieces of evidence and the order you'll present them in.

3. **Produce,** that is, write, your essay on the pages provided in the answer booklet, developing your ideas logically and specifically.

4. **Proofread** your essay, making any necessary changes to clarify your meaning and correcting any obvious errors.

Timing Strategies for the Writing Section

Because you have only 30 minutes to work on your ACT essay, you need to manage your time carefully. A little time spent planning *before* you actually start to write your essay will pay off. You have to understand the question in the prompt, and then think about how you can answer it effectively. This takes a few minutes of planning. Plan what to say before writing and the result will be a focused and organized ACT essay. We recommend taking a couple of minutes to read the prompt carefully and then spending between three and five minutes planning (steps 1 and 2, prompt and plan). This is long enough to read the question, consider possible ways to answer it, and jot down very brief notes about what your two or three main pieces of evidence will be. When you know what you're going to discuss *before* you start writing, you can think about the best order to present your main points in.

The time you spend on step 3, produce, when you actually write your essay in the answer booklet, will go more smoothly if you're working from a well-thought-out written plan. You should spend about 15–20 minutes on the writing stage.

When you've finished writing, use the remaining time, which should be about five minutes, to proofread your essay. At this point you're not looking to make major revisions. You should simply read your essay with a careful eye, looking for small errors or omissions that affect the readability. If you can correct a few grammatical errors, make sure that each sentence clearly conveys what you mean it to, and insert any transitional words or phrases (such as *however, in contrast, in addition,* etc.) that help your argument flow more logically, your proofreading time will be well spent. Leaving time to proofread ensures that your essay is easy for the graders to read and understand, which means you'll get the best score possible.

ACT Writing Section Time Guidelines

Step 1: Prompt–2 minutes

Step 2: Plan–3–5 minutes

Step 3: Produce–15–20 minutes

Step 4: Proofread–5–6 minutes

Chapter Three: **ACT English Overview**

All ACT English questions are passage-based. This means that every decision you make about an answer should be considered in light of the context. The ACT writers divide questions into two broad categories: Mechanics and rhetorical skills. Mechanics questions address grammatical issues, matters such as using the correct pronoun or verb form. Generally, you can determine the correct answer for a Mechanics questions simply by reading a single sentence. Rhetorical Skills questions, on the other hand, often require you to take a larger part of the passage into account. These questions ask you to consider the author's style, tone, purpose, and organizational structure. The ACT mixes both Rhetorical Skills and Mechanics questions together throughout the English section. That fact is what gives rise to step 1 of the Kaplan method for ACT English. As you work through an English passage, you need to constantly ask yourself how much of the passage you need to read (or consider) to determine the best answer to this question.

MECHANICS QUESTIONS

First, let's consider mechanics questions in light of the Kaplan method for ACT English. Step 1 tells you to read until you have enough information to identify the issue. For a Mechanics question, the issue should be apparent as soon as you come to the end of the sentence containing the underlined portion. Sometimes you'll recognize the issue even before you reach the end of the sentence. Step 2 tells you to eliminate answer choices that don't address the issue. In other words, if the underlined part contains an error, eliminate any other answer choice that repeats the error. Step 3 of the Kaplan method tells you to plug in the remaining answer choices and select the most correct, concise, and relevant one.

Recall that the Kaplan method works for all types of ACT English questions. For Mechanics questions, however, the most important word to keep in mind during step 3 is *correct*. Mechanics issues are those that are either correct or incorrect. You can determine the correct answer by knowing which grammar rule to apply. Don't worry, though, you won't need to memorize a lot of rules. The ACT tests a limited set of rules, and this section goes over all of them.

Sentence Sense

Before we discuss how the ACT tests sentence sense, you need to be comfortable with just a few grammatical terms. A *sentence* is a group of words that contains a subject and a verb and expresses a complete thought. A sentence is made up of one or more clauses. A *clause* is a group of words that contains a subject and a verb. A clause may constitute a complete sentence, but it doesn't necessarily have to. If a clause can stand alone as a sentence, it's called an *independent clause.* If a clause cannot stand alone as a sentence, that is, if it doesn't express a complete thought, it's called a *dependent clause.* See if you can label the clauses below as either dependent or independent:

1. _____ because she is my friend
2. _____ she is my friend
3. _____ that I will go to the library
4. _____ I will go to the library
5. _____ if Dana is working tonight
6. _____ Dana is working tonight
7. _____ that all will be well
8. _____ all would be well
9. _____ when I return from vacation next week
10. _____ I return from vacation next week
11. _____ if Dawn and Terri are going skating
12. _____ Dawn and Terri are going skating
13. _____ whereas most people will be driving
14. _____ most people will be driving
15. _____ while my grandmother is visiting over the summer
16. _____ my grandmother is visiting over the summer

In this exercise, all of the even-numbered questions are independent clauses. All of the odd-numbered questions are dependent clauses. In each odd-even pair of problems in the exercise, the independent clause actually contains fewer words than the dependent clause. Take a minute to go back to the odd-numbered questions, and circle the first word in each.

When you see words such as *because, that, if, whereas,* and *while* in an underlined part of an ACT English passage, keep in mind that sentence structure may be one of the issues that problem is testing. Remember, just because a group of words in the passage starts with a capital letter and ends with a period, that doesn't necessarily mean it's a complete sentence. Be on the lookout for a dependent clause that isn't joined to an independent clause. A dependent clause by itself is a *sentence fragment,* which must be revised and corrected.

Another kind of sentence structure error is a *run-on sentence.* A run-on sentence contains two or more clauses that are incorrectly strung together. A well-formed sentence can have more than one clause, but the clauses must be joined in a way that follows the principles of correct sentence structure. Before we review the rules for sentence structure, test your present understanding by considering the following incorrect sentence:

> My history teacher requires us to use at least two books in our research, I have to go to the library this weekend.

Can you tell why the sentence structure is wrong here? Take a minute to see if you can find one or more ways to correct it:

_____

_____

_____

_____

The sentence is a run-on. If a sentence contains two parts that could each stand alone as a sentence (two *independent clauses*), then it's incorrect to join those two parts with just a comma. Doing so creates a run-on sentence. There are several ways to correct a run-on like this one. However, on the ACT, you won't have to choose which one is best; for each question, only one correct choice will be presented.

Run-on Sentence Rules

Use one of these three ways to correctly combine two independent clauses in a single sentence:

1. Use a comma and a FANBOYS word *(for, and, nor, but, or, yet, so)*.
   My history teacher requires us to use at least two books in our research, **so** *I have to go to the library this weekend.*

2. Use a semicolon between the two clauses. After a semicolon, it is not correct to use a FANBOYS word, but it is acceptable to use a word such as *however, moreover,* or *nevertheless.*
   My history teacher requires us to use at least two books in our research; **therefore,** *I have to go to the library this weekend.*

3. Break the run-on into two separate sentences by changing the comma to a period and starting a new sentence.
   My history teacher requires us to use at least two books in our research. I have to go to the library this weekend.

4. Change one of the independent clauses to a dependent clause by adding a word such as *although, because, despite,* or *while.*
   Because *my history teacher requires us to use at least two books in our research, I have to go to the library this weekend.*

In addition to the rules listed here for combining clauses in a sentence, there's one more sentence sense issue that you should be aware of. Fortunately, there's a clue to help you spot it.

> Whenever an underlined portion includes a verb that ends in *–ing*, take note and check that there isn't a sentence sense problem.

Sentence Sense Rule

The verb form ending in *–ing* cannot be used without a helping verb, such as *is, was, has, had,* or *have been*, as the main verb in a clause.

Here's an example. *The monkey swinging from tree to tree* is incorrect because *swinging* is used alone as the main verb in the clause. A helping verb is needed. Depending on the context, you might say something like, *The monkey* is swinging *from tree to tree* or *The monkey* had been swinging from *tree to tree.*

Try these ACT-like questions that test sentence structure:

1.   Two of our team's best players were injured at the beginning of the <u>season, our</u> team has not been doing well.

    (A)   NO CHANGE

    (B)   season, therefore, our

    (C)   season; so our

    (D)   season; therefore, our

The tested issue here is sentence structure: option A makes the sentence a run-on. After identifying this issue, check the answer choices and eliminate those that don't follow the rules for correcting a run-on. Option B is incorrect because a comma cannot join two independent clauses and a word such as *therefore.* Option C is wrong because the semicolon is not the correct punctuation mark to use when you join two independent clauses by a FANBOYS word. Because option C uses *so,* a comma is needed instead of the semicolon here. Option D correctly joins two independent clauses with a semicolon and no FANBOYS word. Recall that it is acceptable to use *therefore* after a semicolon.

2.   The <u>library, which functioning</u> at times as a social center, is more than just an academic resource.

    (F)   NO CHANGE

    (G)   library, functioning

    (H)   library it functions

    (J)   library having the function

The issue here is sentence structure. The sentence as written isn't a run-on, but there is a problem in the way that it's structured. The phrase *which functioning* probably sounds wrong to your ear. Read through the other choices to see if any of the others create sentence structure problems. In this case, you may have to read all three remaining choices into the sentence. Option G doesn't create a problem and is the correct answer. Option H contains the word *it,* which is unnecessary here. Option J doesn't work in the context because it creates the idiomatically incorrect phrase *having the function . . . as.*

3.   My school's French club <u>planning to go</u> to Paris this spring.

    (A)   NO CHANGE

    (B)   planning on going

    (C)   is planning going

    (D)   is planning to go

Did you notice that the underlined portion includes *planning,* an *–ing* verb, without also using a helping verb like such as *has* or *have?* A helping verb is a verb that does not show action by itself, but can "help" the main verb show action. Because this is the case, you should have identified sentence structure as the issue. Option B does not address this issue. Both options C and D address the issue by adding the helping verb *is.* Read each choice into the sentence to determine that the best answer is D.

Sentence structure is one aspect of how sentence sense is tested on the ACT. Another aspect is clarity. For these ACT-like questions, you had to ask yourself if the sentence was constructed properly, and whether its clauses were joined correctly. Now we'll talk about another important consideration: Is the meaning of this sentence clear and unambiguous? If an ACT sentence doesn't make sense or you're not sure what it's supposed to mean, then there's a problem with sentence sense. Whenever you notice that an entire sentence is underlined in an ACT English passage, take that as a clue that it may be testing sentence sense. (The other possibility is that the sentence may be testing relevance, which you will read about in the Rhetorical Skills section.)

Here's an example. Suppose you see this entire sentence underlined in an ACT English passage:

> Tangled in the leash, the door closed on her dog as Samantha was going into the house.

This sentence isn't written in the clearest way possible. Think about what the sentence is trying to say, and see if you can come up with an effective revision here:

_____

_____

As it's originally written, the sentence suggests that *the door* is *tangled in the leash.* If you think about it, you realize that, logically, it's the *dog* that is *tangled in the leash.* Moving that phrase and adjusting the wording slightly creates a more logical sentence. Here's an example of how to correct the sentence: *As they went into the house, the door closed on Samantha's dog, which was tangled in the leash.*

Whenever the sentence that contains an underlined part starts with a verb that ends in *–ed* or *–ing,* that's a clue that the question may be testing sentence sense.

A third consideration about sentence sense on ACT English has to do with how the sentence works in the context of the passage: Is this sentence consistent with the nonunderlined parts of the sentences around it? Verbs and pronouns are the primary issue here. Consider the following excerpt, and see if you can determine how the underlined parts should be corrected:

> When you get ready to travel, there are many things <u>one has to</u> [1._____] take care of in advance. If you're going outside the country, <u>one</u> [2._____] must plan ahead to ensure that you'll get your passport on time. Of course, there <u>was</u> [3._____] the packing to be done, though this can wait until closer to your departure day. If you have pets, however, you should <u>have thought</u> [4._____] ahead about finding a pet-sitter. There is, though, one thing you *must* do at the last minute: Don't forget to lock your door!

You must pay attention to the nonunderlined context to help you make the necessary corrections here. Here is the passage reprinted with correct answers filled in. Notice that certain nonunderlined words are printed in bold, because they are the context clues that help you make the corrections:

> When **you** get ready to travel, there **are** many things <u>one has to</u> [1. you have to] take care of in advance. If **you**'re going outside the country, <u>one</u> [2. you] must plan ahead to ensure that **you**'ll get your passport on time. Of course, there <u>was</u> [3. is] the packing to be done, though this **can wait** until closer to your departure day. If **you have** pets, however, **you** should <u>have thought</u> [4. think] ahead about finding a pet-sitter. There **is**, however, one thing **you** must do at the last minute: Don't forget to lock **your** door!

The following two rules needed to be applied to this exercise.

Sentence Sense Consistency Rules

1. Avoid the *one-you* shift. That is, do not switch needlessly between *one* and *you* within a passage.
2. Make sure the primary verb tense is consistent throughout the passage. If the passage is written primarily in one tense, do not shift to a different tense unless there is a logical reason to do so.

You'll see a reminder about this issue of sentence sense consistency later in the sections on pronouns and verbs.

Punctuation

Some of the easiest questions to recognize are punctuation questions. When you look at the answer choices, you'll see that they all use the same or nearly the same words. This is your clue to think about punctuation rules. The great thing about the ACT is that it tests a limited number of punctuation rules. Comma usage is tested most frequently, followed by semicolon usage.

Comma Rule

Use commas to

1. separate introductory words from the main part of the sentence.
   Before you leave the house, you should make sure you've eaten a healthy breakfast.
2. set off words or phrases that aren't essential to the sentence structure.
   Sonia, who will be playing the role of the lawyer, is a skilled actress.
3. separate two independent clauses when they're joined by a FANBOYS word (*for, and, nor, but, or, yet, so*).
   Many of my friends drink coffee, but I do not.
4. separate items in a series.
   Steps involved in a research paper include choosing a topic, conducting the research, writing a first draft, and doing at least one round of revisions.

These four examples are the only uses of the comma that the ACT tests. Learn to recognize when each rule should be applied, and keep in mind the following additional hint.

Comma Hint

Avoid unnecessary commas. Sometimes your task on an ACT punctuation question is to remove commas that disturb the flow of a sentence.

Semicolon Rule

Use a semicolon to link two independent clauses that are *not* joined by a FANBOYS word.

> I will be missing school to visit colleges; however, my teacher said I will not have to make up the Spanish quiz I will miss.

Be aware of certain words that are frequently used to connect two independent clauses. These words are acceptable to use after a semicolon:

furthermore

however

in fact

indeed

moreover

nevertheless

therefore

thus

Do not use these words after a semicolon:

although

despite

whereas

who

which

where

that

Dash Rule

Use em dashes:

1. To indicate a break in thought.
   You did see the movie—am I right about that?

2. To set off parenthetical information from the main part of a sentence.
   Many people find that small necessary items—a wallet, a cell phone, a transit card—are unfortunately very easy to misplace.

Apostrophe Rule

Use an apostrophe:

1. To take the place of one or more missing letters in a contraction.
   You can't be late.

2. To show the possessive form of a noun.
   My sisters' teams both won games this weekend. (This is correct if you're using the plural form, two sisters who play on two separate teams.)
   My sister's friends are coming to the party. (This is correct if you're using the singular form, one sister.)

As you work through an ACT English passage, notice when a question is testing punctuation. When it is, think about how the various parts of each sentence relate to one another. Ask yourself what the main part of the sentence is, and consider whether some phrases might be nonessential information. If a sentence has more than one clause, think about whether each could stand alone as a sentence. If that's the case, recall the rules about commas and semicolons, and which words are acceptable with each to join two clauses. Keep these ideas in mind as you try the questions below. To increase your understanding, read each answer explanation before you move on to the next question.

I'm unusual among my friends in that I don't <u>like, to drink coffee</u>. I do enjoy going
(1)
with them to coffee <u>shops because, oddly enough,</u> I appreciate the smell of coffee.
(2)
The convivial atmosphere of our local coffee brewer is also quite appealing to <u>me so,</u>
(3)
I enjoy spending time there with friends. Fortunately, I can get a pretty good cup of
tea <u>there, indeed, occasionally</u> I even order hot chocolate. In addition to the socializing
(4)
and <u>refreshment, the coffee shop offers</u> me amusement. I have to laugh at the wide
(5)
array of available coffee drinks—regular, decaf, espresso, cappuccino, latte, to
<u>name just a few,</u> and the amount of time it takes my friends to decide what to order.
(6)
I'm baffled by how my very busy friends can give so much time and attention to
something that, no matter how <u>its' made,</u> still tastes like coffee.
(7)

1. (A)   NO CHANGE
   (B)   like to drink coffee
   (C)   like to drink coffee
   (D)   like to drink, coffee

In this sentence, the comma after *like* disturbs the flow of the clause, *I don't like to drink coffee.* In this question, remember the hint about avoiding unnecessary commas. The correct answer is C.

2. (F)   NO CHANGE

    (G)   shops, because, oddly enough,

    (H)   shops because oddly, enough,

    (J)   shops because oddly enough

Here, the phrase *oddly enough* is nonessential information. If you remove it, the remaining words still make up a correctly formed sentence. Use commas to set off nonessential phrases. The best answer is F.

3. (A)   NO CHANGE

    (B)   me, so

    (C)   me; so

    (D)   me, so,

Think about how this sentence is constructed. It contains two independent clauses, joined by the FANBOYS word *so.* The first clause (*the convivial atmosphere of our local coffee brewer is also quite appealing to me*) can stand alone as a sentence. The second clause (*I enjoy spending time there with friends*) can also stand alone as a sentence. Use a comma after the first independent clause when you're joining two independent clauses with a FANBOYS word. The correct answer is B.

4. (F)   NO CHANGE

    (G)   there indeed, occasionally

    (H)   there: indeed, occasionally,

    (J)   there; indeed, occasionally

Again, think about sentence structure. You have two independent clauses here. The first is *I can get a pretty good cup of tea there.* The second is *I even order hot chocolate.* The word between the two clauses, *indeed,* is not a FANBOYS word, so you need a semicolon rather than a comma to join these two independent clauses. The correct answer is J.

5. (A)   NO CHANGE

    (B)   refreshment, the coffee shop, offers,

    (C)   refreshment the coffee shop, offers

    (D)   refreshment; the coffee shop offers

This sentence contains only one independent clause. This independent clause, *the coffee shop offers me amusement,* forms the main part of the sentence. The earlier part of the sentence (*In addition to the socializing and refreshment*) is not a clause. It is an introductory phrase. Use a comma to set off an introductory phrase from the main part of the sentence. The correct answer is A.

6. (F)   NO CHANGE

    (G)   to name just a few—

    (H)   to name, just a few,

    (J)   to name just a few:

Be careful here. The incorrect punctuation used in option A can make this sentence confusing to read and understand. Take the sentence apart to determine which words make up the main part of the sentence. The independent clause is *I have to laugh at the wide array of available coffee drinks . . . and the amount of time it takes my friends to decide what to order.* The words that follow the nonunderlined dash (*regular, decaf, espresso, cappuccino, latte, to name just a few*) constitute parenthetical information that is not part of the sentence's main clause. A dash must be used at the end of the parenthetical expression to properly set it off. The correct answer is G.

7. (A) NO CHANGE
   (B) its made,
   (C) it's made
   (D) it's made,

This question tests both comma and apostrophe usage. Whenever you see that an underlined portion of an English passage contains an apostrophe, always check that it's used correctly. The spelling *its'* is never correct. If an apostrophe is called for, as it is here, the correct spelling is *it's*. Remember that this spelling is correct whenever it could be replaced by the words *it is*. You have to think about comma rules for this question also. The words *no matter how it's made* are nonessential information. Because you must use commas to set off nonessential information from the rest of the sentence, a comma is required here after *made.* The correct answer is D.

Pronouns

You probably remember this definition: A pronoun is a word that either takes the place of or refers to a noun or another pronoun. Train yourself to spot pronouns immediately in the underlined portion of an ACT English passage. See if you can identify the pronouns in each underlined part of the following paragraph and write them on the lines provided.

My mother and her work friends, nurses in a large emergency room, have many interesting stories <u>about their</u> experiences. Some of these stories are about the
    (1)
challenges patients face, but some of the funniest stories are about interactions
<u>her and the other nurses have</u> with various staff members. Whenever Mom and
    (2)
<u>I have</u> friends over at the same time, my friends and <u>me always wind up</u> laughing at
  (3)   **(4)**
the things we hear. The story about the doctor who thought <u>their cell phone had been</u>
          (5)
"borrowed" by a nurse was hilarious. Mom and her friends have <u>given we</u> teenagers
         (6)
some good advice: One should not go into the medical field <u>if you don't have</u> a good
         (7)
sense of humor.

1. _____
2. _____

3. _____

4. _____

5. _____

6. _____

7. _____

How did you do at picking out the pronouns? Don't worry if you didn't find them all, we'll discuss the pronouns that you'll see on the ACT. Here are the answers:

1. their

2. her

3. I

4. me

5. their

6. we

7. you

Let's do a quick review of what you need to know about pronouns for the ACT. Any pronoun can be described in terms of two things: case and number. Pronoun *case* refers to how the pronoun is used in a sentence—as a subject or an object. In the sentence *I will call you later,* the pronoun *I* acts as the subject, while the pronoun *you* acts as the object. A pronoun's *number* is either singular or plural. Most personal pronouns take a different form (that is, a different word is used) depending on whether they are used as the subject or object in a sentence and depending on whether they are singular or plural. The following table shows the personal pronouns for which you must consider both case and number.

	Singular	**Plural**
Subject	I, he, she, it,	we, they
Object	me, him, her, it	us, them

Generally, your ear tells you which form of a personal pronoun is correct. The ACT often makes a pronoun question trickier by using a personal pronoun in a combination with *and.* You would never say, Me *went to the store.* On the ACT, you might see something such as Me *and Jesse will do the project together.* By reading this sentence without the words *and Jesse* your ear helps you determine that *Me* should be changed to *I* in this sentence.

Examples of correct pronoun usage as subjects and objects:

1. **We** must be respectful in this class, or the teacher will give *us* detention.

2. Kevin and **I** are going skating tonight.

3. The guests said **they** were thankful for the help that *we* volunteers provided.

4. Ginny told **me** there was no need to return the book to *her.*

5. Can you believe my parents said **they** will give *us* the car for the weekend?

Did you notice that the table of personal pronouns above doesn't include the pronoun *you*? The reason for this is that the pronoun *you* takes the same form whether it's used as the subject or object in a sentence. Here's an example:

> *You* must be respectful in the class, or the teacher will give *you* a detention.

However, the ACT does test the pronoun *you* in a different way, by using the word *one* in a sentence that also uses *you.*

Pronoun-Shift Rule

Avoid the *one-you* shift: Do not needlessly shift between the words *one* and *you* in the same sentence or paragraph.

Here's how the *one-you* shift might look on the ACT:

> When <u>one is</u> planning for college, you need to keep many factors in mind.

Here, because the nonunderlined part of the sentence uses the word *you,* the underlined part of the sentence should be corrected to *you are.*

In addition to the personal pronouns and the *one-you* shift, another aspect of pronoun usage that's tested on the ACT is the correct use of *who, whom,* and *which. Who* and *whom* intimidate many people, but it's not hard to use them correctly if you keep in mind the issue of pronoun case. As with the personal pronouns shown in the previous table, the key to using *who* and *whom* correctly is to think about how each word functions in its sentence or clause. Think about whether it is a subject or an object. Here's a hint: If you can correctly substitute the pronoun *he* into a phrase or sentence, then *who* is correct. If you can correctly substitute the pronoun *him* into a phrase or sentence, then *whom* is correct. ACT questions that test *who, whom,* and *which* aren't questions that most people can easily answer just by thinking about what sounds correct. Learn to apply the rule:

Which/Who/Whom Rule
- Use *which* only to refer to things, never to refer to people.
- Use *who* in a sentence context where either *he* or *she* would be correct.
- Use *whom* in a sentence context where either *him* or *her* would be correct.

See if you can circle the correct word in the following sentences:
1. My brother, *who/whom* attends the state university, is majoring in history.
2. The baby, *who/which* is only nine months old, has already started walking.
3. A public speaker should keep in mind the audience *who/whom* she is addressing.
4. The company president is the person *which/whom* you need to contact.
5. The principal said that all students *who/whom* skip the pep rally will receive a detention.

6. The head librarian is the one to *which/whom* you must send your résumé.

7. The painting of *which/whom* I write is the work of an unknown genius.

Here are the correct answers, along with explanations in case you need help applying the rule:

1. *Who* is correct because you'd say He *attends the state university.*

2. *Who* is correct, because *the baby* is a person, not a thing.

3. *Whom* is correct because you'd say *She is addressing* him.

4. *Whom* is correct because you're referring to a person and because you'd say *You need to contact* him.

5. *Who* is correct because you'd say He *skip[s] the pep rally.*

6. *Whom* is correct because you're referring to a person and because you'd say *You must send your résumé to* him.

7. *Which* is correct because you're referring to the painting, a thing, not a person.

Now let's return to the paragraph you saw at the beginning of this section. This time, it's presented as a test-like passage with multiple-choice answers such as those that appear on the ACT. Use it to test your understanding of the various pronoun issues.

My mother and her work friends, nurses in a large emergency room, have many interesting stories <u>about their</u> experiences. Some of these stories are about the
                        (1)
challenges patients face, but some of the funniest stories are about interactions
<u>her and the other nurses have</u> with various staff members. Whenever Mom and
          (2)
<u>I have</u> friends over at the same time, my friends and <u>me always wind up</u> laughing at
  (3)   **(4)**
the things we hear. The story about the doctor who thought <u>their cell phone had been</u>
                                                              (5)
"borrowed" by a nurse was hilarious. Mom and her friends <u>have given we</u> teenagers
                                                          (6)
some good advice: One should not go into the medical field <u>if you don't have</u> a good
                                                            (7)
sense of humor.

11. (A) NO CHANGE

    (B) about there

    (C) on they're

    (D) on their

The possessive pronoun *their* is underlined. It is plural, so it correctly refers to *my mother and her friends.* Following step 2 of the Kaplan method, you can eliminate options B and C, which use the incorrect spelling, *their.* Following step 3 and reading the sentence with options A and D, you should be able to eliminate option D. The correct answer is A.

12. (F)   NO CHANGE
    (G)   her and the other nurses were having
    (H)   she and the other nurses having
    (J)   she and the other nurses have

You should notice immediately that the underlined portion uses the pronoun *her*. Ask yourself if it's used correctly. Remember that you should be especially careful whenever you see an underlined pronoun near the word *and*. Think about how the pronoun sounds in context when you momentarily ignore the word that follows *and*. Does it sound correct to say *interactions* her [has] *with other staff members*? No, you would say *interactions* she *has with other staff members*. The issue here is pronoun case. You can eliminate options F and G. Following step 3, and reading options H and J into the sentence, you should notice a verb error in option H. The correct answer is J.

13. (A)   NO CHANGE
    (B)   I would be having
    (C)   me have
    (D)   me had

Notice the underlined pronoun *I* and determine how it's used in the sentence. Here, *I* is used correctly as the subject of the clause *I have friends over*. Based on pronoun usage, you can eliminate options C and D. Then, if you read option B into the sentence, you can hear that it introduces a verb problem. The correct answer is A.

14. (F)   NO CHANGE
    (G)   I always wind up
    (H)   I always winding up
    (J)   me always winding up

The underlined portion contains the pronoun *me,* so first you should check to see if it's used correctly. It functions as a subject in the clause *me always wind up laughing*. Pronoun usage is definitely the issue here: the subject pronoun *I* is needed instead. Identifying the issue lets you eliminate options F and J. Read the other choices into the sentence, and you'll hear that option H introduces a verb error. The correct answer is G.

15. (A)   NO CHANGE
    (B)   there cell phone had been
    (C)   they're cell phone had been
    (D)   her cell phone had been

There's an error in this sentence as it's written, but it's not an easy one for your ear to detect. This means that you might have difficulty identifying the issue here. Still, you should notice that the pronoun *their* is underlined. Ask yourself what word in the passage it refers to. *Their* refers to the word *doctor*. The problem is *doctor* is singular, but *their* is plural. Because *doctor* is not underlined, you can't change it, so you have to eliminate the pronoun *their*. Notice that options B and C don't eliminate the pronoun; they simply substitute a different word that sounds the same. Only option D correctly uses a singular pronoun (*her*) to refer to the singular noun *doctor*. The correct answer is D.

16. (F) NO CHANGE
    (G) having gave we
    (H) have gave us
    (J) have given us

Your ear might help you easily identify the issue here. If not, notice that the underlined portion contains the pronoun *we,* and determine how it's used in the sentence. The fact that the pronoun immediately follows the verb *given* indicates that it's used here as an object; however, *we* is the form to use for a subject, so *we* is incorrect here. Thus, you can eliminate options F and G. Read the other two options. Both correctly use the objective pronoun *us,* but option H introduces a verb error. The correct answer is J.

17. (A) NO CHANGE
    (B) if they don't have
    (C) without having
    (D) if you aren't having

The issue in this question is the *one-you* shift. That can be a difficult issue to recognize unless you think to look for it. The fact that the underlined portion includes the pronoun *you* should serve as a red flag. Whenever you notice this word underlined, check the surrounding context for consistency. Because the nonunderlined part of the sentence uses the word *one,* it's incorrect to use *you* in the same sentence. Remembering this rule allows you to eliminate options A and D. Read the remaining options into the sentence. Option B uses the plural pronoun *they* to refer to the singular *one,* so it can't be correct. The correct answer is C.

Verbs

You probably remember that a verb is a word, such as *draw, eat,* or *walk,* that expresses an action or a word, such as *is, were,* or *was*, that expresses a state of being. Though it can get pretty complicated to discuss every grammatical point relating to verbs, there are really only three verb usage rules that are tested on the ACT:

1. A verb must agree with its subject.
2. A verb's tense must be logically consistent with time-related phrases in the sentence and other verbs that are used in the passage.
3. Some verbs can form the past tense in a way other than using *–ed*.

An easy way to know if you have to apply one of these rules is to get used to noticing underlined verbs in the ACT English section, and when you do notice one, ask yourself the following questions:

- What is the subject of this verb? Does the underlined verb agree with its grammatical subject?
- Does the tense of the underlined verb make sense in relation to other words in the sentence? Is the underlined verb consistent with other verb tenses used in nearby sentences and the passage as a whole?
- Does this verb form the past tense correctly? Does it sound right?

What is the subject of this verb? Does the underlined verb agree with its grammatical subject?

A key thing to remember is that the noun immediately before the verb may not actually be the verb's subject.

In this example of incorrect subject-verb agreement, see if you can circle the subject and jot down the correction for the underlined verb in the space provided:

> Many of my friends, including everyone in the brass section of
> the band, is [_____] planning to come to my party.

Recall that the subject is who or what is doing the action or being that the verb expresses. In the sentence, you should have circled the word *Many*, which is the subject of this sentence. Detecting the incorrect subject-verb agreement here can be tricky because the subject, *many*, is separated from the verb by several phrases. As you work through English questions, both in your practice and on Test Day, circle the subject that goes with the underlined verb. Then read the subject and the verb without the words that appear between them. When you do this, you'll hear a mistake more easily. You wouldn't say, Many is *planning to come.* The correct subject-verb agreement here is, Many are *planning to come.*

Does the tense of the underlined verb make sense in relation to other words in the sentence? Is the underlined verb consistent with other verb tenses used in nearby sentences and the passage as a whole?

To determine if an underlined verb makes sense within its own sentence, watch for time-related phrases and nonunderlined verbs. In the following example of illogical verb tense usage, circle the time-related word, and write down the correct verb tense in the space provided:

> Before my parents will let me take the car by myself, I <u>had to</u>
> [_____] improve my grade-point average considerably.

Here you should have circled the time-related word *before* and the nonunderlined verb *will let*. If you focus on these words, you should see that the underlined *had*, in the past tense, is not logical in this sentence. Possible corrections are *have to*, *must*, and *will have to*. On the ACT, only one correct answer will be presented among the answer choices

Does this verb form the past tense correctly? Does it sound right?

See if you can make the necessary correction in this sentence:

> Hemingway, along with several other Americans, <u>had went</u>
> [_____] to Paris to write.

The verb error in this sentence could be corrected in two ways, depending on the context. The key thing to spot here, though, is that *had went* is never correct. It's a good idea to train your ear to recognize several past tense forms that are common errors. The following forms are never correct: *had did, had flied, had wrote, had took.* You don't need to memorize every verb that forms the past tense irregularly (that is, with a spelling other than simply adding *–ed),* but you should be aware that this type of error is sometimes tested on the ACT.

Word-Choice Questions

Many of the Mechanics questions on the ACT hinge on verb and pronoun usage, but there are a couple of other word-choice issues that you need to be aware of: modifiers, comparatives and superlatives, and idiomatic usages.

A *modifier* is something that describes or provides more information about a word. Two different parts of speech, adjectives and adverbs, function as modifiers. In addition to these single-word modifiers, phrases can also serve as modifiers. Let's look at the two modifier rules that are tested on the ACT.

Single-Word Modifier Rule

An adjective must be used only to modify a noun or a pronoun. An adverb must be used only to modify either a verb, an adjective, or another adverb.

Try the following exercise. Underline the adjective or adverb, and circle the word it logically modifies. Then determine whether the modifier is used correctly. If it isn't, put an *X* in the space provided.

1. _____Caitlin drove careful on the highway.
2. _____Carlos worked diligently on the project.
3. _____I am certainly that the show starts at 8:00.
4. _____Sarah found it was extreme cold in the tent.
5. _____Sonnesh is extremely happy.
6. _____Diligent work leads to success.

You should have identified questions 1, 3, and 4 as being incorrect. Question 1 incorrectly uses the adjective *careful* to modify the verb *drove.* (It should be *carefully.)* Question 3 incorrectly uses the adverb *certainly* to modify the pronoun *I. (Certain* is correct here.) Question 4 incorrectly uses the adjective *extreme* to modify the adjective *cold. (Extremely* is called for here.) The other questions are correct. Question 2 uses the adverb *diligently* to modify the verb *worked.* Question 5 uses the adverb *extremely* to modify the adjective *happy.* Question 6 uses the adjective *diligent* to modify the noun *work.*

Modifying Phrase Rule

A modifying phrase should be placed as close as possible to the word it modifies. Specifically, when a sentence begins with a modifying phrase, the next noun or pronoun in the sentence must be the word that phrase logically modifies.

> You can easily spot most introductory modifying phrases because they usually begin with a verb that ends in *–ed* or *–ing*.

You can easily spot most introductory modifying phrases because they usually begin with a verb that ends in *–ed* or *–ing*. If you remember this, you'll have no trouble at all with introductory modifiers on the ACT. Let's look an example:

18. Having just returned from three weeks of primitive camping, <u>sleeping in his own bed was what Matt looked forward to most</u>.

    (A)   NO CHANGE

    (B)   being home in his own bed was what Matt looked forward to most.

    (C)   Matt most looked forward to sleeping in his own bed.

    (D)   the thing Matt looked forward to most was sleeping in his own bed.

If you notice that the sentence starts with a modifying phrase (*Having just returned from three weeks of primitive camping*), and you ask yourself who or what this phrase logically describes, you'll find this question easy to get right! Logically, the introductory phrase can only be modifying *Matt*. Therefore, *Matt* must immediately follow the phrase, so you can eliminate all choices except option C. The key here is paying attention to the nonunderlined context of the sentence and using it to determine what the best answer is.

Like some modifier questions, another issue tested on the ACT also relates to adjectives. This is the issue of *comparative* and *superlative* adjectives. Generally, comparative adjectives end with *–er*, and superlative adjectives end in *–est*. You determine whether the comparative or superlative form of an adjective is correct by asking how many items are being compared.

Comparative and Superlative Rule

Use the comparative form of an adjective (for example, *older* or *shorter*) when only two people or things are being compared. Use the superlative form of an adjective (for example, *oldest* or *shortest*) when comparing three or more people or things.

Because the ACT cannot include a question without an unambiguously correct answer, the context surrounding a comparative or superlative must always make it clear how many things are being compared. In the following question, look for a phrase that clues you in on, or indicates, how many people are involved. Here's an example:

19. Of all my friends, I think Johanna is the <u>most likely to become a doctor</u>.

    (A)   NO CHANGE

    (B)   more likely to become a doctor

    (C)   most likely becoming a doctor

    (D)   most likeliest to become a doctor

If you focused on the word *all*, good for you! The phrase *of all my friends* tells you that three or more people are being discussed here. This means that the superlative form *most* is correct. Eliminate option B and plug the remaining choices in. Option C correctly uses the superlative *most likely*, but it creates a sentence sense problem by changing the verb to *becoming* so eliminate option C. You should eliminate option D because the idea of the superlative is already included in the word *most*, so it's incorrect to change *likely* to *likeliest*. Thus, you can eliminate option D.

The other word-choice issue that's tested on the ACT is idiomatic usage. An *idiom* is an expression that is conventionally phrased in a particular way. Most often, correct idiomatic usage hinges on prepositions. For example, you would never say, "I'm traveling *at* school." You'd say, "I'm traveling *to* school." In different contexts, though, a different preposition can be correct. For example:

> I'm in the math club _____ school.

Your ear should tell you that *at* is correct here. In fact, for idioms, it is indeed your ear that you must rely on to get the correct answer. Idioms, by definition, are not constructed by following any general rules. Idiomatic usage isn't heavily tested on the ACT, and, in any case, the English language includes so many idioms that it would be impossible to give you a complete list to memorize. Instead, keep the following guideline in mind: Whenever you notice that the underlined portion includes a preposition, think about how it sounds in context to make sure it's idiomatically correct.

> Whenever you notice that the underlined portion includes a preposition, think about how it sounds in context to make sure it's idiomatically correct.

Sometimes, when you've eliminated two answer choices and are trying to choose the better one of the remaining two, thinking about correct idiomatic usage will help you select the correct answer.

RHETORICAL SKILLS QUESTIONS

Rhetorical Skills questions on the ACT demand a different approach from the Mechanics issues previously discussed. You can think of Mechanics questions as those that have black-and-white answers, governed by specific conventions that you can learn and apply. Rhetorical Skills questions, on the other hand, are not as simple.

To determine the best answer for a Rhetorical Skills question, you have to call upon some of the same skills you use for the Reading Comprehension questions in the ACT Reading section. Often, for Rhetorical Skills questions, you need to take a big-picture view of the passage. Whereas Mechanics questions can be answered by looking at a small part of the passage, often one sentence, and determining what is right and wrong, Rhetorical Skills questions demand that you consider broader aspects of the passage. As you determine the best answer for a Rhetorical Skills question, you may need to consider one or more of these points:

- What is the author's purpose in writing this passage?
- What effect does choosing one word or phrase instead of another create for the reader?
- What is the overall organizational structure of the passage?
- Would changing the order of sentences in a paragraph or the order of paragraphs in the passage make the writing easier to follow and understand?

As you'll see when you work on the Reading practice in this workbook, you'll need to address some of these same questions in order to choose the best answer for a Reading Comprehension question. Thus, it may be helpful to think of Rhetorical Skills questions as Reading questions that just happen to appear in the ACT English section.

Recognizing a Rhetorical Skills Question

If the fact that the test maker puts Reading-like questions in the English section seems intimidating at first, don't worry. It is true that one of the biggest challenges of the ACT English section is that Mechanics and Rhetorical Skills questions are interspersed. As you begin your English practice, one thing you'll have to get used to is determining how much of the passage you need to consider when answering a given question. The first step of the Kaplan method for ACT English— read until you have information to identify the issue—illustrates how important it is to know *how much of the passage you must consider* in order to get to the best answer.

There is, however, a general guideline that will help you greatly. While Mechanics questions are usually presented with just the question number and the four multiple-choice answers, Rhetorical Skills questions very often appear with a question stem, that is, something you must read between the question number and the multiple-choice answers. Therefore, you should take the presence of a question stem in the English section as a strong clue that the question is likely a Rhetorical Skills question, requiring you to consider the author's purpose and methods instead of right-or-wrong grammar and usage issues. One notable exception to the rule that Rhetorical Skills questions generally come with question stems is the category of questions that we call *Connections*. We will discuss more about Connections questions in the next section.

Writing Strategy Questions

Writing Strategy questions always appear with a question stem. A Strategy question asks you to choose which phrasing most effectively accomplishes a particular purpose. The most important thing you need to do is to *consider the question stem carefully!* You must read actively, and often it helps to "think with your pencil." When you read the question stem, think about which words most clearly express what the particular question is asking for. Quickly underline those words to help you focus. When you focus clearly on what the question is asking, the best answer will usually stand out among the offered choices.

In the following Strategy question, underline the key words in the stem *before* looking at the answer choices:

> The biologist <u>worked painstakingly for more than a year</u> before her research project
> **(20)**
> yielded any publishable results.

20. Which of the following options most effectively conveys that the biologist relied on cooperation with other scientists?

   (F)   NO CHANGE
   (G)   needed to discuss methodology with her colleagues
   (H)   planned many experiments
   (J)   needed to order several pieces of costly equipment

If you focused on the words *conveys that the biologist relied on cooperation with other scientists,* it's likely that option G jumped out as the best answer. Options F, H, and J are not incorrect for any grammatical reasons, but they do not fulfill the purpose identified by this question stem. When you're answering Writing Strategy questions, it's helpful to know that, for these questions, the test maker doesn't put ungrammatical or otherwise incorrect language in the answer choices. If you read through the answer choices looking for what sounds best, you won't get very far. The question stem of a Strategy question is crucial, so read it carefully before you look at the answer choices.

> For most Writing Strategy questions, you can find a key phrase in the question stem. Get in the habit of looking for a key phrase and underlining it to help you focus on what the question is asking for.

Two kinds of Writing Strategy questions for which you will *not* find a key phrase to underline in the question stem are questions that ask about the effect of adding or deleting a certain phrase or sentence. For questions that ask about deletion, focus on the given phrase, asking yourself what effect it creates for you as a reader. Consider the example:

> The construction site was littered with debris. Scraps of wood, drywall, and various types of nails were scattered on the ground. Even large sheets of roofing materials, some still packaged as they came from the supplier, were lying against the unfinished exterior walls. [21]

21. The author is considering deleting the following sentence:

    Scraps of wood, drywall, and various types of nails were scattered on the ground.

    What would be lost if the author made this deletion?

    (A) Information about how long the building site had been unattended.

    (B) A description of what materials are needed in construction.

    (C) A suggestion about how to clean the site.

    (D) Specific details that provide information about what the site looks like.

To answer this question, consider the given sentence in the context of the passage. The previous sentence describes the site as *littered with debris,* and the sentence in question lists items that make up that debris. Because it offers specific details describing the debris, option D is the best answer. If you focus on the given sentence's relation to the sentences around it and how it adds to your understanding of the author's purpose, you shouldn't fall for the wrong answer traps.

> For Writing Strategy questions that ask about the effect of deleting information, consider the context and determine how the information contributes to the writer's purpose.

Organization Questions

Organization questions test your understanding of logical sequence. It's easy to recognize an Organization question, because it usually involves sentences or paragraphs that are labeled with bracketed numbers in the text of the passage. Some Organization questions ask you to rearrange the order of the sentences within the paragraph (think of these as scrambled sentences questions) or the order of the paragraphs within the whole passage (think of these as scrambled paragraphs questions). Other Organization questions present a sentence to be added to the passage, and then ask you to determine the best location for it.

The important thing to keep in mind about Organization questions is that *they are based on logic.* The test maker can't present an Organization question unless there is a clearly discernable order to the particular paragraph or passage. Remember that each question on the ACT can have only one possible correct answer. Therefore, the way to succeed with an Organization question is, first, to recognize that it's testing logical sequence, and then to search carefully in the passage for particular words and phrases that provide the key to the correct sequence.

Sometimes a passage is organized according to a rough outline structure. For example, in a passage on nutrition, you might find separate paragraphs that discuss proteins, carbohydrates, fats, and antioxidants. If you were asked where to add a sentence about the antioxidant potential of a particular fruit, you'd put it in the fourth paragraph, the one focusing on antioxidants. Remember to use your reading skills to help you find the best answer to a question like that.

Another organizational format is the chronological sequence. As you read through an English passage that includes an organization question, be alert for specific dates and time references, such as *in 1750* or *before the American Revolution.* Dates and time references can serve as key clues when you need to determine the best location to add new information.

Another organizational format, similar to the chronological one, is the description of stages in a process. As you read, notice words such as *first, second, then, next, last,* and *finally.* These words serve as clues to help you keep track of sequencing and can be useful if you need to find the best spot in the passage to add information.

As you work on this ACT-like Organization question, underline key words that help you determine the logical sequence as in the example:

> [1] If you're like most people, you may find that applying to college is a complicated process. [2] This in itself can be time-consuming; you need to search through guide-books, learn about colleges from their websites, and talk to admissions officers at college fairs. [3] You also need to take standardized tests and continue to maintain your high school grade point average. [4] Then, by the fall of your senior year, you must actually start filling out applications and arranging to have supporting documentation sent to the colleges.

22. Upon reviewing the paragraph and realizing that some information has been left out, the writer composes the following sentence:

    The first challenge is to narrow down a list of places you'd like to study.

    The most logical placement for this sentence would be

    (F)   before sentence 1.

    (G)   after sentence 1.

    (H)   after sentence 2.

    (J)   after sentence 3.

Did you find any words to underline in the paragraph? The word *then* in sentence 4, is one indicator of sequence. The sentence to be added, which is stated in the question stem, also contains a sequence clue: *first.* This word indicates that the sentence should most likely be added somewhere near the beginning of the paragraph. Plug the new sentence into the passage at the locations described by the answer choices, and think about how it sounds in each context. Notice that sentence 1 introduces the topic of the paragraph. Therefore, it wouldn't make sense to place the additional sentence before that. Read the new sentence after sentence 1, and continue reading sentence 2. The additional sentence fits perfectly here because sentence 2 lists several things that must be done in order to *narrow down a list of places.* You can quickly plug the sentence in at the other locations if you have time, but you should feel pretty confident that you've found the best answer in option G.

When you notice that a passage is presented with numbered paragraphs (the numbers will be in brackets, centered above each paragraph), be aware as you're working through the passage that the paragraphs may not be printed in the most logical order. The other possibility when a passage is printed with numbered paragraphs is that a later question will ask where in the passage is most appropriate to add extra information. If such a question is present for the passage, the paragraphs will be printed in the most logical order, and you will not see a scrambled paragraphs question for this passage.

For an Organization question that asks you to determine the best ordering of paragraphs, there are several points you should consider. First, glance at each paragraph to determine its topic. You might want to make a brief note in the margin or circle a word or phrase in each paragraph to help you identify the main idea. Second, ask yourself which of the paragraphs sounds like it would make the best introduction to the passage. Third, ask yourself which paragraph sounds most like a concluding paragraph. Usually, simply identifying the most logical introductory and concluding paragraphs is enough to let you determine the best sequence for all the paragraphs. Sometimes, you may have to consider the topics and relationships among the body paragraphs as well.

Consider the following scrambled paragraphs question. Even though we give you only the skeleton of a passage to work with, you should be able to find clues that allow you to determine the best sequence for the paragraphs.

[1]

Carbohydrates in food . . .

[2]

Protein comes from several sources . . .

[3]

With each passing decade, scientists learn more about how the components of food affect our health. Nutrition researchers have been aware of the basic building blocks, fats, carbohydrates, and proteins, for years. Fats are . . . .

[4]

While nutritionists have been studying the three building blocks of food for years, they frequently turn their attention to new areas. Cholesterol, for example, came to the attention of nutritionists in the 1970's. It was discovered that heart disease . . .

[5]

In another development in nutrition, antioxidants began creating a stir in 2000 when . . .

Question 23 asks about the preceding passage as a whole.

---

23. For the sake of logic and coherence, paragraph 3 should be placed

   (A) where it is now.
   (B) before paragraph 1.
   (C) after paragraph 1.
   (D) after paragraph 5.

Remember, an Organization question is testing your reading skills. Start by thinking about how paragraph 3 relates to the topics of the other paragraphs. Paragraph 1 discusses carbohydrates; paragraph 2 discusses proteins; paragraph 4 treats cholesterol; and the topic of paragraph 5 is antioxidants. Now read paragraph 3 carefully. Notice the second sentence: it mentions *carbohydrates* and *proteins*, topics of two of the other paragraphs. Therefore, paragraph 3 would make a good first paragraph because it introduces, at least partially, the rough outline structure of the passage. The best answer is option B.

Connections Questions

Connections questions differ from the other types of Rhetorical Skills questions in that they generally don't appear with a question stem. Therefore, one of the most helpful things you can do to answer Connections questions correctly is to learn to recognize certain connections words and phrases that appear frequently on the ACT. To find the best connections word or phrase to use in a specific context, you must read carefully in the nonunderlined part of the passage. Sometimes you need to read only the sentence that contains the underlined portion, but sometimes you must go back and carefully read the sentence before it as well.

Connections words and phrases are those that express a relationship between ideas. The two most common types of connections tested on the ACT are cause and effect connections and contrast connections. Other connections that are tested are sequence and emphasis. You should thoroughly familiarize yourself with the words and phrases in the following table. Whenever you see a connections word underlined, you can expect that the other answer choices will also be various connections words and phrases. Spotting a connections word on the ACT is a red flag that you need to think about logical relationships.

Connections Words and Phrases	
Connections that show addition, continuation, emphasis, or examples	additionally
	and
	for example
	for instance
	furthermore
	indeed
	in addition
	in fact
	likewise
	moreover
Connections that show cause and effect	as a result
	because
	consequently
	leading to
	since
	so
	therefore
	thus

Connections that show contrast	although
	but
	despite
	even though
	however
	nevertheless
	on the other hand
	rather
	though
	whereas
	while
Connections that show sequence	finally
	first
	if . . . then
	last
	later
	next
	second
	then

Let's look at some examples of how connections words and phrases are tested on the ACT.

24. Many of my friends enjoy team sports; <u>however</u>, I prefer individual activities such as running and yoga.

   (F)   NO CHANGE
   (G)   but
   (H)   therefore
   (J)   in addition

If you train yourself to recognize the connections words and phrases shown in the table, you'll have no trouble identifying that this question tests connections. Whenever you notice that a connections word or phrase is underlined, read carefully in the surrounding context to determine how the ideas are related. This sentence has two parts. The first is *many of my friends enjoy team sports.* The second is *I prefer individual activities.* Ask yourself how the two ideas are related. Because *team sports* are different from *individual activities,* the relationship is one of contrast. When you first read the sentence it should sound logical because *however* is a contrast connection. Indeed, option F is the best answer here. You can eliminate options H and J because they do not express contrast. Option G does express contrast, but it is not appropriate here because a semicolon is used between the two independent clauses.

25. <u>Although</u> she has a strong interest in Renaissance art, Elizabeth is eagerly anticipating her trip to Rome.

    (A)   NO CHANGE
    (B)   While
    (C)   Because
    (D)   Indeed

The presence of an underlined connections word here should alert you that you need to consider the relationship between ideas in the sentence. There are two ideas here: Elizabeth's interest in Renaissance art and her eager anticipation of her trip to Rome. Ask yourself how these ideas are connected. There is a lot of Renaissance art in Rome, so Elizabeth's interest in it leads her to be excited about visiting there. The relationship is one of cause and effect. You can eliminate option A because it's a contrast connection. Eliminate option B for the same reason. Eliminate option D because it's an emphasis connection. Option C is the best answer.

26. Restricting sodium in the diet is important to protecting one's health. A main source of dietary sodium is that found in canned, microwavable, and other prepared foods. <u>Despite this</u>, another source is the salt people add to their own food at the table.

    (F)   NO CHANGE
    (G)   However
    (H)   In addition
    (J)   For example

The underlined portion here is a connections phrase, one that shows contrast. Read the surrounding context carefully to determine if that is the appropriate kind of connection here. In this case, you must read not only the sentence that contains the underlined portion, but the sentence before it as well. The previous sentence lists one source of dietary sodium. The sentence containing the underlined segment lists *another source*. The appropriate connection here is one that expresses addition or continuation. Option H is the only one of the answer choices that expresses continuation, so it's the best answer. Eliminate options F and G because they're contrast connections. Eliminate option J because it indicates an example rather than addition or continuation.

27. I would have called you, <u>rather</u> I couldn't because I lost my cell phone.

    (A)   NO CHANGE
    (B)   but
    (C)   moreover
    (D)   while

What do you do when you notice a connections word underlined? You're right, you read the sentence looking for the relationship between ideas! Here, ask yourself how losing the cell phone is related to not calling. The writer is saying that *if* she'd had her cell phone, she would have called. Not having the phone prevented the calling. The appropriate kind of connection here is contrast. This question illustrates the importance of reading the answer choices into the sentence. Notice that option A, *rather*, is indeed a contrast connection, but it doesn't sound right here. Option D, *while,* is also a contrast connection that doesn't work in the context. Option B, a contrast connection that fits perfectly in the context, is the best answer. Eliminate option C because it's not a contrast connection.

Once you learn to recognize the various connections words, you should have no trouble with Connections questions on the ACT. Just let the presence of any underlined connections word remind you to consider the kind of logical relationship expressed in the sentence. Don't worry if a question includes more than one choice that's in the right category of connections. If that's the case, your ear will tell you which one is appropriate.

Wordiness Questions

Wordiness questions on the ACT can be tricky if you're not prepared for them. As you work through the English section, it's important to remember that *concise writing is valued on the ACT.* In other words, sometimes one answer choice will be better than another *simply because it's shorter.* It can be easy to lose sight of this fact when you're working through the English section encountering so many questions—such as the Mechanics questions—that seem to have clear right-or-wrong answers.

There are two types of wordiness errors you can expect to see on the ACT. The first type is *redundancy.* Redundancy means saying the same thing twice, not literally, but saying something one way and then repeating the meaning in different words. For example:

> My little brother worked hard on and put a lot of effort into
> building his sand castle.

You probably noticed here that *worked hard on* and *put a lot of effort into* mean pretty much the same thing. Only one phrase or the other should be used, not both. Remember, when you say the same thing twice *and you repeat yourself,* you're being redundant!

Fortunately for you, many redundancy questions come with a built-in clue that wordiness is the tested issue: the "OMIT the underlined portion" answer choice. Whenever you see that "OMIT" is provided as an option, always start by asking yourself: Is the underlined portion truly necessary and would anything valuable be lost if the underlined portion were taken out? If the answers to these questions are "no," then you can confidently select OMIT as the best answer choice. You should note that OMIT, if it's offered as an answer choice, always appears as the fourth option. (Remember, the ACT is highly predictable!)

Questions with OMIT as the last option come with an added bonus. They can save you time! It means you often have to consider only two, not four, answer choices. If you read through a question and notice that OMIT is a choice, and if you determine that the underlined portion can indeed be omitted, then that's your answer. If you're going to leave something out, you don't have to choose the best way to word it, so you don't need to consider the middle two answer choices. Let's look at an example here:

28. My older sister, <u>who is a sibling of mine,</u> is studying to be a surgeon.

    (F)   NO CHANGE
    (G)   who is of course one of my relatives,
    (H)   one of my siblings,
    (J)   OMIT the underlined portion.

First notice that OMIT is an answer choice. Remember, that's your clue to ask yourself whether the underlined portion is necessary! Read around the context to see if the underlined information is already expressed by other, nonunderlined words. That is the case here, because a sister, by definition, is a sibling. You can eliminate option F and know that option J is the best choice *without even taking the time to read* options G and H.

Now let's consider another kind of Wordiness question, one that is not always as easy to recognize. This second kind of question is the Wordiness question for which OMIT is not offered as an answer choice. For this kind, you don't have the handy red flag to alert you that wordiness is the issue. Generally, instead of redundancy, this type of question tests *verbosity.* Verbosity means using more words than are necessary. Verbosity results when a long, drawn-out expression is used in place of a shorter one. Read this verbose sentence, and come up with a shorter way of expressing its meaning:

> The student council held a meeting for the purpose of determining what would be the most profitable kind of fund-raising event.

_____

_____

_____

Here's a more concise way to express the idea: The student council met to determine the most profitable kind of fund-raising event. You may have come up with a different version. The key thing is to notice the wordy phrases that could be replaced with shorter alternatives. Here's how a verbosity question might look on the ACT:

29. Jonathon wanted to write his history paper in the <u>amount of time that would be the shortest possible</u>.

    (A)   NO CHANGE
    (B)   way that would take up the smallest amount of his time possible
    (C)   in the least possible time
    (D)   time that would be the least he could possibly spend on it.

You may or may not notice wordiness as the issue here when you read the underlined portion. The problem with a wordy construction isn't grammatical (and grammatical issues are often easier to spot). Wordiness is a style issue, and that's more subtle. Therefore, you should always work through an English passage remembering that the best ACT style is *concise.* While there's no OMIT choice to serve as a warning here, there is another clue you might notice: option C is considerably shorter than the other answer choices. When this is the case, it's often an indication that the issue is wordiness. If you can't determine anything really wrong with one or more answer choices, choose the shortest one. There's a good chance you'll be right. In this question, option C is the correct answer because it's most concise. Eliminate the three other options because they're verbose.

Let's look at one more example of an ACT Wordiness question. In this one, the sentence is wordy because it's redundant, but you won't find OMIT as an answer choice:

30. The intricate figures along the edge of the garden were <u>created and sculpted by</u> the owner of the house.

    (F)   NO CHANGE

    (G)   sculpted by

    (H)   were the creative work of a sculptor who is

    (J)   the original creation of

Let's look at some ways you can identify that this question tests wordiness, even though OMIT is not the last answer choice. First, if you're reading carefully, your ear will tell you that *created and sculpted* is redundant, so you can eliminate option F. Here, although *created* doesn't mean exactly the same thing as *sculpted,* the idea of *created* is part of the definition of *sculpted.* Second, you should notice that option G is shorter than all the others are. Remember, when the meaning of the options is basically the same, you should always go with the most concise one. Option G is the best answer here. Eliminate option H because it's both redundant (using *creative* and *sculptor,* similarly to option F) and verbose. Eliminate option J because it's not as concise as option G.

Passives

Like wordiness, the issue of passives relates to writing style. For matters of style, you have to use judgment to determine which choice sounds best; you can't simply apply a rule. Most sentences in English are worded in what we call the *active voice.* When a sentence is in the active voice, the subject of the sentence is the person or thing doing whatever action the verb expresses. On the other hand, when a sentence is in the passive voice, the subject of the verb is *receiving* the action instead of *doing* it. In other words, when an active sentence is written in the passive, the subject becomes an object. Some examples will make the difference clear. In the following sentences, the subjects are printed in upper case and the objects are underlined.

        Active Voice: My FAMILY packed the <u>car</u> carefully before we left for vacation.
        Passive Voice: The CAR was packed carefully by my <u>family</u> before we left for
                vacation.
        Active Voice: My AUNT gave me a new <u>phone</u>.
        Passive Voice: A new PHONE was given to me by my <u>aunt</u>.

Most of the time, we speak and write in the active voice. The active voice puts the emphasis on the subject, which is desirable most of the time. Occasionally, a speaker or writer who wants to emphasize the object, rather than the subject, chooses to use the passive voice. Generally speaking, however, it's preferable to use the active voice. Once in a while, you may come across an ACT question that tests whether you can recognize this. Here's an example:

31. <u>Her knowledge of knitting having been taught to me by my grandmother, I have expanded my skills even further.</u>

    (A)   NO CHANGE
    (B)   My grandmother taught me everything she knows about knitting, and I have expanded my skills even further.
    (C)   Having been taught everything she knows by my grandmother, my knowledge of knitting has been expanded even further.
    (D)   My grandmother taught me everything she knows about knitting, and my knowledge has been expanded by my own reading.

In option A, the preposition *by* alerts you to check for the passive voice. The verb in the first part of the sentence is *taught.* The grammatical subject is *knowledge.* The person doing the teaching, however, is *my grandmother.* Because the subject is not doing the action, this is a passive construction. Examine the answer choices to see if an active voice wording is offered. It is. In option B, both the first and second parts of the sentence are written in the active voice, so option B is the best answer. In option C, in the second part of the sentence, the verb is *has been expanded* and the subject is *knowledge,* but it's not knowledge that is doing the expanding. The same thing is true in the second part of option D, which also has *knowledge* as the subject and *has been expanded* as the verb.

You should note that while the active voice is preferable if all other things are equal, there are some situations in which other grammatical issues make the passive voice the only correct choice. The most common instance is in a sentence that begins with a modifying phrase. Consider this example:

32. Tattered and worn after years of use, <u>the old book of poems was still treasured by my grandfather.</u>

    (F)   NO CHANGE
    (G)   the poems in the old book were still treasured by my grandfather
    (H)   my grandfather still treasured the old book of poems
    (J)   the poems were treasured by my grandfather in the old book.

The word *by* in the underlined portion is a clue that the expression is in the passive voice. Remember, though, it's not an absolute rule that the passive voice is always wrong. Sometimes, as in this question, the nonunderlined part of the sentence leaves you with no choice but to go with a passive construction. Option F is actually the best answer here. Let's look at the other options to see what's wrong with them. Option G starts with *the poems.* Think about this in light of the context. The opening part of the sentence, *tattered and worn after years of use,* is an introductory modifier. Remember from the Mechanics section that it *is* a rule that when a sentence opens with a modifier, the thing it logically describes must be the next noun in the sentence. Eliminate option G because it is not *the poems* that are *tattered and worn,* but the *book.* Similarly, option H, although written in the active voice, creates an illogical situation. (The meaning here is not that it's *my grandfather* who is *tattered and worn after years of use.*) Consider option J. Like option F, it is written in the passive voice, but the phrase *in the old book* is not placed where it should be, after *poems.* For all these reasons, option F is the best answer.

Chapter Four: **English Practice Set I**

Directions: In the following passage, certain words and phrases have been underlined and numbered. You will find alternatives for each underlined portion in the column to the right. Select the one that best expresses the idea, that makes the statement acceptable in standard written English, or that is phrased most consistently with the style and tone of the entire passage. If you feel that the original version is best, select "NO CHANGE." You will also find questions asking about a section of the passage or about the entire passage. For these questions, decide which choice gives the most appropriate response to the given question. For each question in the test, select the best choice, and fill in the corresponding space on the answer folder. You may wish to read each passage through before you begin to answer the questions associated with it. Most answers cannot be determined without reading several sentences around the phrases in question. Make sure to read far enough ahead each time you choose an alternative.

THE WEDDING CAKE HOUSE

Locals in Kennebunk, Maine, have built up a legend around <u>an unusually 19th-</u>
<u>century house</u> in that seaside town. <u>In contrast to</u> the frothy white ornamentation that
(1)
(2)
covers much of the house's exterior, it is known as the Wedding Cake House. Building
on this name, <u>the wooden carvings were made, the legend suggests, by a newly-wed</u>
(3)
<u>sea captain</u>, who plied his woodworking talent <u>during lonely hours at sea</u>
(4)
to surprise his bride upon his return home.

The <u>reality is that the</u> truth about the house departs from the appealing legend
(5)
about the lovelorn sailor. The owner of the house, shipbuilder George Washington
<u>Bourne, brought his bride, Jane</u>, to the house in 1825. The original house was an
(6)
example of the balance and <u>typifying symmetry on</u> the Federalist architecture of the
(7)

KAPLAN

time. The two-story house, with a low hipped roof, multiple large casement windows spanning the front facade, and <u>the area above the front door taken up by a large</u>
(8)
<u>Palladian window</u>, exemplified geometrical balance. The elaborate frosting-like designs <u>being</u> a later addition to this neoclassical house, though they didn't come about in the
(9)
way the romantic legend describes.

[1] The transformation of the house from an example of neoclassic restraint to a building with so many Gothic overlays that it looked like a wedding cake <u>resulting from</u>
(10)
an accident. [2] In 1852, <u>a fire destroyed the barn and shed</u> that were connected to the
(11)
house. [3] The shipbuilder, now retired, <u>decided on spending</u> his leisure hours carving
(12)
wooden trim that he could apply to the main house so that its style, on the surface at least, <u>would harmonize with</u> the style of his new Gothic barn. [4] Thus, the Wedding
(13)
Cake House is technically not an example of the Gothic architecture it appears to emulate; <u>moreover,</u> it remains a neoclassical Federal style house that displays multiple touches of
(14)
Gothic <u>styling: buttresses arches cornices, and pinnacles.</u> ⌐16⌐
(15)

1.   (A)   NO CHANGE
     (B)   a house unusually of the 19th century
     (C)   a house unusual of the 19th century
     (D)   an unusual 19th-century house

2.   (F)   NO CHANGE
     (G)   Because of
     (H)   Despite
     (J)   A consequence of

3.   (A)   NO CHANGE
     (B)   a newly-wed sea captain, the legend suggests, made the wooden carvings
     (C)   the legend suggests that the elaborate wooden carvings were made by a newly-wed sea captain
     (D)   it has been suggested according to the legend that the wooden carvings were made by a newly-wed sea captain

4. The author is considering deleting the underlined phrase. If this deletion were made, the essay would primarily lose

    (F)   a fact that describes the house.

    (G)   a detail that enhances the romantic nature of the legend.

    (H)   relevant information about the sea-captain's job

    (J)   a historical detail.

5.   (A)   NO CHANGE

    (B)   reality of the situation is that

    (C)   actual honest

    (D)   OMIT the underlined portion.

6.   (F)   NO CHANGE

    (G)   Bourne, brought, his bride Jane,

    (H)   Bourne brought his bride Jane,

    (J)   Bourne brought his bride, Jane

7.   (A)   NO CHANGE

    (B)   symmetry that was typical on

    (C)   symmetrical type of

    (D)   symmetry that typified

8.   (F)   NO CHANGE

    (G)   a large Palladian window occupying the area above the front door

    (H)   the area above the front door being occupied by a large Palladian window

    (J)   taking up the area by above the front door, a large Palladian window

9.   (A)   NO CHANGE

    (B)   were being

    (C)   were

    (D)   making up a

10.   (F)   NO CHANGE

    (G)   was being caused by

    (H)   had been causing by

    (J)   was the result of

11.   (A)   NO CHANGE

    (B)   the barn and shed were destroyed by a fire

    (C)   the barn and shed burning down

    (D)   a fire destroying the barn and shed

12. (F) NO CHANGE
    (G) decided to spend
    (H) decided that to spend
    (J) deciding he would spend

13. (A) NO CHANGE
    (B) be in harmony to
    (C) create the appearance of harmony with
    (D) harmonizes with

14. (F) NO CHANGE
    (G) however
    (H) rather
    (J) therefore

15. (A) NO CHANGE
    (B) styling; buttresses, arches, cornices, and pinnacles
    (C) styling, buttresses: arches, cornices, and pinnacles
    (D) styling: buttresses, arches, cornices, and pinnacles

16. Upon reviewing this paragraph and finding that some information has been left out, the writer composes the following sentence incorporating that information:

    Bourne, well-traveled and an admirer of the Gothic architecture he had seen in Europe, rebuilt the barn with five tall pinnacles reminiscent of those on the Milan cathedral.

    This sentence most logically be placed after sentence

    (F) 1.
    (G) 2.
    (H) 3.
    (J) 4.

    Question 17 asks about the preceding passage as a whole.
    ---

17. Suppose the writer's goal had been to write a brief essay describing a house with features of two different architectural styles. Would this essay fulfill that goal?

    (A) Yes, because the Wedding Cake House includes elements from both the Federalist and the Gothic styles.
    (B) Yes, because the original Federalist style house was associated with a legend.
    (C) No, because the Wedding Cake House was originally built in the Federalist style.
    (D) No, because the carvings that gave the Wedding Cake House its name are in only the Gothic style.

ANSWERS AND EXPLANATIONS

1. D
2. G
3. C
4. G
5. D
6. F
7. D
8. G
9. C
10. J
11. A
12. G
13. A
14. H
15. D
16. G
17. A

1. **The best answer is D.** The issue is word choice. Option A incorrectly uses the adverb *unusually* to modify the adjective *19th-century.* If you recognize this error, your eye will probably be drawn to option D, which corrects the modifier error. Just to make sure, plug in the other two choices. Eliminate option B because it incorrectly uses the adverb *unusually* to modify the noun *house.* Eliminate option C because *unusual of* is the wrong idiom (*unusual for* is correct) and because it's wordy.

2. **The best answer is G.** The issue is connections. You should recognize that the underlined segment, *in contrast to,* is a connections phrase. That's a signal to read the sentence carefully for meaning and look for what the logical connection between ideas is. Here, *the frothy white ornamentation* on *the house's exterior* provides the reason that the house is called the Wedding Cake House. The relationship is one of cause and effect. Having identified this, you can eliminate options F and J, both of which are contrast connections. To decide between options G and J, plug them into the sentence. Option J is not as concise as option G, so option G is the best of the four choices.

3. **The best answer is C.** The issue is sentence sense. Pay attention here to the nonunderlined context. Ask yourself what the introductory modifier, *building on this name,* is describing. Logically, that word must come next in the sentence. It is *the legend* that builds *on this name.* Only option C makes legend follow the phrase that describes it, so option C is correct.

4. **The best answer is G.** The issue is writing strategy. Think about the meaning expressed by the phrase under consideration, *during lonely hours at sea.* Read through the answer choices to see which one works. Option F is wrong because the phrase does not describe the house. Option G is the best because it makes the reader think of the sea captain missing his bride.

Option H may be tempting, because the sea captain's job does include *lonely hours at sea,* but the paragraph's focus is more on the sea captain and his bride than it is on his job. Option J is wrong because the phrase does not include a historical detail.

5. **The best answer is D.**   The issue is wordiness. Remember, whenever OMIT is an option, consider it first. The sentence makes sense without the underlined phrase. Indeed, the word *reality* in options A and B repeats the idea of *truth* in the nonunderlined portion. Option C is also redundant. There is no need to say *actual honest* before *truth.* Option D is the best answer.

6. **The best answer is F.**   The issue is punctuation. This sentence contains two nonessential phrases that must be set off by commas. The basic part of the sentence is *The owner of the house . . . brought his bride . . . to the house in 1825.* The descriptive phrase *shipbuilder George Washington Bourne* and the name *Jane* are both nonessential information. Option F correctly uses commas to set off this nonessential information. A comma in option G incorrectly separates the verb *brought* from its object *his bride.* Option H is incorrect because it leaves out the two necessary commas after *Bourne* and *bride.* Option J is incorrect because it omits the necessary comma after *Bourne.* The best answer is option F.

7. **The best answer is D.**   The issue is word choice. The phase *symmetry on* is not idiomatically correct here. Identifying that lets you eliminate options A and B. Read the other two choices into the sentence. Though the phrase *symmetry of* would be the correct idiom, option C *symmetrical type of* doesn't make sense. Option D is the best answer.

8. **The best answer is G.**   The issue is sentence sense, specifically parallelism. Check the nonunderlined context. This sentence includes a list that starts *a low hipped* **roof,** *multiple large casement* **windows.** *. . .* Because the list is made up of nouns that describe features of the house, parallelism is best established by putting *large Palladian* **window** next in the list. If you recognize this, you can eliminate every option except option G. Option H repeats the parallelism error in option F. Option J is better than options F and H, but it still doesn't establish parallelism as clearly as option G. Option G is the best answer.

9. **The best answer is C.**   The issue is sentence sense. Whenever you notice an *–ing* verb underlined, check to make sure that, if it is used as the main verb in a clause, it has a helping verb with it. Option A is incorrect because *being* is used here without a helping verb as the main verb of the sentence. Eliminate option D for the same reason. Plug the remaining choices into the sentence. Eliminate option B because *being* is not necessary with *were.* Option C is the best answer.

10. **The best answer is J.**   The issue is sentence sense. Option F uses the *–ing* verb *resulting* as the main verb of the clause without a helping verb, so eliminate it. Read the other choices. Option G is wordy because the word *being* is not necessary here. Option H is wrong because *had been causing* is not the right verb form in context. Option J is the best answer.

11. **The best answer is A.**   The issues are sentence sense and passives. The best answer is option A. Option B is not the best answer because the statement is in the passive voice. Eliminate option C because it uses *burning,* an *–ing* verb, without a helping verb, as the main verb in a clause. Eliminate option D because it also uses an *–ing* verb, *destroying,* as the main verb without a helping verb.

12. **The best answer is G.**   The issues are sentence sense and idioms. You should be able to recognize that option F, *decided* **on spending,** is not the correct idiomatic usage. Option G, *decided*

to spend, corrects the idiom error and is the best choice. Read option H into the sentence. You should hear that it creates sentence structure problems. Eliminate option J because it uses the *–ing* verb *deciding* as the main verb of a clause. The best choice is option G.

13. **The best answer is A.** The issues are idioms, wordiness, and sentence sense. There is no error in option A, so it is the best answer. Read the other choices into the sentence to confirm this. Option B contains incorrect idiomatic usage, *be in harmony to*, and is wordy. Option C is wordy. Option D uses the present tense *harmonizes* and so is not consistent with the context of the passage, which requires a past tense verb here.

14. **The best answer is H.** The issue is connections. Whenever you notice a connections word underlined, such as *moreover* here, remember that you need to read the sentence carefully for meaning to determine the best logical connection. Option F, *moreover,* is a transition that expresses emphasis, which is not appropriate here. The first part of the sentence states that the Wedding Cake House is not an example of Gothic architecture. The second part states that the house's style is neoclassical federal. This calls for a contrast connection. Eliminate option J, *therefore,* because it is a cause-and-effect connection. Options G and H are both contrast transitions, but you must read them in the sentence to tell which is best. Option H, *rather,* sounds best in the context here.

15. **The best answer is D.** The issue is punctuation. Notice that option A uses a colon to introduce a list. This is correct, but there is another problem here. The word *buttresses,* one of the items in the list, needs to be followed by a comma. Eliminate option A. Having identified that the colon is correct, you should be drawn to option D as the best answer. It corrects the comma problem in option A. Option B is incorrect because it uses a semicolon when what follows is not an independent clause. Option C is incorrect because it puts the colon in the wrong place.

16. **The best answer is G.** The issue is organization. The best way to handle a question like this is to read the sentence to be added into the passage at the locations indicated by the answer choices. Option F seems a possibility, but it is not the best answer. Option G is the best. The additional sentence introduces Bourne's Gothic-style barn, so it makes sense to add this sentence *before* the existing mention of the *new Gothic barn.* Eliminate option H because the *new Gothic barn* has already been mentioned in sentence 3. Eliminate option J because sentence 4 discusses the house, not the barn. Option G is the best answer.

17. **The best answer is A.** The issue is writing strategy. The key words to focus on in the question stem are *describing a house with features of two different architectural styles.* The essay certainly does this, so eliminate options C and D. Now look at the reasons given in options A and B. The reason provided in option A relates directly to the question asked in the question stem, so option A is the correct answer. The reason given in option B is true according to the essay, but it doesn't address the question in the question stem.

Chapter Five: **English Practice Set II**

Directions: In the following passage, certain words and phrases have been underlined and numbered. You will find alternatives for each underlined portion in the column on the right. Select the one that best expresses the idea, that makes the statement acceptable in standard written English, or that is phrased most consistently with the style and tone of the entire passage. If you feel that the original version is best, select "NO CHANGE." You will also find questions asking about a section of the passage or about the entire passage. For these questions, decide which choice gives the most appropriate response to the given question. For each question in the test, select the best choice, and fill in the corresponding space on the answer folder. You may wish to read each passage through before you begin to answer the questions associated with it. Most answers cannot be determined without reading several sentences around the phrases in question. Make sure to read far enough ahead each time you choose an alternative.

FANTASY LITERATURE: IT'S MORE THAN HARRY POTTER

[1]

J. K. Rowling, author of the immensely popular Harry Potter series, has wrought her own special magic in the fantasy genre. Though she may be the best-known fantasy writer to the current <u>generation, she</u> is hardly the first. A number of others, <u>many of which,</u>
(1)   (2)
like Rowling, are British, were writing fantasy novels before J. K. Rowling was born.

[2]

One such writer is George MacDonald, a Scottish minister, best known for his novels *Phantastes* and *Lilith*. MacDonald's work, <u>similar to Rowlings',</u> showed that fantasy
(3)
literature could hold appeal for older children and even adults. In *Phantastes*, a young man named Anodos journeys through a fantasy land where he experiences magical adventures. <u>While</u> *Phantastes* is a relatively light story, *Lilith*, a much later work by MacDonald, is a
(4)
<u>more darker and more provocative</u> tale. In this <u>novel a character, called</u> Mr. Vane travels
(5)   (6)

through a fantasy land. There he encounters Lilith, an attractive but troubling fairy princess. In describing Mr. Vane's experiences, MacDonald explores the questions of <u>how meaning is found in the condition of being human</u> and how redemption might be possible.
(7)

[3]

<u>Another British fantasy writer,</u> C. S. Lewis, acknowledged <u>the fact that he felt indebted to</u>
(8) (9)
George MacDonald. It was MacDonald's mythmaking, rather than his writing style, that Lewis admired. Lewis's *Chronicles of Narnia*, a tale with mythic power, is a group of seven books tied together <u>more than</u> the fictional world they describe than by the
(10)
narration of a particular character's experiences. Narnia is a magical place where animals can talk and <u>time seemed to progress</u> at its own rate. Like Harry Potter and his
(11)
mates at Hogwarts, the characters <u>whom inhabit</u> Narnia struggle with the conflicting
(12)
forces of good and evil.

[4]

Yet another fantasy series, occupying fewer printed pages <u>but</u> treating its material in
(13)
the same broad scope that Rowling does, is J. R. R. Tolkien's *Lord of the Rings*. Here, the tension <u>between good and evil are</u> played out in epic scale; the series describes a
(14)
fellowship of seven characters who journey together in a quest to dispose properly of the ring in the title. As Lewis does with Narnia, Tolkien <u>was inventing</u> a universe,
(15)
which he calls Middle Earth, and peoples it with a range of characters from mortal humans to <u>immortal elves</u> and horrifying creatures called "orcs" and "uruk-hai."
(16)

1. (A) NO CHANGE
   (B) generation: she
   (C) generation; she
   (D) generation. She

2. (F) NO CHANGE
   (G) of which many
   (H) many of whom,
   (J) many being those whom

3. (A) NO CHANGE
   (B) like Rowling's
   (C) as with Rowlings'
   (D) like with Rowling's

4. (F) NO CHANGE
   (G) Because
   (H) Despite that
   (J) Given that

5. (A) NO CHANGE
   (B) most provocatively dark
   (C) darker and most provocative
   (D) a darker and more provocative

6. (F) NO CHANGE
   (G) novel, a character called
   (H) novel a character called
   (J) novel, a character called,

7. (A) NO CHANGE
   (B) human nature and what that means
   (C) what it means to be human
   (D) how being human has meaning

8. The writer is considering deleting the underlined portion. If this deletion were made, the paragraph would primarily lose
   (F) a description of C. S. Lewis's work.
   (G) a fact about C. S. Lewis's ethnic origin.
   (H) a phrase that relates C. S. Lewis to the novelists discussed above.
   (J) a description showing contrast between C. S. Lewis and George MacDonald.

9. (A) NO CHANGE
   (B) his feelings of owing a debt
   (C) his feeling of indebtedness
   (D) that indeed he felt indebted

10. (F) NO CHANGE
    (G) rather more than
    (H) more by
    (J) more with

11. (A) NO CHANGE
    (B) time progresses
    (C) time would be progressing
    (D) the progress of time is

12. (F) NO CHANGE
    (G) which inhabits
    (H) who inhabits
    (J) who inhabit

13. (A) NO CHANGE
    (B) and
    (C) however
    (D) thus

14. (F) NO CHANGE
    (G) among good and evil is
    (H) between good and evil is
    (J) between good or evil are

15. (A) NO CHANGE
    (B) inventing
    (C) invents
    (D) invented

16. (F) NO CHANGE
    (G) elves who are immortal
    (H) more immortal elves
    (J) elves being immortal

Question 17 asks about the preceding passage as a whole.

---

17. Suppose that the writer had been assigned to write a brief essay describing the influence of earlier fantasy novelists on J. K. Rowling. Would this essay successfully fulfill that goal?

    (A) Yes, because three fantasy authors are discussed along with J. K. Rowling.

    (B) Yes, because the issue of an author's indebtedness is discussed.

    (C) No, because J. K. Rowling is the most recent of the writers discussed, and she is the only woman.

    (D) No, because the essay mentions other fantasy novelists but does not discuss particular ways that J. K. Rowling was influenced by them.

ANSWERS AND EXPLANATIONS

1. A
2. H
3. B
4. F
5. D
6. G
7. C
8. H
9. C
10. H
11. B
12. J
13. A
14. H
15. C
16. F
17. D

1. **The best answer is A.** The issue is punctuation. Option A correctly uses a comma to set off introductory information from the main part of the sentence. If you don't spot this right away, plug the other choices into the sentence. Option B incorrectly uses a colon to introduce something that is not a list, example, or explanation. Eliminate option C because it incorrectly uses a semicolon after a dependent clause. Eliminate option D because it puts a period after a dependent clause. This is incorrect because a dependent clause cannot stand alone as a sentence. Option A is the correct choice.

2. **The best answer is H.** The issue is pronouns. Whenever you see a pronoun underlined, check to see that it's used correctly. In option F, the pronoun *which* is used incorrectly to refer to people. Recognizing this, you can eliminate options F and G. Plug in the other choices to determine the best one. Option J is awkward and certainly wordy compared to option H. Option H is the best answer.

3. **The best answer is B.** The issue is punctuation, specifically the apostrophe. Eliminate option A because *Rowling,* a singular noun, does not form the possessive by adding *s'*. Knowing this, you can also eliminate option C. Plugging the remaining choices into the sentence, you should be able to tell that option D is wordy, leaving option B as the best answer choice.

4. **The best answer is F.** The issue is connections. When the underlined portion includes a connections word like *which,* determine the logical relationships that the sentence is expressing. The sentence here conveys the contrast between a *light story* and a *darker and more provocative tale*. Option F is appropriate because *while* expresses this contrast. Eliminate options G and J because they are both cause-and-effect connections. Option H is a contrast

connection, but it is not suitable in this particular context. Option F is the best answer.

5. **The best answer is D.** The issue is word choice. When you see a comparative adjective (one that ends in –er) underlined, check to make sure it's used correctly. Here, using the comparative *darker* instead of the superlative *darkest* is correct, because two things are being compared. However, a comparative adjective should never be preceded by the word *more*. Eliminate option A. This line of thinking should also help you eliminate options B and C, which incorrectly use the superlative *most*. Option D is the best answer.

6. **The best answer is G.** The issue is punctuation. In option F, you should notice that the sentence contains the introductory phrase *in this novel,* which should be set off by a comma. Knowing this, you can eliminate options F and H. Plug options G and J into the sentence. Option J is incorrect because it uses a comma after *called,* incorrectly separating a verb from its object. The correct answer is option G.

7. **The best answer is C.** The issue is wordiness. Option A is wordy. If you don't recognize this immediately, plug in the other choices. Option B is awkward and also a bit wordy. Option C is concise and is the best answer. Option D is wordy and awkward.

8. **The best answer is H.** The issue is writing strategy. When a question stem asks about what would be lost by deleting a portion, read that portion carefully and consider how it functions in its context. Also, note that the question stem includes the word *primarily.* This means you should determine the most important aspect of the underlined portion. Here, you can eliminate option F immediately, because the underlined portion says nothing about Lewis's work. Option G is tempting, because the phrase does indicate Lewis's ethnic origin. Option H, however, is even better than option G. The phrase in question opens the paragraph, and the word *another* shows continuity between Lewis and the writers discussed in earlier paragraphs. Eliminate option J because the phrase does not indicate any contrast. Option H is the best answer.

9. **The best answer is C.** The issue is wordiness. As with many wordiness problems, you may not immediately identify the issue simply by reading option A. Still, read the other choices in the sentence. Option C is slightly shorter and more direct than the others are, so it is the best choice.

10. **The best answer is H.** The issue is idioms. Option F uses an incorrect idiomatic expression, *tied together . . . than.* Recognizing this, you can eliminate options F and G. The correct idiom here is *tied together by.* If you know this, you can recognize option H is the best answer. If not, read options H and J in the sentence. Chances are your ear will hear the idiom error in option J. The best answer is option H.

11. **The best answer is B.** The issue here is sentence sense, particularly as it relates to verb tenses. Whenever you notice an underlined verb, one of the things to check for is whether its tense is consistent with the other tenses in the surrounding context. In option A here, the past tense verb *seemed* is inconsistent with the present tense verbs *is* and *describe* used elsewhere in the sentence. Knowing this, you can spot the inconsistency in option C, as well, which uses *would be.* Having eliminated options A and C, you should plug the other two into the sentence. Options B and D both correctly use the present tense, but option B is the better choice because option D is wordy.

12. **The best answer is J.** The issue is pronouns. When you notice an underlined pronoun, one of the things to check for is that it is the correct form for how it functions in the sentence. Here, *whom* is used incorrectly as the subject of the verb *inhabit.* The pronoun form

who is required here. You can eliminate option G because the pronoun *which* is used only to refer to things, never to people. Read the remaining options in the sentence to decide which is better. The pronoun *who* can refer to nouns that are either singular or plural. In this case, *who* refers to *characters,* which is plural. The correct verb form, therefore, is *characters who **inhabit**.* Option J is the best answer.

13. **The best answer is A.** The issue is connections. Whenever you notice a connections word underlined (here, *but*), consider carefully the relationship between the ideas around it. This sentence sets up a contrast: Tolkien's series is shorter, in terms of page count. Still, it treats its material in a broad scope. The word *but* nicely expresses this contrast. Consider the other options. Option B, *and*, is a simple joining word; it doesn't express contrast, so eliminate it. Option C correctly expresses contrast, but it doesn't work in the structure of this particular sentence. Eliminate option D because *thus* is a cause-and-effect, rather than a contrast, connections word. The best answer is option A.

14. **The best answer is H.** The issues are word choice and verb usage. When you notice that the word *between* is underlined, pause to ask yourself how many things are being talked about. Here, two things, *good and evil*, are being discussed, so *between* is correct. Notice, also, though, that the underlined portion includes the verb *are*. One thing to check for when you see an underlined verb is subject-verb agreement. Ask yourself what the subject of *are* is. It is *tension,* so the correct verb form here is *is*. Knowing that *between* is correct here and that the correct verb is *is,* you can eliminate options F, G, and J.

15. **The best answer is C.** The issue is sentence sense, especially as relates to verb tense. When you see an underlined verb, remember to check that its tense is consistent with the tense used in the surrounding context. In the nonunderlined part of this sentence, you find the present tense verbs *does* and *calls*. This is an indication that a present tense verb is needed. Eliminate option A because it uses a past tense. Eliminate option B because it uses an *–ing* verb alone as the main verb of a clause. Eliminate option D because it uses the past tense. The best answer is option C.

16. **The best answer is F.** The issue is wordiness. You may not be able to identify this issue until you read all of the answer choices. Option F is clearly the most concise, so it is the best answer.

17. **The best answer is D.** The issue is writing strategy. The key words to focus on in the question stem are *describing the influence of earlier fantasy novelists on J. K. Rowling.* Ask yourself what the purpose of the essay is. It mentions three fantasy writers who worked before Rowling, but it doesn't specifically describe how they influenced her. Knowing this, you can eliminate options A and B. Now consider the reasons provided in options C and D. In option C, the fact that Rowling is the most recent of the writers does not mean that the influence of the previous writers must be discussed, and the fact that Rowling is a woman is irrelevant. The reason given in option D specifically addresses the question posed by the question stem. Option D is the best answer.

Chapter Six: **English Practice Set III**

Directions: In the following passage, certain words and phrases have been underlined and numbered. You will find alternatives for each underlined portion in the column on the right. Select the one that best expresses the idea, that makes the statement acceptable in standard written English, or that is phrased most consistently with the style and tone of the entire passage. If you feel that the original version is best, select "NO CHANGE." You will also find questions asking about a section of the passage or about the entire passage. For these questions, decide which choice gives the most appropriate response to the given question. For each question in the test, select the best choice, and fill in the corresponding space on the answer folder. You may wish to read each passage through before you begin to answer the questions associated with it. Most answers cannot be determined without reading several sentences around the phrases in question. Make sure to read far enough ahead each time you choose an alternative.

GAMELAN MUSIC

The gamelan is an Indonesian musical ensemble traditionally heard <u>in variously</u>
(1)

<u>ritualistic settings</u>. Unlike a symphony orchestra, which <u>being composed of</u> the same
(2)

kinds of instruments as those used in any other symphony orchestra, each gamelan is made up of a unique set of instruments. These instruments are <u>made</u> and tuned to be
(3)

played together in a particular grouping. An instrument made for one gamelan,
<u>however</u>, cannot be used in a different gamelan.
(4)

Percussion instruments play a significant role in any <u>gamelan; and</u> some of these
(5)

have a melodic component as well. However, the main melody of a piece is carried by stringed instruments, such as the rebab, or by wind <u>instruments. Such</u> as the bamboo
(6)

flute. Whereas in a symphony orchestra all melodic instruments are tuned to the same key, melodic <u>instruments in a gamelan are</u> tuned to be complementary with, but not
(7)

necessarily to match, the tuning system used by other instruments in the gamelan. In addition to the wind instruments, parts for the human voice <u>may be present additionally</u>
                                                                                            (8)
in a gamelan composition.

   <u>Gongs are an important component of a gamelan.</u> These include metallophones,
                              (9)
gong chimes, hanging gongs, xylophone-like instruments called gambang, and drums. The metallophones, used for both percussion and melody, <u>consists in</u> a series of tuned
                                                                        (10)
metal bars that are struck with a mallet. Gong chimes are <u>gong sets largely placed on</u>
                                                            (11)
<u>horizontal stands</u>, while hanging gongs drop vertically from a stand. Gambang are similar to metallophones, but with keys made of wood rather than metal. A gamelan's drums are constructed in asymmetrical pairs, <u>with the larger one of the pair</u> on the
                                                      (12)
right. The drums are typically played with the hands.

   <u>While</u> gamelan music today is frequently performed <u>of its</u> own sake at concerts,
     (13)   (14)
it was traditionally intertwined with social life. The gamelan was a part of various ritual activities, <u>between</u> theatrical performances, shadow puppet plays, and coming-
                     (15)
of-age ceremonies. Gamelan music also <u>accompanied, dances at religious temples, the</u>
                                        (16)
<u>royal court,</u> and village festivals.

1. (A) NO CHANGE
    (B) in various ritual settings
    (C) in settings that are varied and ritualistic
    (D) ritually in variously settings

2. (F) NO CHANGE
    (G) composing
    (H) is composed of
    (J) had been composing of

3. (A) NO CHANGE
    (B) constructed, made
    (C) built, made
    (D) constructed and built

4. (F) NO CHANGE
    (G) therefore
    (H) on the contrary
    (J) as a consequence of this

5. (A) NO CHANGE
   (B) gamelan, some
   (C) gamelan and
   (D) gamelan, and

6. (F) NO CHANGE
   (G) instruments: such
   (H) instruments; such
   (J) instruments, such

7. (A) NO CHANGE
   (B) instruments in a gamelan were
   (C) instruments' in a gamelan were
   (D) instrument's in a gamelan are

8. (F) NO CHANGE
   (G) may be present
   (H) being also present
   (J) likewise being included

9. Which choice would make the most effective and appropriate introductory sentence
   for this paragraph?

   (A) NO CHANGE
   (B) Several types of percussion instruments are used in a gamelan.
   (C) The hand and the mallet are two methods of playing.
   (D) There is not a set number of instruments in a gamelan.

10. (F) NO CHANGE
    (G) consist in
    (H) consists in
    (J) consist of

11. (A) NO CHANGE
    (B) standing large gongs set horizontally in places
    (C) sets of large gongs that are placed horizontally on stands
    (D) horizontal placed large gong standing sets

12. (F) NO CHANGE
    (G) with the larger one of the pair being
    (H) with the largest one of the pair
    (J) the largest one of the pair being

KAPLAN

13. Which of the following choices would NOT be acceptable as an alternative to the underlined portion?

   (A)   Whereas

   (B)   Although

   (C)   Because

   (D)   Even though

14.   (F)   NO CHANGE

   (G)   for its

   (H)   of its'

   (J)   for it's

15.   (A)   NO CHANGE

   (B)   including

   (C)   among them

   (D)   which would include

16.   (F)   NO CHANGE

   (G)   accompanied dances, at religious, temples, the royal court,

   (H)   accompanied dances: at religious temples, the royal court

   (J)   accompanied dances at religious temples, the royal court,

---

Question 17 asks about the preceding passage as a whole.

---

17. Suppose the writer's goal had been to write an essay persuading the reader that gamelan music is more complex than symphonic music. Would this essay fulfill that goal?

   (A)   Yes, because various aspects of both the symphony orchestra and the gamelan are discussed in the essay.

   (B)   Yes, because the writer describes several differences between the gamelan and the symphony orchestra.

   (C)   No, because the essay is descriptive only and does not attempt to persuade the reader.

   (D)   No, because only complexities of the symphony orchestra are described.

ANSWERS AND EXPLANATIONS

1. B
2. H
3. A
4. G
5. D
6. J
7. A
8. G
9. B
10. J
11. C
12. F
13. C
14. G
15. B
16. J
17. C

1. **The best answer is B.** The issue is modifiers. Logically, the adverb *variously* is not meant to modify the adjective *ritualistic.* Identifying the issue allows you to eliminate options A and D. Then plug the remaining choices into the sentence. Option B is the best. The two adjectives *various* and *ritual* both modify the noun *settings.* Option C is not the best because it's wordy.

2. **The best answer is H.** The issue is sentence sense. The verb form *being composed of* is not an acceptable form for the way it's used in the dependent clause beginning with *which.* If you notice that the problem is with the –*ing* form of the verb, you can also eliminate options G and J. The best answer is H because it uses the correct verb form in the dependent clause.

3. **The best answer is A.** The issue here is redundancy, but you may not be able to identify it right away because the underlined part doesn't contain an error. If you don't notice the redundancy as you look through the answer choices, try plugging each into the sentence. Options B, C, and D all introduce redundancy, because *built, made,* and *constructed* all mean roughly the same thing.

4. **The best answer is G.** Notice that the underlined word *however* is a connections word. Whenever you see such a word underlined, that's a clue that you should read the nonunderlined context carefully to determine the logical relationship between two ideas. Think about the meaning of the sentence before this one: If the instruments are designed to be used together in a *particular* grouping, then the instruments for *one* grouping cannot be used in a *different* grouping. You need a connections word that expresses cause and effect. Eliminate options F and H because they both express contrast. Because options G and J both express cause and effect, you must read each into the sentence to determine which is best. You should eliminate option J because it's wordy, leaving option G as the best answer.

5. **The best answer is D.**   The issues here are punctuation and sentence structure. You should be able to recognize that option A is wrong because the semicolon cannot be used with the word *and* to join two independent clauses. Read the other choices into the sentence to test them for correctness. Option B is wrong because it creates a run-on by joining two independent clauses with only a comma. Option C creates a punctuation problem, because a comma is required before *and,* a FANBOYS word, when it's used to join two independent clauses. Option D is best because it correctly uses *and* with the comma.

6. **The best answer is J.**   The issues here are punctuation and sentence structure. Option F is incorrect because it punctuates *Such as the bamboo flute* as a complete sentence when it's just a phrase. If you recognize this, you may be able to spot immediately that option J, using the comma, is correct. If not, plug each choice in. Option G is wrong because what follows the colon is not an explanation. Option H is wrong because what follows the semicolon is not an independent clause.

7. **The best answer is A.**   The issues are punctuation (the apostrophe) and sentence sense. Option A avoids the incorrect apostrophe used in options C and D. Option A also correctly uses the present tense verb *are,* which matches the overall tense of the passage. Options B and D incorrectly use the past tense verb *were.*

8. **The best answer is G.**   The issue is redundancy, though this may be hard to spot at first. The underlined word *additionally* unnecessarily repeats the meaning of the nonunderlined phrase *in addition* at the beginning of this sentence. Eliminate options H and J, because they both create redundancy with the words *likewise* and *also.* Option G is the best answer because it eliminates the redundancy.

9. **The best answer is B.**   The issue is organization. Because the question asks about the best introductory sentence, you should read through the whole paragraph before deciding on your answer. As you read through the paragraph, you can answer questions 10, 11, and 12 and then come back to answer question 9. What is the topic of this paragraph? This paragraph describes some of the percussion instruments used in a gamelan. Option B is the most general of the choices; it is broad enough to relate to everything in the paragraph. Option A is too specific: gongs are mentioned in the paragraph, but so are other instruments. Option C does relate to the paragraph's topic of percussion instruments, but if you read it into the context, it doesn't flow smoothly with the sentence that follows. Option D is too general and doesn't lead into the paragraph's focus on percussion instruments. Option B is the best answer.

10. **The best answer is J.**   The issues are verb usage and idioms. When you notice an underlined verb, one of the things you should check for is agreement with its subject. The subject here is *metallophones,* which is plural. Thus, the verb form needed is *metallophones con-sist.* Identifying this issue lets you eliminate options F and H. Plug options G and J into the sentence. The idiomatically correct phrase here is *consist of.* Plugging option G into the sentence should help you hear this. Option J is the best answer.

11. **The best answer is C.**   When you read through the sentence as written, it should sound confusing. The issue here is sentence sense. The adverb *largely* doesn't really modify *placed,* so the word order is mixed up. Read the other choices back into the sentence to determine which makes the most sense. Option B also sounds confusing. Option C, even though in this case it's longer than the other choices, is the most sensible, logical wording. *Large* correctly modifies *gongs,* and *horizontally* modifies *placed.* You should be able to eliminate option D because it's not correct for the adjective *horizontal* to modify the verb *placed.* Option C is best.

12. **The best answer is F.** The issue is superlative and comparative adjectives. Whenever you notice that a word ending in –er or –est is underlined, that's a red flag that you should ask yourself how many things are being compared. Here, the phrase *of the pair,* which is used in all four options, clearly indicates that two items are being compared. For two items, the comparative form, *larger,* is correct. Recognizing this lets you eliminate options H and J. Plugging option G into the sentence, you should notice that it is slightly longer than option F. Because it's more concise than option G, option F is the better answer. (Note that of all *four* options, we would say that option F is the *best* answer.)

13. **The best answer is C.** Be careful when an English question stem includes the word *NOT.* For most English questions, you're looking for the choice that sounds best. For this question, you need to determine which option does *not* sound correct. Notice that the underlined word here, *while,* is a connections word. This is a signal that you must pay attention to the meaning and logic of the sentence. This sentence expresses contrast, the difference between gamelan music as it's played *today* and how it was played *traditionally.* Options A, B, and D would all fit acceptably here because they're all contrast connections. Option C would not be acceptable because it's a cause-and-effect transition. Thus, option C is the best answer.

14. **The best answer is G.** The issues here are idioms and punctuation (the apostrophe). Start with the punctuation. You know contractions are tested on the ACT, so whenever you see the words *its, it's,* or even *its'* (which is never correct) underlined, check the context to determine the correct spelling. In the context here, *its own sake,* the word *its* is correctly spelled for use as a possessive pronoun. Recognizing this lets you eliminate options F and J. You should also recognize that the spelling used in option H, *its',* is never correct. Even if you're unsure about the correct spelling of *its* here, your ear may tell you that the phrase *performed of* is idiomatically incorrect, allowing you to eliminate options F and H. However you get to it, option G is the best answer.

15. **The best answer is B.** The issue is word choice. When you notice that either *between* or *among* is underlined, that's a signal to check the context to determine how many things are being talked about. In this context, a list of three things follows: *...performances,...plays, and...ceremonies.* The word *between* is not correct here, so you can eliminate option A. Plug the other options into the sentence. You might think that option C, with *among,* would be correct, because more than two things are discussed, but it's not the best wording here. Option C is a little awkward and not as concise as option B. You can eliminate option D because it's wordy. The best answer is option B.

16. **The best answer is J.** The issue is punctuation. Notice that the underlined portion and its surrounding context include a list: *religious temples, the royal court, and village festivals.* Commas are needed to separate the items in this list, but nowhere else in the sentence. Eliminate option F because the comma after *accompanied* incorrectly separates the verb from its object, *dances.* Eliminate option G because the commas around the phrase *at religious* incorrectly break up the flow of the sentence. Eliminate option H because the colon is unnecessary and breaks up the flow of the sentence. Option J is the best choice.

17. **The best answer is C.** The issue is writing strategy. The key words in the question stem are *persuading the reader that gamelan music is more complex than symphonic music.* Think about the tone of the essay, and consider whether it is persuasive. No, it is not. The essay does make some comparisons between gamelan music and symphonic music, but the writer makes no attempt to say that one is more complicated than the other is. Thus, you can eliminate options A and B. Now look at the reasons in options C and D. Option C is the best answer because it acknowledges that the tone of the essay is not persuasive.

Chapter Seven: **English Practice Set IV**

Directions: In the following passage, certain words and phrases have been underlined and numbered. You will find alternatives for each underlined portion in the column on the right. Select the one that best expresses the idea, that makes the statement acceptable in standard written English, or that is phrased most consistently with the style and tone of the entire passage. If you feel that the original version is best, select "NO CHANGE." You will also find questions asking about a section of the passage or about the entire passage. For these questions, decide which choice gives the most appropriate response to the given question. For each question in the test, select the best choice, and fill in the corresponding space on the answer folder. You may wish to read each passage through before you begin to answer the questions associated with it. Most answers cannot be determined without reading several sentences around the phrases in question. Make sure to read far enough ahead each time you choose an alternative.

IT'S THE LITTLE THINGS THAT MATTER

[1]

I've <u>lived, in New York City for my entire life,</u> and I'm not happy to be leaving it,
    (1)
even <u>if the reason is</u> that my mom got a great new job three states away. <u>Theirs a lot</u>
     (2)   **(3)**
about my life here that I'll miss. It will be awful having to do senior year in a <u>strange</u>

<u>place without my friends.</u> That's only part of it, though. <u>Being that cell phones and</u>
     (4)   **(5)**
<u>computers are so common,</u> it's easier than ever to communicate over a distance, and I
know my buddies and I will stay in touch.

[2]

Moving means leaving more than my friends. I'll be <u>leaving and abandoning</u> my
                                                                                   (6)
childhood home behind. It may be hard for someone <u>who's never lived</u> in a city to
                                                                            (7)

understand, but my neighborhood is far from impersonal. It really does have the feel of a village. There are lots of people <u>who, though not exactly friends are</u> a regular part
(8)
of my life. Unlike my friends, these aren't people I know well enough <u>staying in contact</u>
(9)
with after I move. This may sound odd, but I'll miss them.

[3]

There's Joe, the old guy who's been the superintendent of my apartment building ever since I can remember. He's always out sweeping the hallway or cleaning the laundry <u>room, and</u> he's just a call away to fix a clogged sink or change a lightbulb in a
(10)
tall fixture. Joe has a warm smile and is incredibly nice. I have to admit, I love that he always keeps a few fun-size chocolate bars in his tool box, and he's happy to share his stash with my <u>sister and I as well</u>. Sure, I can come back and check on Joe when I visit
(11)
New York, <u>and</u> it just won't be the same.
(12)

[4]

I'll also miss Gen, the quiet woman <u>which runs</u> the green grocer on the corner.
(13)
<u>I think most New Yorkers would agree that the corner grocery is indispensable.</u>
(14)
Whenever I run in for a drink or a snack, it seems she's there at the cash register with her lively kindergarten son, Tang, and now her new baby. I feel like I've watched Tang grow up. <u>How old when I come back to visit, who knows, will his baby sister be?</u>
(15)
Will the family even still be here? It's so strange to think that <u>people who are now seen</u>
(16)
<u>by me</u> every day may just vanish from my life. I'll miss these small connections with people almost as much as I'll miss my friends.

1. (A) NO CHANGE
   (B) lived in New York City for my entire life
   (C) lived in, New York City, for my entire life
   (D) lived in New York City for my entire life,

2. (F) NO CHANGE
   (G) the reason being
   (H) being for the reason
   (J) because of the reason

3. (A)   NO CHANGE
    (B)   Their's a great deal
    (C)   There's a lot
    (D)   Theirs a lot

4. All of the following choices would appropriately convey the writer's concerns about a new school EXCEPT
    (F)   NO CHANGE
    (G)   different place where I won't know anyone.
    (H)   different state.
    (J)   new place with unfamiliar classmates.

5. (A)   NO CHANGE
    (B)   Cell phones and the computer being so common,
    (C)   Among cell phones and the computer,
    (D)   Between cell phones and the computer,

6. (F)   NO CHANGE
    (G)   saying goodbye to
    (H)   leaving
    (J)   parting with and leaving

7. (A)   NO CHANGE
    (B)   never having lived
    (C)   who hadn't ever lived
    (D)   which hasn't ever lived

8. (F)   NO CHANGE
    (G)   who, though not exactly friends, are
    (H)   who, though not exactly, friends, are
    (J)   who though not exactly friends, are

9. (A)   NO CHANGE
    (B)   to stay in contact
    (C)   so that staying in contact
    (D)   for the keeping in touch

10. (F)   NO CHANGE
    (G)   room. And
    (H)   room; and
    (J)   room,

11. (A)   NO CHANGE
    (B)   me and my sister
    (C)   my sister and I
    (D)   I and also my sister

12. (F)   NO CHANGE
    (G)   so
    (H)   but
    (J)   despite that

13. (A)   NO CHANGE
    (B)   who runs
    (C)   who had run
    (D)   which had been running

14. (F)   NO CHANGE
    (G)   For most New Yorkers, the corner grocery store is a great convenience.
    (H)   The average New Yorker probably could not live with the convenient corner grocery.
    (J)   OMIT the underlined portion

15. (A)   NO CHANGE
    (B)   Who knows how old his baby sister will be when I come back to visit?
    (C)   When his baby sister comes back to visit, who knows how old I will be?
    (D)   Who knows, when his baby sister comes back to visit, how old I will be?

16. (F)   NO CHANGE
    (G)   people I have been now seeing
    (H)   people I now see
    (J)   I'm now seeing people

> Question 17 asks about the preceding passage as a whole.

17. For the sake of logic and coherence, paragraph 3 should be placed

    (A)   where it is now.
    (B)   before paragraph 1.
    (C)   after paragraph 1.
    (D)   after paragraph 4.

ANSWERS AND EXPLANATIONS

1. D
2. F
3. C
4. H
5. D
6. H
7. A
8. G
9. B
10. F
11. B
12. H
13. B
14. J
15. B
16. H
17. A

1. **The best answer is D.** The issue is punctuation. Option A uses a comma after *lived* that incorrectly breaks up the flow of the sentence. The comma after *life,* however, is used correctly to connect two independent clauses joined by the FANBOYS word *and.* Knowing that this second comma is called for, you can eliminate options B and C. Option D is the best answer.

2. **The best answer is F.** The issue is word choice. The word *if* used in option F is appropriate because what follows describes a condition. None of the other options uses *if.* In addition, options G and H incorrectly use the verb form *being.* Option J is redundant: there is no need to say *the reason* with *because.* Option F is the best answer.

3. **The best answer is C.** The issue is word choice. Whenever you see *theirs* underlined, check that it's used correctly. The word *theirs* is a possessive pronoun, which is incorrect in this sentence. The word needed here is *there's* because its meaning is *there is.* Recognizing this, you should eliminate all choices except option C, which is the correct answer.

4. **The best answer is H.** The issue is writing strategy. The key words to focus on in the question stem are *the writer's concerns about a new school.* Options F, G, and J all include phrasing that expresses the writer's nervousness about going to school with a different group of students. Option H does not, and because this question asks for the one choice that does not express the writer's concerns, option H is the best answer.

5. **The best answer is D.** The issue is word choice. Beware whenever you see the phrase *being that* on the ACT. *Being that* is not an acceptable way to say *because.* You can eliminate option A and plug in the other choices to look for something better. Eliminate option B because it uses the *–ing* verb *being* without a helping verb as the main verb in a clause. Eliminate option C because it incorrectly uses *among* when only two things are being

discussed. Option D, which correctly uses the word *between* when two things are discussed, is the best answer.

6. **The best answer is H.**   The issue is wordiness. Eliminate option F because *leaving* and *abandoning* mean the same thing, so the phrase is redundant. Eliminate option J for the same reason. Plug in the remaining choices. Options G and J probably both sound okay to your ear, but option H is the better choice because it's more concise.

7. **The best answer is A.**   The issues are pronouns and verb tense. Address the pronoun issue first: whenever you see *who's* underlined, make sure that it's in a context in which either *who is* or *who has* makes sense. In this sentence, *who's* correctly stands for *who has*. Now look at verb tense. In this sentence, the past tense verb *has…lived* is correct. Check the other options just in case. Eliminate option B because it uses the *–ing* verb *having* without a helping verb as the main verb in the clause. Eliminate option C because the past tense verb *had…lived* is not the appropriate one here. Eliminate option D because it incorrectly uses the pronoun *which* to refer to a person. The best answer is indeed option A.

8. **The best answer is G.**   The issue is punctuation. Think about how the sentence is structured and where the commas are needed. The main part of the sentence is *there are lots of people…who are a regular part of my life*. The phrase *though not exactly friends* is nonessential information and should be set off with commas. Eliminate option F because it doesn't place a comma after *friends*. Eliminate option H because, though it correctly sets off the nonessential phrase, it unnecessarily inserts a comma after *exactly*, which breaks up the flow of the sentence. Eliminate option J because it doesn't use a comma after *who*. The best answer is option G.

9. **The best answer is B.**   The issue is idioms. There is an error in option A because the correct idiomatic usage here is *enough **to stay** in contact*. Eliminate option A. If you identified the idiom issue, option B should stand out as the best choice. If not, plug in the remaining choices. Option C introduces a sentence structure problem with *so that,* which doesn't lead to a complete thought. Option D uses the awkward phrasing *for the keeping in touch.* Option B is the best answer.

10. **The best answer is F.**   The issues are sentence structure and punctuation. Option F correctly uses a comma and the FANBOYS word *and* to join two independent clauses. Option G incorrectly begins a sentence with *and.* Option H incorrectly uses a FANBOYS word with a semicolon to join two independent clauses. Option J creates a run-on sentence by using only a comma, without a FANBOYS word, to join two independent clauses. The best answer is option F.

11. **The best answer is B.**   The issue is pronouns. Whenever you spot an underlined pronoun, check to make sure it's used correctly. In option A, the pronoun *I* is used incorrectly as the object of the preposition *with.* Recognizing this, you should eliminate options A, C, and D. Option B correctly uses the object pronoun *me* and so is the best answer.

12. **The best answer is H.**   The issue is connections. Option F uses *and,* which is a generic connections word that doesn't express any particular logical relationship. Read the sentence carefully to see if a more specific connections word would be appropriate. There are two ideas in this sentence. First is that the writer can come back to visit, and second is that it won't be the same. The second idea expresses some disappointment, so a contrast connections word is appropriate. Eliminate option G because *so* expresses cause and effect. Options H and J both convey contrast. Read each in the sentence. Option H works best here.

13. **The best answer is B.**   The issues are pronouns and verb tenses. When you notice the word *which* underlined, remember that it should refer only to things, never to people. Here, *which* is used incorrectly to refer to *Gen.* Recognizing this, you can eliminate options A and D. Notice that options C and D use different verb tenses, and plug these choices into the sentence. Pay attention to the broader context of the passage. The predominant tense is the present, so eliminate option C, which uses a past tense. Option B is the best choice.

14. **The best answer is J.**   The issue is wordiness, specifically relevance. Whenever you notice that an entire sentence is underlined, check to see if OMIT is offered as an answer choice. If it is, that's a clue that you should ask yourself whether the sentence is relevant to the topic of the paragraph. The focus of this paragraph is how much the writer will miss the family at the green grocer. Therefore, a sentence about how most New Yorkers find the green grocer indispensable is not relevant. Option J is the best answer choice. Having determined this, you don't even need to worry about options G and H. If a sentence is irrelevant, don't consider the best way to word it; simply take it out.

15. **The best answer is B.**   The issue is sentence sense. If an entire sentence is underlined and OMIT is not offered as an answer choice, that's a clue that you need to find the choice that is most logical and easy to understand. Pay attention to the order of the words and phrases. Option A probably sounds confusing when you read it, another good clue that sentence sense is the issue. Option B is clear and makes sense, but you should consider the other options just in case. Options C and D are both misleading because it is the writer, not the *baby sister*, who will come *back to visit.* Option B is the best choice.

16. **The best answer is H.**   The issue is sentence sense. Option F is probably not going to be the best choice because it uses the passive voice. Read through the answer choices looking for the active voice. Option H is written in the active voice. Option G is wrong because it inappropriately uses a past tense that isn't consistent with the context. Option J is wrong because it uses a present tense *(am seeing)* that isn't consistent with the simple present and future tenses that are used in the context. Option H is the best answer.

17. **The best answer is A.**   The issue is organization. To answer a question that asks you to determine the best ordering of paragraphs, think about which would make the best introduction and which would make the best conclusion. Here, paragraph 1 introduces the topic and serves as the best introduction. Paragraph 4—especially the last two sentences—make it the best conclusion for the essay. Recognizing this lets you eliminate options B and D. To decide between options A and C, consider the relationship between paragraphs 2 and 3. Paragraph 2 discusses in general the people the writer will miss. Paragraph 3 discusses, Joe, a specific one of those people. Therefore, it makes sense to keep paragraph 3 after paragraph 2, making option A the best answer.

Chapter Eight: **English Practice Set V**

Directions: In the following passage, certain words and phrases have been underlined and numbered. You will find alternatives for each underlined portion in the column on the right. Select the one that best expresses the idea, that makes the statement acceptable in standard written English, or that is phrased most consistently with the style and tone of the entire passage. If you feel that the original version is best, select "NO CHANGE." You will also find questions asking about a section of the passage or about the entire passage. For these questions, decide which choice gives the most appropriate response to the given question. For each question in the test, select the best choice, and fill in the corresponding space on the answer folder. You may wish to read each passage through before you begin to answer the questions associated with it. Most answers cannot be determined without reading several sentences around the phrases in question. Make sure to read far enough ahead each time you choose an alternative.

NEW DEVELOPMENT IN PSYCHOLOGY

[1]

In recent years, however, a number of psychologists have turned there attention
(1)
away from illness and depression, choosing to focus instead on health and happiness.
Their work has gained the attention of that group of people we call the public. Kay
(2)
Redfield Jamison, in *Exuberance: The Passion for Life*, describes exuberance as a temperamental trait. Through a series of biographical sketches of both famous and less
(3)
well-known figures, Jamison explores the nature of exuberance. Her subjects, what
(4)
they have in common being energy, passion, and a sense of play and joy that guides
their work and even recreation throughout their lives.

[2]

At one time, the word psychologist may have evoked an image of a bespectacled
(5)

and bearded doctor encouraging a reclining patient to explore her deepest fears, <u>desires
that felt repressed</u>, and darkest dreams. The groundbreaking work of Dr. Sigmund Freud
    (6)
did indeed have a negative orientation, focused on treating <u>patients who's</u> behavior
                              (7)
showed symptoms of emotional or mental illness. This orientation toward pathology
directed the work of psychologists for many decades.

[3]

<u>Another investigating psychologist, who finds value in healthy mental states, Martin</u>
                               (8)
<u>Seligman is one.</u> Seligman's work is guided by the idea that the role of the psychologist is
not simply to help people <u>in the effort of avoiding</u> pain and pathology, but to help them
                           (9)
attain feelings of happiness, engagement, and fulfillment. Seligman <u>has encouraged</u> his
                              (10)
colleagues in academic psychology to focus research on these areas. He has also written
books <u>accessible to</u> a lay audience, including *Authentic Happiness, Learned Optimism,*
    (11)
and *The Optimistic Child.* [12]

[4]

Academic interest in happiness continues to <u>grow, not only for those, in the field of</u>
                           (13)
<u>psychology, but,</u> also for students in other fields. Recently a course <u>that students have</u>
                           (14)
called "Positive Psychology," taught by Harvard Professor Tal-Ben Shahar, has drawn
more students than a <u>popularly perennial economics introduction</u> class. Shahar's class,
                           (15)
while grounded in rigorous <u>research; encourages</u> students to reflect on their own
                           (16)
assumptions about happiness.

1. (A) NO CHANGE
    (B) turning their
    (C) have turned their
    (D) who have turned there

2. (F) NO CHANGE
    (G) people known as
    (H) those we call
    (J) OMIT the underlined portion

3. (A) NO CHANGE
    (B) sketches of both famous, and, less well-known figures, Jamison
    (C) sketches of both famous and less well-known figures, Jamison,
    (D) sketches, of both famous, and less well-known, figures Jamison

4. (F) NO CHANGE
    (G) What her subjects have in common are
    (H) The common thing for her subjects is
    (J) Having this in common, her subjects are

5. (A) NO CHANGE
    (B) had been evoking
    (C) may have been evoking
    (D) is evoking

6. (F) NO CHANGE
    (G) repressed desires
    (H) those desires that had been repressed
    (J) desires that she had been repressing

7. (A) NO CHANGE
    (B) patients' who's
    (C) patients whose
    (D) patient's whose

8. (F) NO CHANGE
    (G) Martin Seligman, also finding value in healthy mental state investigation, is another psychologist.
    (H) Another psychologist, Martin Seligman, is one who finds value in investigating healthy mental states.
    (J) Another psychologist who finds value in investigating healthy mental states is Martin Seligman.

9. (A) NO CHANGE
    (B) avoid
    (C) who need to avoid
    (D) in the avoidance of

10. (F) NO CHANGE
    (G) which has encouraged
    (H) who has encouraged
    (J) encouraging

11. Which of the following alternatives to the underlined phrase would NOT be acceptable?

    (A) accessible on
    (B) that are accessible to
    (C) accessible for
    (D) that can be understood by

12. At this point the writer is considering adding the following sentence:

    In fact, it was a casual remark by a child that inspired Seligman to write *The Optimistic Child*.

    Assuming this statement is true, would it be a relevant and appropriate addition to the essay?

    (F) Yes, because it explains where Seligman got the title for *The Optimistic Child*.
    (G) Yes, because child development is an important branch of psychology.
    (H) No, because casual remarks are not mentioned anywhere else in the essay.
    (J) No, because it distracts from the focus of the paragraph.

13. (A) NO CHANGE
    (B) grow not only, for those in the field of psychology, but
    (C) grow, not only for those in the field of psychology but
    (D) grow not only, for those in the field of psychology but,

14. (F) NO CHANGE
    (G) that is
    (H) that some have
    (J) OMIT the underlined portion

15. (A) NO CHANGE
    (B) perennially popular introductory economics
    (C) economically popular perennially introductory
    (D) popular perennial and introductory economics

16. (F) NO CHANGE
    (G) research: is encouraging
    (H) research, encourages
    (J) research—encourages

> Question 17 asks about the preceding passage as a whole.

17. For the sake of logic and coherence, the best order for the paragraphs in this essay is

   (A)   as they are now.
   (B)   2, 1, 3, 4.
   (C)   1, 4, 2, 3.
   (D)   3, 2, 1, 4.

ANSWERS AND EXPLANATIONS

   1. C
   2. J
   3. A
   4. G
   5. A
   6. G
   7. C
   8. J
   9. B
   10. F
   11. A
   12. J
   13. C
   14. J
   15. B
   16. H
   17. B

1. **The best answer is C.**   The issues are pronouns and sentence sense. When you see *there* underlined, make sure it is not being used incorrectly in place of the possessive pronoun *their*. That is indeed the case here. Eliminate options A and D. Plug the remaining choices into the sentence. You should hear the error in option B: it incorrectly uses an *–ing* verb without a helping verb as the main verb in a clause. Option C is the best answer.

2. **The best answer is J.**   The issue is wordiness. Remember to check for wordiness whenever you notice that OMIT is offered as an answer choice. The underlined words are unnecessary, so the best answer is option J.

3. **The best answer is A.**   The issue is punctuation. When you can tell that commas are being tested, as is the case here, consider the sentence structure. The first part of the sentence, *Through a series of biographical sketches of both famous and less well-known figures,*

is an introductory phrase and so should be separated from the rest of the sentence by a comma. Option A correctly does this. Eliminate option D because it does not. Option B is wrong because the commas around *and* disturb the flow of the sentence. Option C is wrong because the comma after *Jamison* incorrectly separates the subject from the verb *explores.* The best choice is option A.

4. **The best answer is G.**   The issue is sentence sense. This sentence lacks a proper verb, so eliminate option F. Eliminate option H because it's awkward. Eliminate option J because it doesn't flow smoothly with the remainder of the sentence. The best choice is option G.

5. **The best answer is A.**   The issue is verb tense. You can probably tell that option A doesn't seem to contain an error. Nevertheless, consider the other choices, just to be sure. Option B incorrectly uses *had been evoking,* a verb tense that should be used only to describe an action that took place prior to another past action. Option C incorrectly uses *may have been evoking*, a form that should be used only for an action that continues into the present. Option D is incorrect because it uses the present tense *is evoking,* which is not consistent with the phrase *at one time* used in this sentence.

6. **The best answer is G.**   The issue is wordiness. You may not spot this issue immediately, but considering all the answer choices should make it apparent. Notice that option G is much shorter than the others are. Option G makes sense in the context and it's the most concise, therefore, it is the best answer. Options F, H, and J are all wordy.

7. **The best answer is C.**   The issues are punctuation (the apostrophe) and pronouns. Whenever you notice an underlined word that contains an apostrophe, check that it's being used correctly. Here, it doesn't make sense to substitute *who is* or *who has* for *who's,* so eliminate option A. Eliminate option B for the same reason. Now consider options C and D, reading them into the sentence. It doesn't make sense for the word *patient's* to be possessive here, so eliminate option D. The best answer is option C.

8. **The best answer is J.**   The issue is sentence sense. When an entire sentence is underlined and OMIT is not offered as an answer choice, you must think carefully about the meaning of the sentence and choose the wording that is clearest and most logical. Eliminate option F because of the way the sentence is constructed. Starting with *another* and ending with *is one* is awkward. Eliminate option G because the focus of the sentence is at the end, *is another psychologist,* and this doesn't fit with the focus of the passage, which is psychologists who investigate *healthy mental states.* Option H is better than options F and G, but it is not as good as option J. Option J, because it uses *who* instead of *is one* is a more direct and concise statement.

9. **The best answer is B.**   The issue is wordiness. When one answer choice is considerably shorter than the other three, it is the best answer if no significant meaning is lost. This is the case here. Options A, C, and D are all wordy. Option B is the best answer.

10. **The best answer is F.**   The issue is sentence sense. Option F is correct. Eliminate options G and H because it is incorrect in this context to put a pronoun such as *who* or *which* between the subject and the verb. (Another red flag for option H is that *which* should never be used to refer to a person.) Eliminate option J because it incorrectly uses *encouraging* without a helping verb as the main verb in the sentence.

11. **The best answer is A.**   The issue is idioms. When an English question stem includes the word *NOT,* remember that you are looking not for an answer that sounds good, but for one that sounds bad. Read all choices into the sentence to find the one that is not acceptable for

some reason. Option A, even though it is shorter than options B and D, is the answer you're looking for. Option A is incorrect because *accessible **on*** is incorrect idiomatic usage. Either *accessible **to*** or *accessible **for*** would be acceptable here. The correct answer is option A.

12. **The best answer is J.**   The issue is writing strategy. When you're asked if an additional sentence would be relevant, consider the main topic of the paragraph. This paragraph focuses on Seligman's interest in positive psychology and his role in promoting it among colleagues and the public. The mention of the book *The Optimistic Child* is as supporting detail, so it would not be relevant to add a sentence that explains the source of inspiration for it. Eliminate options F and G.

13. **The best answer is C.**   The issue is punctuation. When commas are underlined, think about how the sentence is structured. The main part of this sentence is *academic interest in happiness continues to grow.* What follows, *not only for those in the field of psychology but also for students in other fields,* is considered nonessential information and so should be set off by commas. Knowing this, you can eliminate options B and D. Eliminate option A because the flow is disturbed by the commas after *those* and *psychology*. Option C is the best answer.

14. **The best answer is J.**   The issue is wordiness. Always consider wordiness when you notice that OMIT is one of the answer choices. Because the sentence reads smoothly and makes sense without the underlined portion, option J is the best answer.

15. **The best answer is B.**   The issue is sentence sense. Often when adverbs and adjectives are underlined in the same question, it's a clue that sentence sense is the issue. Eliminate option A because it doesn't make sense for the word *popularly* to modify *perennial.* Eliminate option C because it creates even more confusion with modifiers. It doesn't make sense for *economically* to modify *popular* or for *perennially* to modify *introductory.* Eliminate option D because it uses *perennial* to modify *economics,* which doesn't make sense. Option B is the best answer because it correctly uses *perennially* to modify *popular* and *introductory* to modify *economics.*

16. **The best answer is H.**   The issues are sentence structure and punctuation. Option F uses a semicolon. To determine if that is correct, consider whether the word that come before and the words that come after the semicolon each stand alone as sentences. The answer here is no; in fact, neither grouping of words forms a complete sentence. Eliminate option F because the semicolon is used incorrectly. Think about the structure of the sentence to determine what punctuation is needed. The main part of the sentence is *Shahar's class . . . encourages students to reflect on their own assumptions about happiness.* The phrase *while grounded in rigorous research* is nonessential information and so should be set off by commas. Knowing this, you can spot that H is the best answer.

17. **The best answer is B.**   The issue is writing strategy. When you're asked about the order of paragraphs, start by determining which would make the best introduction and which would make the best conclusion. Notice the chronological element in this passage. The passage discusses psychology from *Freud* to *recent years.* It makes sense, then, to organize this passage chronologically, putting the paragraph that discusses Freud first. Only option B does this. Option B also puts paragraph 4, which treats the present (as evidenced by the words *continues to grow* and *recently*) last, which makes sense in the chronological sequence. Option B is the best answer.

Chapter Nine: **English Practice Set VI**

Directions: In the following passage, certain words and phrases have been underlined and numbered. You will find alternatives for each underlined portion in the column on the right. Select the one that best expresses the idea, that makes the statement acceptable in standard written English, or that is phrased most consistently with the style and tone of the entire passage. If you feel that the original version is best, select "NO CHANGE." You will also find questions asking about a section of the passage or about the entire passage. For these questions, decide which choice gives the most appropriate response to the given question. For each question in the test, select the best choice, and fill in the corresponding space on the answer folder. You may wish to read each passage through before you begin to answer the questions associated with it. Most answers cannot be determined without reading several sentences around the phrases in question. Make sure to read far enough ahead each time you choose an alternative.

MY WILDERNESS EXPERIENCE

My camping trip <u>in the wilderness land of Canada</u> was everything I'd expected and
                          (1)
more. I had known <u>their would be</u> challenges: I'd have to carry heavy supplies, face
                        (2)
some difficult hiking trails, and, of course, <u>deal with</u> wildlife and the unpredictability
                                                    (3)
of the weather. <u>With</u> my previous camping experience and the training I'd done for
                    (4)
cross-country, I felt well-prepared.

I now realize that the only challenges I'd anticipated were outside myself. Annoying bugs, heavy <u>rains. The</u> exertion of miles of hiking every day for a week—I'd thought
                          (5)
about all these things and knew that I would push myself to get through them. As it turned out, <u>nonetheless</u>, the most significant challenges weren't the physical ones I'd
                        (6)
been prepared for, but the emotional ones that <u>happened to catch even me by surprise</u>.
                                                        (7)

A city kid, I <u>who had lived in urban areas my whole life,</u> found that the beauty of
(8)

nature was utterly overwhelming. I'd been in the woods before, but I'd never been in
a vast area of pristine wilderness. It's hard for me to describe what I saw without resorting to clichés and exaggeration. ⑨ The snow-covered mountains, trees with foliage or
<u>needles in at least a thousand different</u> shades of green, a sky that
(10)

looked bluer and cleaner than any I'd ever seen, and the graceful flight of eagles high
overhead—words feel so inadequate <u>for the purpose of conveying</u> my experience,
(11)

but I'm not sure photographs or videos would do much better. To really understand,
you have to experience it.

When you're exposed to beauty like this, <u>one starts to realize</u> how magnificent
(12)

nature is and how human beings aren't really in control the way we like to think we
are. At times on my trip, I <u>felt spine-tingling chills</u> and a light-headed panic. The
(13)

ultimate stillness, <u>punctuated only by the wind's slow movement of the leaves</u>, and
(14)

the occasional clear, piercing bird call, even the freshness of the air, moved me beyond
belief. The feeling of being <u>overpowered at</u> nature changed how I see myself. My
(15)

simple camping trip did indeed <u>turn out, to be humbling, but in ways</u> I never expected.
(16)

1. (A) NO CHANGE
   (B) at the Canadian wilderness
   (C) in the Canadian wilderness
   (D) to the wilderness at Canada

2. (F) NO CHANGE
   (G) there would be
   (H) their might have been
   (J) there are challenges

3. (A) NO CHANGE
   (B) I'd also have to deal with
   (C) dealing with
   (D) to deal with

4. Which of the following alternatives to the underlined portion would be LEAST acceptable?

    (F)   As a result of

    (G)   Despite

    (H)   Because of

    (J)   Owing to

5.   (A)   NO CHANGE

    (B)   rains: the

    (C)   rains; the

    (D)   rains, the

6.   (F)   NO CHANGE

    (G)   moreover

    (H)   however

    (J)   consequently

7.   (A)   NO CHANGE

    (B)   caught me by surprise

    (C)   were very surprising to me

    (D)   surprised me

8.   (F)   NO CHANGE

    (G)   who had lived my entire life in a single urban area,

    (H)   accustomed to urban experiences,

    (J)   OMIT the underlined portion.

9. The writer is considering deleting the following sentence:

    It's hard for me to describe what I saw without resorting to clichés and exaggeration.

    If the writer were to make this deletion, the essay would primarily lose

    (A)   a reason that that the writer valued the time in the wilderness.

    (B)   an indication that the writer has given some thought to how the reader will react to the description.

    (C)   a contradiction of the statement made in the previous sentence.

    (D)   an explanation of what a cliché is.

10.   (F)   NO CHANGE

    (G)   needles, in at least a thousand, different

    (H)   needles in at least a thousand, different

    (J)   needles in, at least a thousand, different,

11. (A) NO CHANGE
    (B) to convey
    (C) to convey and express
    (D) in the attempt at conveying

12. (F) NO CHANGE
    (G) one becomes aware of
    (H) you became aware of
    (J) you start to realize

13. (A) NO CHANGE
    (B) was aware of chills causing tingling along my spine
    (C) felt a chilled feeling that tingled my spine
    (D) experienced a feeling of spine-tingling chills

14. Which of the following phrases provides the MOST specific detail about sounds the writer experienced?
    (F) NO CHANGE
    (G) along with the color of the leaves
    (H) in addition to the moss I saw on the trees
    (J) reminding me of a peaceful dream

15. (A) NO CHANGE
    (B) overpowered by
    (C) taken over by the power of
    (D) overpowered with

16. (F) NO CHANGE
    (G) turn out to be humbling, but in ways
    (H) turn, out to be humbling, but in ways
    (J) turn out to be, humbling but in ways

Question 17 asks about the preceding passage as a whole.

---

17. Suppose the writer's goal had been to write a brief essay describing an experience of a human battling nature. Would this essay successfully fulfill that goal?

   (A)   Yes, because the essay mentions bugs and rainfall.

   (B)   Yes, because the essay discusses the writer's anticipation of facing wildlife.

   (C)   No, because the essay focuses more on the writer's internal, not external, experience of nature.

   (D)   No, because the essay mentions only aspects of nature that exist in the Canadian wilderness.

ANSWERS AND EXPLANATIONS

1. C
2. G
3. A
4. G
5. D
6. H
7. D
8. J
9. B
10. F
11. B
12. J
13. A
14. F
15. B
16. G
17. C

1. **The best answer is C.**   The issues are wordiness and idioms. Option A unnecessarily uses the word *land,* and the preposition *in* is not idiomatically correct in this context. Options B and D, using *to* and *at,* also form incorrect idioms. Option C uses the idiomatically correct preposition *in* and is appropriately concise.

2. **The best answer is G.**   The issues are word choice and verb tense. *Their* is a possessive pronoun and is not interchangeable with *there.* Option G addresses this issue. Option H incorrectly uses *their* and also introduces a verb tense problem. Option J correctly uses *there* but incorrectly changes *would be* to the present tense *are.*

3. **The best answer is A.** The issues are wordiness and parallelism. Option B is wordy. Option C doesn't use parallel structure because *dealing* doesn't match the form of *carry* and *face* that are in the nonunderlined part of the passage. Option D is likewise not parallel because it adds the word *to* before *deal.*

4. **The best answer is G.** The issue is transitions. Options F, H, and J all include a word or phrase that correctly expresses the relationship of cause and effect. Option G is wrong because it inappropriately uses a contrast word, *despite.*

5. **The best answer is D.** The issue is punctuation. Option A uses a period when no complete sentence is present. Option B uses the colon incorrectly because what follows the colon here is not an explanation. Option C is wrong because the semicolon should be used only to join two independent clauses. Option D correctly uses a comma after *rains,* the second item in the series *bugs…rains…exertion.*

6. **The best answer is H.** The issue is connections. Option F uses the appropriate kind of connection, a contrast word, but this particular word doesn't fit in this context. Option H, *however,* works better. Option G is incorrect because *moreover* is not a contrast word. Option J is wrong because *consequently* is not a contrast word.

7. **The best answer is D.** The issue is wordiness. Options A and C are unnecessarily wordy. Option B is better, but it is not as concise as option D.

8. **The best answer is J.** The issue is redundancy. Option F is not the best answer because the phrase *who had lived my whole life in urban areas* repeats the meaning expressed by the nonunderlined phrase *a city kid.* Options G and H simply reword the redundant phrase. Only option J eliminates the redundancy.

9. **The best answer is B.** The issue is writing strategy. Focus on the sentence in question: *It's hard for me to describe what I saw without resorting to clichés and exaggeration.* Here the writer is self-consciously reflecting on what the reader will think of his words. Only option B comes close to getting at this idea. Option A doesn't answer the specific question posed in the question stem. Option C is wrong because there is no contradiction here. Option D is wrong because the sentence in question doesn't define *cliché.*

10. **The best answer is F.** The issue is punctuation. Option F is correct because it does not use any unnecessary commas. All other options insert unnecessary commas that inappropriately break up the flow of the sentence.

11. **The best answer is B.** The issue is wordiness. Option A uses the filler phrase *for the purpose of,* which causes this version to be wordy. Option C is redundant because *convey* and *express* mean the same thing. Option D unnecessarily uses the phrase *in the attempt,* which leads this version to be wordy.

12. **The best answer is J.** The issue is word choice. Option F is wrong because the nonunderlined part of the sentence uses the word *you.* Therefore, *one* is incorrect in this sentence. Option G is wrong because it also uses *one.* Option H corrects the *one-you* shift but introduces a new error with the past tense *became.*

13. **The best answer is A.** The issue is wordiness. Option B uses the extraneous phrases *was aware of* and *along my spine* that lead to this version being longer than necessary. Option C uses unnecessary repetition with *felt…a feeling.* Option D is wordy because of the phrase *experience a feeling.*

14. **The best answer is F.** The issue is writing strategy. Pay attention to the question stem. It helps to underline the words *most specific details about the sounds the writer experienced* to help you focus on what the question is asking for. Only option F, with the words *punctuated* and *wind,* addresses the issue of sound. Option G, with *color,* addresses only something that can be seen. Option H explicitly uses the phrase *I saw.* Option J provides no details related to sound.

15. **The best answer is B.** The issue is idioms. Options A and D use *at* and *with,* both incorrect prepositions with the word *overpowered.* Option C is not idiomatically incorrect, but it's not as concise as option B.

16. **The best answer is G.** The issue is punctuation. Option G correctly uses a comma to separate the nonessential phrase *but in ways I never expected* from the main part of the sentence. Options F and H use a comma to set off the nonessential phrase, but they also introduce other unnecessary commas that disturb the flow of the sentence. Option J fails to use the necessary comma and inserts an unnecessary one elsewhere.

17. **The best answer is C.** The issue is writing strategy, so pay attention to the question stem. You should have underlined the phrase *describing an experience of a human battling nature.* This question asks you to think about the purpose of the passage. The main point is the writer's surprise at his emotional response to the wilderness. Thus, you can eliminate options A and B. Option D is wrong because the question stem doesn't ask about nature in any specific geographic area. Option C is best because the word *internal* accurately describes the author's emotional response that forms the centerpiece of this passage.

Chapter Ten: **Introduction to ACT Reading**

The ACT Reading section is passage-based, and all the information you need to answer the questions correctly is found in the passage. This means the ACT is an open-book test. Nevertheless, it does not mean that it's easy. Getting through the Reading section in the time allowed is a challenge for most people. You, however, will find it much less intimidating because you're using this Kaplan workbook. After doing the practice exercises and the sample passages, you'll know what to expect on Test Day in terms of passage topics and structure, question types, and typical wrong answer traps. This chapter fills you in on all those aspects of the Reading section.

Remember from chapter 2 that for each section of the ACT, we have a Kaplan method designed specifically to help you maximize your score in that section. As you practice for the Reading section, don't hesitate to refer to chapter 2 for the Kaplan strategies for ACT Reading. Applying the Kaplan method as you do the practice passages is crucial to your success, so you'll find references to it throughout this chapter.

THE KAPLAN METHOD FOR ACT READING

Pause for a moment to write down what you can remember about the Kaplan method for Reading:

1. _____
2. _____
3. _____

Here's a quick review:

1. **READ** the passage, taking notes as you go.
2. **EXAMINE** the question stem, looking for clues.
3. **SELECT** the answer choice that best matches your prediction.

Handling step 1 well is the foundation of answering each reading question correctly, so let's look at what you should be thinking about as you read the passage and take notes. The key is to read actively.

ACTIVE READING

Take a minute to consider what you think "active reading" might mean. Write down your ideas:

_____

_____

_____

_____

Perhaps one thing that occurred to you is that active reading is not passive. Reading actively means doing something. What you need to do on your first reading is ask yourself questions and look for certain elements that you'll be expecting in an ACT passage. We do recommend that you actually read the passage, not merely skim it, but in your first reading you should focus more on some aspects of the passage than on others.

Guide to Active Reading

1. Focus on the big picture; note the purpose of each paragraph, and do not get bogged down in details.
2. Pay close attention to the first and last paragraphs. They often give great clues for determining the purpose of the passage as a whole.
3. Notice phrasing that indicates an example such as *an illustration of, for example, for instance, this . . . can be seen when,* and *to illustrate.* Remember that the example is a detail, but the general statement or principle it's illustrating is more general and could be a main idea.
4. Ask yourself questions as you read:
   a. What is the writer's purpose? Is he merely describing and explaining, or does he try to persuade the reader? Notice whether the writer is taking a side on an issue.
   b. What is the tone of the passage? Do you notice any phrasing that is approving, critical, or sarcastic?

   c. What is the internal logic of the passage? Do you notice features of a chronological structure or an outline structure or some of each?

5. Read for contrast, noting when the writer points out differences and contradictions. Pay attention to connections words and phrases that show contrast such as *although, appears, but, by claims, despite, even though, however, in spite of, on the other hand, some . . . others, though* and *yet.*

6. Read for comparison; note when the writer points out similarities in two things.

7. Notice where and when the writer states an opinion.

8. Notice where and when the writer makes an argument. What is her evidence? What point is the evidence supporting? Notice words that direct the flow of an argument such as *as a consequence, as a result, because, consequently, resulting in, therefore* or *thus.*

The idea behind active reading is that it puts *you* in charge. When you learn to read actively for the ACT, you're not at the mercy of the test maker's choice of complicated passages about unfamiliar topics. With practice, you'll know a lot about what to expect in an ACT Reading passage. On Test Day, you don't have time to read each passage as slowly and carefully as you might like to. You need to read the passage only to get a sense of the writer's purpose and determine its structure. You don't have to understand every detail the author discusses.

No matter what the author's purpose for writing the passage is, *your* only purpose for reading it is to understand the passage well enough to be able to answer the ten questions about it. The ACT is not a memory test; the passage is right there in the test booklet for you to refer to as you answer the questions. On your first reading, you need only to get a sense of what is where. Step 1 of the Kaplan method directs you to make notes so that you can more easily locate the information you need when you go to answer the questions. The principles of active reading guide your note-taking and tell you what to focus on during your first read-through.

There's a reason this chapter refers to your first "read-through" instead of your first "reading" of the passage. What we mean by "read-through" is a delicate balance of the words *reading* and *skimming.* We don't advise you to skip the passage all together, or merely skim it, and go right to the questions. On the other hand, we don't advise you to read the whole passage slowly and thoroughly. If you read too slowly, you won't have time to make it through the entire Reading section.

Instead, we recommend that you do a quick read-through of the passage before you start answering the questions. Use a combination of skimming and reading to read some parts of the passage more slowly than you do others. At the beginning of the passage, you should read carefully, just until you're confident you've got a sense of what the writer is trying to do. Look for repetition of key words and ideas. After that, you probably won't have to read the rest of the passage slowly, word for word. If you can tell how a paragraph relates to the one that came before it, jot down your passage map note and move on. You don't have to eyeball every word of that paragraph. As a general—though not absolute—rule, it's often a good idea to read the first and last sentences of the middle paragraphs fairly carefully. Those sentences tend to give you the purpose of the paragraph and make connections with the previous and succeeding paragraphs.

If you're surprised to hear that you shouldn't read each paragraph carefully before you look at the questions, remember, the passage isn't going anywhere. It's right there in the test booklet for you to refer to as you answer the questions, and you *should* refer to it. You'll score the most points on Test Day if you let the questions themselves direct you to the parts of the passage you need to read and understand thoroughly in order to answer the questions.

UNDERSTANDING THE STRUCTURE OF THE PASSAGE

As you'll recall from chapter 1, one feature of a standardized test is its predictability. The ACT writers can't pick any random piece of writing and create ACT Reading questions for it. Only a passage that has a clearly discernible organization and internal logic will appear as one of the three nonfiction passages on the ACT. (See the section on prose for information about the structure of a fiction passage.) Determining this structure is your task in step 1 of the Kaplan method.

Organizational Structures in ACT Reading Passages: Outline and Chronological Development

On your first read-through, you should read actively, asking yourself questions about the writer's purpose and viewpoint. Understanding the structure helps you to determine the writer's purpose. Therefore, you should get in the habit of noticing key words and phrases that are clues to the passage's structure. Two key organizational structures to keep in mind are the outline structure and the chronological structure. By "outline" we don't mean the highly structured notes you may have had to prepare before writing a paper for school. For our purposes here, *outline structure* simply means that one broad topic is divided into several narrower aspects. A *chronological structure* is in place when a writer treats the topic in terms of development over time, most often starting with an earlier time period and moving toward more recent time periods.

Here's an exercise to help you think about the organizational structure of a passage. Consider each sentence and decide whether it points to a chronological or an outline structure. Underline key words or phrases that help you decide.

1. _____ In the middle ages, few ordinary people knew how to read and write.

2. _____ Three American writers exhibited this fascination with nature in their poetry.

3. _____ By the early twentieth century, various groups had become interested in promoting women's right to vote.

4. _____ A turning point came in 1859 when Charles Darwin published *Origin of Species.*

5. _____ By the beginning of the next decade, the vaccine had become almost universal.

6. _____ Another aspect of residential architecture to be considered is the use of stained glass windows.

7. _____ The second factor in the education debate is funding.

8. _____ The musician's works can be classified as belonging to one of three major periods.

This exercise should have you thinking about which words to pay attention to on a first reading in order to help you identify a passage's structure. Here are the answers:

1. chronological; *in the middle ages*
2. outline; *three American writers*
3. chronological; *by the early twentieth century*
4. chronological; *a turning point, 1859*
5. chronological; *by the beginning of the next decade*
6. outline; *another aspect of*
7. outline; *the second factor*
8. chronological; *can be classified; three major periods*

Of course, not every ACT Reading passage you encounter will have a simple outline or chronological structure. A writer might combine the two or use a different kind of organizational format that allows for an effective development of the topic. Still, you should always be alert on your first read-through for any time-related words, phrases, and key words that indicate a writer is dividing a larger topic into smaller subtopics. In addition, words that express contrast and logic can also provide quick clues about a passage's organizational structure.

Other Structural Factors to Consider: Logic and Contrast

While some ACT passages feature a strictly chronological flow or follow a basic outline format, not every passage can be described so simply. However, you can expect each nonfiction passage to have its own internal logic. To determine this internal logic, you need to pay attention to words and phrases that express relationships between ideas. The very same words and phrases described under the Connections heading in the English Introduction also appear in passages in the Reading section. When you spot these words in your first read-through of an ACT Reading passage, take note. It's even a good idea to underline them. They provide important clues about the author's purpose and the structure of the passage. Refer to the following table for a list of some of these words:

Key Words That Indicate Cause and Effect and Contrast

Cause and Effect	Contrast
as a result	but
as shown by	claims (may suggest that a "claim" isn't true)
because	difference
consequently	however
evidence shows	in contrast
for this reason	nevertheless
it follows that	on the other hand
so	some . . . others
therefore	whereas
thus	while

Of course, the words in the table don't form an exhaustive list, but they do give you an idea of the kinds of words to pay attention to when you need to determine the logical flow and notice what contrasts the writer presents. One thing to notice is that these words are not subject-specific. This is precisely why connections words and phrases are so important. They show up repeatedly in all three nonfiction ACT passages, no matter what topic the passage discusses. You can't predict the exact content of the Reading passages you'll see on Test Day, but you can be certain that cause-and-effect and contrast words and phrases will be present and crucial to your understanding of the passage.

ACT READING QUESTION TYPES

A crucial part of scoring points on the ACT is *understanding what the particular question is asking.* You'll read more about typical wrong answer traps later on, but for right now, you should know that the test maker includes details from the passage among the wrong answer choices. You won't necessarily find the correct answer to a question correctly simply by selecting an answer that is familiar from the passage. To find the right answer, you have to make sure it answers the question posed by the question stem. It's for this reason that we've broken down ACT Reading questions into six different types: Detail questions, Inference questions, Generalization questions, Function questions, Writer's View questions, and Vocabulary-in-Context questions. As you read about these common question types, remember, you don't score points for correctly identifying a question type. The purpose of recognizing different question types is to help you understand *what each question is asking* because that's the first step in determining the best answer.

Detail Questions

A Detail question asks about a specific detail in the passage. These questions are very straightforward. You don't have to draw a conclusion or make an interpretation; you simply have to locate the particular detail in the passage and restate it. Sometimes the correct answer choice for a Detail question uses virtually the same wording that's used in the passage. At other times, the correct answer is a paraphrase of the wording from the passage.

Certain phrases in the question stem serve as clues that a particular question is asking about a detail directly from the passage. These phrasings include:

- *As stated in the passage,*
- *According to the author,*
- *According to the passage,*
- *The passage states that*
- *The writer states that*
- *All are the following are cited in the passage EXCEPT*

What all these phrasings have in common is that they refer you back to the passage, and they ask about something that is stated directly rather than something that's implied.

Although Detail questions are easy to answer when you know where in the passage to look, it can be challenging to locate the part of the passage that contains the answer. Therefore, it's very important to take good notes for your passage map on your first read-through of the passage. Remember that passage map notes should not include specific details but instead should note the location of details. For example, if a paragraph discusses the career of an artist, don't take notes about specific paintings and critical reactions. Instead, write a short note that describes the general purpose of the paragraph, such as *early career—critics admired.*

For such a paragraph, some people like to underline the names of specific paintings or critics on the first reading. You might find as you practice that this kind of underlining helps you. However, we recommend that you underline sparingly. Each ACT reading passage includes many details, but the test presents only ten questions for each passage. Many of the details in a given passage will not be relevant to any of the ten questions. The purpose of your first read-through is to *focus on the big picture.* Do *not* try to psyche out the test maker by trying to guess which details will show up in the question and underlining them. Though this advice may seem counterintuitive at first, the best way to score points on Detail questions is by not getting too wrapped up in particular details on your first read-through of the passage.

Keep Detail questions in perspective. Of all the question types, they appear most frequently on the ACT Reading section: Roughly one-third of the questions are Detail questions. If you're attacking the questions and you have difficulty locating a particular detail, don't sweat it. Just circle the question number in your test booklet and make an initial guess. If you have time before the section ends, you can come back to the circled question. Remember that you don't have to answer every single question correctly to get a good score. This is especially important to keep in mind for Detail questions. Do your best, but don't obsess. No single question is worth more of your time than any other is.

Inference Questions

Inference questions ask about something that is implied, or suggested, in a small part of the passage. You may be tempted to think that such questions are a matter of opinion, that *anything* could be implied, but this is not the case. Although it's true that Inference questions, unlike Detail questions, ask you to draw a conclusion that's not directly stated in the passage, the correct answer to an inference question will not be a huge logical step away from what is stated in the passage. In other words, to answer an Inference question correctly, do not go too far beyond what's in the passage. You do have to make an inference, but you can't get carried away. The best answer to an Inference question, like the best answer to all ACT Reading questions, is strongly grounded in the words of the passage.

You can learn to recognize Inference questions by spotting key phrases in the question stem. Common wordings used in Inference questions include:

- *It may be inferred from lines . . . that*
- *The author implies about . . . that*
- *The phrase . . . suggests that*
- *In lines . . . the author most likely means that*
- *It is most reasonable to infer from lines . . . that*

Notice from these phrasings that an Inference question refers you to a specific line, phrase, or location in the passage. To answer an Inference question, you must read that part of the passage and come up with a prediction based on what is stated there. Thus, Inference questions refer to a small, localized part of the passage.

Generalization Questions

Generalization questions look a lot like Inference questions. The two are similar in that they both require you to draw a logical conclusion based on what you read in the passage. The difference between them lies in how much of the passage you need to consider for each. We've defined Inference questions as those that refer to a small, particular part of the passage, such as a phrase or sentence. An Inference question stem tells you exactly what part of the passage it's asking about. A Generalization question, on the other hand, asks you about a larger part of the passage, which may or may not be clearly identified by the question stem. It may address a whole paragraph, or the passage as a whole. To answer a broadly worded Generalization question, you sometimes need to draw on material from multiple parts of the passage, say the beginning, middle, and end. In this case, keep the overall purpose of the passage in mind. Whenever a question stem refers to the passage as a whole, you must choose an answer that fits with the passage as a whole, not with just one part of the passage, such as a single sentence or paragraph.

The same key words that appear in the question stem for an Inference question are also used for Generalization questions. For both question types, you'll see words such as *probably, most likely, implies, inferred,* and *suggests*. When you spot these words in a question stem, don't worry about explicitly determining whether you're dealing with an Inference or a Generalization question. Remember, identifying question types doesn't score points on the ACT; answering questions correctly does! We distinguish between Inference and Generalization questions only to remind you that the first refers to a smaller, narrower part of the passage, while the second refers to a larger part of the passage or to the passage as a whole. The main point for you is that you always need to read the question stem carefully. (Remember step 2 of the Kaplan method: Read the question stem looking for clues.) With a careful reading of the question stem, you'll know what the question is asking you to do (for both Generalization and Inference questions, that's drawing a conclusion) and how much of the passage you should consider when you make your prediction.

Writer's View Questions

A Writer's View question asks about something in the passage from the point of view of the writer (or possibly, in the case of a prose fiction passage, the narrator). Writer's view questions refer to *the author, the writer, the narrator,* or *the point of view.* Here are some phrasings you might encounter in a Writer's View question:

- *The author would most likely agree that*
- *The view of the narrator regarding . . . appears to be*
- *The author's view of . . . is*
- *The writer's attitude toward*

A Writer's View question, like both Inference and Generalization questions, asks you to make an inference that's based on the passage. Two things you should keep in mind in answering a Writer's View question are:

1. **Keep straight who says what**. If the passage describes multiple viewpoints, make sure you know which viewpoint the author supports or agrees with.
2. **Pay attention to the tone of the passage**. Even a single word such as *fortunately, unfortunately,* or *regrettably* can be a big clue in helping you determine the author's view.

Vocabulary-in-Context Questions

A Vocabulary-in-Context question asks about the meaning of a word (or, occasionally, of a phrase) as it's used in the passage. The word or phrase is always printed in italics, and a line number reference is always provided. The line reference is a terrific help; the question stem tells you exactly where in the passage you need to look to answer the question. The following steps will help you answer Vocabulary-in-Context questions:

1. Look in the line referenced by the question stem, and pretend that the word you're looking to define is actually a blank line in the sentence.
2. Read that sentence and look for clues to help you determine what word or phrase would make sense in the blank. Use that word or phrase as your prediction for this question.
3. Look at the answer choices and choose the one closest to your prediction.

Here are some other points to help you with Vocabulary-in-Context questions:

- Do *not* skip the prediction! Words used for Vocabulary-in-Context questions are often chosen because they have more than one meaning. The first meaning that comes into your mind or the most common meaning is not necessarily the appropriate meaning in the context of the passage. As its name suggests, the Vocabulary-in-Context question relies on the context of the word as it's used in *this* passage.
- Occasionally predicting seems tough: You may not find any clues within the sentence where the word is used. If that's the case, look at the sentences before and after it. In nearly every case, one of these three sentences contains specific clue words to let you predict the meaning of the "blank."
- Connections words and phrases are often the key to making your prediction. Pay particular attention to words such as *yet, but,* and *however.* These contrast clues may tell you that your prediction should be the opposite of another word that's used in the sentence.

You should learn to love Vocabulary-in-Context questions. They don't appear frequently on the ACT (you'll probably see between one and three on any given Test Day), but they're easy to spot and fairly easy to answer quickly once you know how. Because of this, always look for Vocabulary-in-Context questions and try to answer them. If you have to guess on any question, guess on a harder question that would take you more time to answer. Make use of any Vocabulary-in-Context questions you find in order to rack up a few easy points quickly.

TYPICAL WRONG ANSWER TRAPS ON THE ACT READING SECTION

Think for a minute about one of the most important things you're learning about the ACT: It is predictable. You can prepare and know what to expect on Test Day precisely because the ACT is a standardized test. You've learned that the format is always the same and the question types are predictable. Now we'll look at how you can even know what to expect when it comes to incorrect answer choices! The test maker uses several types of wrong answer choices. We call these wrong answer traps. If you know what kinds of traps to expect, you'll be better prepared to avoid falling for them. We call these wrong answer traps misused details, distortions, extremes, contradictions, and out-of-scope answers.

Misused Details

A misused detail refers to a detail that actually is used in the passage. When you spot a misused detail among the answer choices, it may jump out at you and look very tempting because it concerns something you remember reading about in the passage. If it's used in the passage, then why is it wrong? Remember that you have to choose the best answer to the question posed in this particular question stem. If a detail doesn't directly answer the question you're dealing with, it can't be the best answer to this question, even though it may be a true statement according to the passage. Remember step 2 of the Kaplan method for ACT Reading: Predict the answer in your own words *before* you look at the answer choices. Predicting, along with reading the question stem carefully, is your best defense against falling for misused details.

Distortions

The distortion is a wrong answer choice that uses a detail from the passage but phrases the detail in such a way that it's distorted, or twisted, into something that doesn't match what's in the passage. A distortion may combine two details from the passage in an inaccurate way, or it may combine a detail from the passage with something else that doesn't appear in the passage at all. As with misused details, it's much easier to avoid falling for a distortion if you make a prediction about the best answer to the question before you even read the answer choices.

The distortion trap is similar in some ways to the misused detail trap. You may be wondering how to tell the difference between these two. That's a good question, but you shouldn't worry if you can't identify a particular wrong answer as either a distortion or a misused detail. Remember, on the ACT, you don't score points for correctly labeling the kinds of wrong answer traps. You score points for correctly identifying the correct answer!

Extremes

As its name suggests, an extreme answer choice uses language that's too extreme. This means that the answer choice may be something that is along the right lines to answer the question but is worded in a way that goes too far. Certain kinds of words appear frequently in extreme answer traps. Here are some words and phrasings that can indicate extreme answer traps:

- *absolutely*
- *always*

- *all*
- *best*
- *certainly*
- *ever*
- *in every case*
- *largest*
- *never*
- *no*
- *none*
- *smallest*
- *worst*
- *without a doubt*

An answer choice that contains words or phrases like those listed is not *necessarily* the wrong answer. However, if an answer choice does contain extreme language, you should consider it a trap unless the extreme language is also used in the passage. For example, suppose a writer says, "Isaac Newton was one of the one most brilliant scientists of his time," and you encounter a question that asks about the writer's opinion of Newton. Consider the following answer choices. Circle any extreme words you notice, and see if you can pick out which one is correct and which are extreme:

(A)   Isaac Newton was the most brilliant scientist ever to have lived.

(B)   Isaac Newton displayed much brilliance in his scientific work.

(C)   Isaac Newton was more brilliant than any of his contemporaries were.

(D)   Isaac Newton was the most brilliant scientist of his day.

What did you identify for extreme language? You should have spotted the following words:

(A)   *most ... ever*

(B)   no extreme words

(C)   *more ... than any*

(D)   *most*

If you noticed the extreme language, it should be easy to see that option B is the correct choice.

Contradictions

A contradiction is a wrong answer trap that goes against what's stated in the passage. We sometimes call this an *opposite* answer trap. Think about why an opposite trap would be a tempting answer choice. It addresses something that is indeed found in the passage, so it will contain words that may tempt you much as a misused detail or distortion does. A contradiction trap doesn't come out of left field; it's clearly related to the topic of the passage. The problem with a contradiction is that it completely turns around what is stated in the passage. To avoid contradiction traps, read carefully both in the passage as you make your prediction and in the answer choices when you look for a match for your prediction. Little words such as *no* and *not* are sometimes the key to spotting a contradiction. They reverse the meaning of a sentence, giving it a 180-degree turn.

Out-of-Scope Answers

The *scope* of a passage refers to what information is covered in the passage. A passage that touches on a few key aspects of a large topic has a scope that is broad. A passage that treats a smaller topic in greater depth and detail has a scope that is narrow. Because the correct answer to an ACT Reading question is always based on what is in the passage, you should pay close attention to the scope of the passage when you're considering answer choices and looking for the one that best matches your prediction.

An out-of-scope trap goes beyond what is stated in the passage. If you see an answer choice that brings up something you don't even remember seeing in the passage, you can usually eliminate that as an out-of-scope trap. (Occasionally, the best answer to a generalization question may appear to bring up something that isn't directly in the passage. Remember to read the question carefully to determine what it's asking.) Let's consider some choices that are wrong because they go beyond the scope of the passage. Generalization questions that ask about the passage as a whole frequently include this trap among the answer choices. Suppose you see a passage that discusses two medieval philosophers followed by this question:

> The primary purpose of this passage is to
>
> (A)   give an overview of medieval philosophy.
>
> (B)   discuss the merits of a medieval philosopher.
>
> (C)   argue that medieval philosophy has been more influential than ancient Greek philosophy.
>
> (D)   describe the work of two medieval philosophers.

Did you spot three out-of-scope answer traps here? Option A is out-of-scope because it's too broad. A passage that discusses only two philosophers can't be an overview of all of medieval philosophy. On the other hand, option B is too narrow. While one or more paragraphs does concern a single medieval philosopher, option B addresses only part of the passage and so is out-of-scope. Option C cannot be correct because the passage discusses only medieval philosophy, not ancient Greek philosophy. Because Greek philosophy isn't addressed at all in the passage, it can't be part of the best answer for this question. Option D is the best answer here.

THE FOUR DIFFERENT PASSAGE TYPES

In addition to knowing the kinds of questions to expect and the kinds of wrong answer traps you'll see repeatedly on the test, it helps to have some familiarity with the different passage types. Generally, the three nonfiction passage types will be organized according to a clearly identifiable structure that is based on an outline, chronology, or logical argument. Occasionally, you'll encounter a nonfiction passage written in a more narrative structure that has something in common with the prose fiction. Here, we'll look at the passage types in the order in which they appear on the ACT.

Prose Fiction

The prose selection is taken from a novel or short story. Because the prose passage is centered on characters' thoughts, moods, behaviors, and relationships, it's quite different from the three nonfiction passages. As you do the practice passages in this book, get a feel for your own comfort level with prose passages. Do you find them as easy as or even easier than the other three passages? If so, then jump right into the ACT Reading section at the beginning and work on the prose passage first. On the other hand, if you're generally less comfortable with the prose passage, it would be wise for you to work through the other three passages first and come back to do the prose passage last. Remember that you need to manage your time carefully during the Reading section if you want to answer each question. If you attempt to do the prose passage first even though you're not comfortable with prose, chances are that you'll get bogged down and spend too long on it. This leaves less time to work on passage types that may be easier for you. You don't want to run out of time and wind up guessing on questions for a passage type that would have been easy for you to answer if only you'd had more time to spend on it.

One aspect of the prose passage that can be challenging is that you must infer much of the meaning. Typically, fiction writers don't come right out and make explicit statements. They tend to *show* rather than *tell.* Thus, your ability to understand a prose passage hinges largely on your ability to make appropriate inferences. If you find this challenging, think about watching a movie. The writer and director don't often tell you what to think. Instead, they show you a situation. The music, lighting, and camera angles all affect how you interpret what the characters say and do. Obviously, a piece of literature doesn't use music and cinematography to impart meaning. Nonetheless, a prose passage may be easier for you to understand if you try to visualize it as a movie. Trying to visualize the characters as if they were on film, and not just as words on a page, can help you develop a fuller understanding of the prose passage.

Recall that scoring points on this ACT section requires you to read actively, which means asking yourself questions as you read. For the prose section, the questions you need to keep in mind are different from the questions that help you understand a nonfiction passage. Ask yourself:

- Who are the characters?
- What do specific details about a character help you understand about that person? The ways the character looks, moves, and speaks can give you important clues.
- How are the characters related? You can think of this first in a literal way: Are they friends, relatives, acquaintances, or strangers who are meeting here for the first time? You can also think of this in a more psychological way, asking what connects them: Are they accepting and approving of each other, or are they tied together by a more negative emotion?
- What is the overall tone of the passage? Is the mood upbeat and joyful or serious and reflective? Do any words create a sense of tension, drama, or excitement?
- What contrasts does the passage present? Is one character portrayed as being sharply different from another in personality, background, or values?

Often the ACT prose passage focuses on only a few main characters, but it may include several minor characters as well. As you read through the prose passage, one of the most important things you must do is develop your understanding of the main characters. If you come across a character that seems more minor, you can underline the name, but don't get distracted by giving equal attention to all the characters. Focus on the most important ones.

Social Science

The social science passage always appears second in the ACT Reading section. It may cover a topic relating to history, anthropology, archaeology, education, psychology, political science, biography, business, geography, sociology, or economics. Because social science is a nonfiction passage, remember to apply the active reading questions listed at the beginning of this chapter. Look for the connections words that illustrate the logical progression of the passage. Topics you might see in a social science passage include:

- A reinterpretation of the traditional understanding of a historical event
- A discussion of several scholars who've done work in the field and similarities and differences in their viewpoints
- A presentation of one scholar's view on a topic and argument explaining why the writer disagrees with that view
- An explanation of a concept or idea and why it's important in the field of study
- A discussion of the causes of a historical event
- An overview of the work of an important person in the field

This list is merely representative; it certainly doesn't include everything you might find in a social science passage. No matter what the topic, your task on your first read-through is to grasp the author's purpose for writing. As you read each paragraph, ask yourself how it broadly contributes to the overall purpose. Don't focus on particular details until later, when a question directs you to do so.

Humanities

The humanities passage is always the third passage in the ACT reading section. Broadly speaking, you can think of the humanities as areas that relate to human creativity. Obviously, the visual arts, such as drawing, painting, and sculpture, fall into this category, but so do other areas, such as literature, theatre, music, dance, philosophy, language, communications, film, literary criticism, radio, television, and architecture. As you read the humanities selection, you should apply all of the active reading questions that you'd use for any nonfiction selection. Some examples of topics that you might be likely to find in a humanities passage include:

- A discussion of the style of one or more artists, and characteristics of the artist's work that make it noteworthy or unique
- A discussion relating to the development of a particular art form, what the origin of the form was, and how it changed over time as different artists used it
- A critical assessment of the work of a particular artist, how the artist's work was received in his own lifetime, and whether scholars in the field have maintained that view or come to a different view

- A chronological tracing of a particular artist's work over time, what the characteristics of the artist's early work were, what periods or stages scholars use to categorize the artist's work, and whether the work of a particular period is valued more highly than work from the other periods is

Again, this list is not exhaustive. Notice, however, that the outline form and the chronological structure appear in some way in each example. Even though you can't predict the topic you'll see in the humanities passage, and you may find yourself on Test Day facing a topic you have little familiarity with, you don't need to be intimidated. The practice you get in this workbook looking for the main purpose and the relationships among ideas will prevent you from getting lost in the details.

Natural Science

The natural science passage is always the fourth (and last) passage type in the ACT Reading section. Areas that might appear in a natural science passage include botany, zoology, natural history, biology, chemistry, earth sciences, physics, anatomy, astronomy, ecology, geology, medicine, meteorology, microbiology, physiology, and technology. Don't worry if a science passage includes technical terms that you aren't familiar with. If you need to understand a technical term to answer a question correctly, then that term will be explained somewhere in the passage. Some examples of the way a topic might be treated in an ACT science Reading passage include:

- A concept is introduced and several different understandings of it are presented. (Remember to keep straight who says what.)
- A historical view of a scientific concept is contrasted with a contemporary view.
- Several different ways of investigating a particular phenomenon are discussed.
- A first-person narrative discusses personal experience investigating a scientific concern.
- A detached presentation of facts discusses what is known in a particular field.
- A description of the current understanding of a concept is discussed, and suggestions of what researchers might investigate next are presented.

While a science passage may seem challenging if you don't know much about the particular topic, you should be especially careful with passages that address topics you *are* familiar with. If you've just studied a particular group of elements in your chemistry class and you find a passage that discusses those elements, your first read-through of the passage will go pretty quickly and comfortably because you've had some previous exposure to the material. When you attack the questions, however, don't rely on your previous knowledge. The correct answer is always based on something that's stated in the passage. Even when you're familiar with a topic (in fact, *especially* when you're familiar with it), it's very important to carefully read the question stem and make sure that your prediction is grounded in this passage.

If you've attacked the passages in the order in which they appear on the test, you may be feeling tired and rushed by the time you get to the science passage. Don't lose sight of the big picture. Read the passage through once quickly looking only to discern the writer's main purpose. Make brief passage map notes, and get to the questions as soon as possible. Avoid spending time trying to understand every detail in the passage. You score points only for answering questions correctly, not for coming to a complete and thorough understanding of the passage.

ACT READING REVIEW AND WRAP-UP

What are some of the most important things to take away as you move on to practice with the sample questions in this workbook? How can you work with these guidelines in a way that will maximize your chances of answering questions correctly? Take a moment to skim through this chapter and note some of the suggestions that you think will be most helpful to you:

_____

_____

_____

_____

Now, try our quiz to make sure you can recall the Kaplan method and other strategies.

Review Quiz

1. The Kaplan method for ACT Reading is:

    Step 1: Read the _____, taking _____ as you go.

    Step 2: Examine the _____, looking for _____.

    Step 3: _____ the answer in your own words, and _____
    the answer choice that _____

2. What should you do on your first read-through of the passage? _____
    _____
    _____.

3. What should you do when you can't easily locate the right lines to answer a question?
    _____
    _____.

4. What kinds of words and phrases tell you that a chronological structure is important in the passage? _____
    _____

5. What kinds of words tell you that the passage is organized like an outline? _____
    _____
    _____

6. What kind of logical relationship is indicated by words such as *because, thus, consequently,* and *therefore*? _____
    _____

7. What kind of logical relationship is indicated by words such as *on the other hand, however, but, while,* and *although*? _____
    _____

8. True or False? The details are the most important part of any ACT Reading passage.

9. What question type is each of the following phrasings associated with?

    a. *According to the author,* _____

    b. *The primary purpose of this passage is to* _____

    c. *The author uses the phrase . . . in order to* _____

    d. *As used in the passage, . . . most nearly means* _____

    e. *It may be inferred from lines . . . that* _____

    f. *Which of the following statements would the author most likely agree with?* _____
_____

10. List the five common wrong answer traps that the test maker includes among the answer choices:

    a. _____

    b. _____

    c. _____

    d. _____

    e. _____

Answers to Review Quiz

1. Step 1: passage; notes

   Step 2: question stem; notes

   Step 3: Predict; select; best matches your prediction

2. Focus on the big picture, determine the author's purpose for writing; avoid getting bogged down by details.

3. Drop it and move on! Circle the question number in your test booklet, fill in a guess when you grid answers for that page, and come back to take a second look at the question if you have time left when you've finished the section.

4. Dates and time-related phrases such as *during the 1800s, after the Revolutionary War,* and *before the 20th century*

5. A sentence near the beginning of the passage that breaks a large topic into smaller parts, such as *Beethoven's work can be divided into three periods;* words such as *groups, categories,* and *classification* also suggest an outline structure.

6. Cause and effect

7. Contrast

8. False: The details are important only if they help you determine the author's purpose or if a particular question asks about a detail.

9. a. Detail

   b. Generalization

   c. Function

   d. Vocabulary-in-Context

   e. Inference

   f. Writer's view

10. a. Misused detail

    b. Extreme

    c. Opposite or contradiction

    d. Distortion

    e. Out-of-scope

Reading Wrap-up

We trust you did well on the quiz. Now try your hand at the sample practice passages in the next chapters. Practice using the Kaplan method just as you will on Test Day. Because the passage map notes are so crucial to your success, we've included suggested passage map notes as part of the Answers and Explanations for each passage. Your own notes need not match these exactly to be effective, but your note for each paragraph should address the purpose of the paragraph as a whole and not recite details.

Some of the practice passages here may be slightly longer than the ones you'll see on the actual ACT. To give you extra opportunities for practice, our passages include 12 questions instead of the 10 questions per passage that you'll see on Test Day.

To get the most benefit from the practice passages, don't just answer the questions and correct them. Give some attention to the questions you get wrong. Read the answer explanation and try to determine *why* you got the question wrong. Some questions to consider include:

- Did you read the question stem carefully?
- Did you find the most appropriate part of the passage to refer back to before making your prediction?
- Were you focusing on the wrong words when you referred to the passage?
- Did you try to answer the question from memory or skip the prediction step?

Occasionally, a particular question may give you trouble because you don't know the meaning of a word used in the passage. If this happens to you, don't panic. You don't always need to know the meaning of every word in the passage to answer all the questions correctly. If you think you do need to know a word's meaning, see if you can deduce the meaning from the other words around it (just as you do to answer a Vocabulary-in-Context question). If you find yourself stumbling over a lot of unfamiliar words, plan to add some vocabulary study to your ACT prep time. A great way to start is to look up any unfamiliar words in the practice passage. You can keep a running vocabulary list, write the words on flashcards, or add them to an electronic device that you can use for study and review. However, don't let vocabulary study distract you from working through practice passages and applying the Kaplan method and strategies. While some vocabulary study can be helpful for everyone, the most effective way to get ready for the ACT is to spend time working on practice passages.

We hope you've gotten a sense that the ACT Reading section is like a game with easily identifiable rules that you can learn and apply. As with any game, you are sure to improve with practice. Have fun!

Chapter Eleven: **Reading Practice Set I— Prose Fiction**

Directions: This test contains a passage, followed by several questions. After reading the passage, select the best answer to each question. You are allowed to refer to the passage while answering the questions.

PROSE FICTION

This passage is adapted from the novel The House of Mirth, *written by Edith Wharton and published in 1905. This excerpt concerns Mr. Gryce and Miss Lily Bart and other guests who are visiting at Bellomont, the home of the Trenors.*

The observance of Sunday at Bellomont was chiefly marked by the punctual appearance of the smart omnibus destined to convey the household to the little church at the gates. Whether any one
Line got into the omnibus or not was a matter of secondary importance,
(5) since by standing there it not only bore witness to the orthodox intentions of the family, but made Mrs. Trenor feel, when she finally heard it drive away, that she had somehow vicariously made use of it.

It was Mrs. Trenor's theory that her daughters actually did go
(10) to church every Sunday, but their French governess's convictions calling her to the rival fane, and the fatigues of the week keeping their mother in her room till luncheon, there was seldom any one present to verify the fact. Now and then, in a spasmodic burst of virtue—when the house had been too uproarious over night—Gus
(15) Trenor forced his genial bulk into a tight frock-coat and routed his daughters from their slumber, but habitually, as Lily explained to Mr. Gryce, this parental duty was forgotten till the church bells were ringing across the park, and the omnibus had driven away empty.
(20) Lily had hinted to Mr. Gryce that this neglect of religious observances was repugnant to her early traditions, and that during her visits to Bellomont she regularly accompanied Muriel and Hilda to church. This tallied with the assurance, also confidentially imparted, that, never having played bridge before, she had been

(25) "dragged into it" on the night of her arrival and had lost an appalling amount of money in consequence of her ignorance of the game
and of the rules of betting. Mr. Gryce was undoubtedly enjoying
Bellomont. He liked the ease and glitter of the life and the luster
conferred on him by being a member of this group of rich and con-

(30) spicuous people. However, he thought it a very materialistic society;
there were times when he was frightened by the talk of the men and
the looks of the ladies, and he was glad to find that Miss Bart, for
all her ease and self-possession, was not at home in so ambiguous
an atmosphere. For this reason, he had been especially pleased to

(35) learn that she would, as usual, attend the young Trenors to church
on Sunday morning. As he paced the gravel sweep before the door,
his light overcoat on his arm and his prayer-book in one carefully-
gloved hand, he reflected agreeably on the strength of character
which kept her true to her early training in surrounds so subversive

(40) to religious principles.

For a long time Mr. Gryce and the omnibus had the gravel
sweep to themselves, but, far from regretting this deplorable indif-
ference on the part of the other guests, he found himself nourishing
the hope that Miss Bart might be unaccompanied. The precious

(45) minutes were flying, however. The big chestnuts pawed the ground
and flecked their impatient sides with foam. The coachman seemed
to be slowly petrifying on the box and the groom on the doorstep,
and still the lady did not come. Suddenly, however, there was a
sound of voices and a rustle of skirts in the doorway, and

(50) Mr. Gryce, restoring his watch to his pocket, turned with a nervous
start, but it was only to find himself handing Mrs. Wetherall into
the carriage.

The Wetheralls always went to church. They belonged to the vast
group of human automata who go through life without neglecting

(55) to perform a single one of the gestures executed by the surrounding
puppets. It is true that the Bellomont puppets did not go to church,
but others equally important did—and Mr. and Mrs. Wetherall's
circle was so large that God was included in their visiting list. After
them Hilda and Muriel struggled, yawning and pinning each oth-

(60) er's veils and ribbons as they came. They had promised Lily to go to
church with her, they declared, and Lily was such a dear old duck
that they didn't mind doing it to please her, though for their own
part they would much rather have played lawn tennis with Jack and
Gwen, if she hadn't told them she was coming. The Misses Trenor

(65) were followed by Lady Cressida Raith, a weather-beaten person in
Liberty silk and ethnological trinkets, who, on seeing the omnibus,
expressed her surprise that they were not to walk across the park.
At Mrs. Wetherall's horrified protest that the church was a mile
away, her ladyship, after a glance at the height of the other's heels,

(70) acquiesced in the necessity of driving, and poor Mr. Gryce found
himself rolling off between four ladies for whose spiritual welfare
he felt not the least concern.

It might have afforded him some consolation could he have
known that Miss Bart had really meant to go to church. She had
(75) even risen earlier than usual in the execution of her purpose. She
had an idea that the sight of her in a grey gown of devotional cut,
with her famous lashes drooped above a prayer-book, would put
the finishing touch to Mr. Gryce's subjugation and render inevi-
table a certain incident which she had resolved should form a part
(80) of the walk they were to take together after luncheon. Her intentions in short had never been more definite, but poor Lily, for all
the hard glaze of her exterior, was inwardly as malleable as wax. She
was like a water-plant in the flux of the tides, and today the whole
current of her mood was carrying her toward Lawrence Selden.
(85) Why had he come to Bellomont? Was it to see herself?

1. As used in line 33, the word *ambiguous* most nearly means:

   (A) misty.
   (B) contradictory.
   (C) wealthy.
   (D) unclear.

2. From the third paragraph, it can be inferred that Mr. Gryce is attracted to Lily because

   (F) she embodies the ease and luster that he enjoys at Bellomont.
   (G) he is intrigued by her ambiguous behavior and the apparent complexity of her intellect.
   (H) she does not appear to fit in completely in her surroundings.
   (J) she learns to play games quickly.

3. In this passage, Mr. and Mrs. Trenor are primarily characterized as being

   (A) widely known for their generous hospitality.
   (B) somewhat hypocritical in their concern for appearances.
   (C) overly concerned about the religious practices of their guests.
   (D) unreasonably controlling of their two daughters.

4. The phrase *It was Mrs. Trenor's theory* (line 9) is used primarily to indicate that

   (F) Mrs. Trenor doesn't care whether or not her daughters attend church.
   (G) Mrs. Trenor's understanding and that of the French governess contradict each other.
   (H) Mr. and Mrs. Trenor have different beliefs about how best to manage their daughters.
   (J) Mrs. Trenor would like to believe that Muriel and Hilda attend church regularly.

5. The author uses the phrase *spasmodic burst* (line 13) in order to emphasize that

    (A) Mr. Trenor's overweight condition is affecting his health.
    (B) the Trenors are consistent in providing their guests with transportation to church.
    (C) parties given by the Trenors are known to be uproarious.
    (D) Mr. Trenor does not regularly attend church.

6. Lily's admission to Mr. Gryce that she *had lost an appalling amount of money . . . betting* (lines 25–26) is used in the passage mainly as

    (F) an indication that Lily's financial status is significantly lower than that of her hosts.
    (G) a detail that Mr. Gryce uses to justify his admiration of Lily.
    (H) evidence of the contrast between Lily, who is not at home at Bellomont, and Mr. Gryce, who enjoys his visit there.
    (J) an example of the Trenors' tendency to manipulate Lily.

7. According to the passage, which of the following statements accurately describe the Wetheralls' attitudes and habits regarding church attendance?

    I. They attend church regularly.

    II. They view Sunday church attendance as a pressing moral obligation.

    III. They feel that church attendance is expected of them.

    IV. They view going to church as something similar to making a social visit.

    (A) I, II, III, IV
    (B) II, III, IV
    (C) III only
    (D) I, III, IV

8. It can be inferred from the last paragraph that

    (F) Lily never had any intention of meeting Mr. Gryce for church.
    (G) Lily is conscious of trying to appear attractive to Mr. Gryce.
    (H) Lily's inflexibility can create social problems for her.
    (J) Lily's outward appearance of malleability belies her actual resoluteness.

9. The main focus of this passage is

    (A) the hypocrisy of the Trenors and their guests.
    (B) the uncomfortable interaction between Mrs. Wetherall and Lady Cressida Raith.
    (C) Mr. Gryce's interest in Lily Bart.
    (D) the manners and morals of the upper classes.

10. The author includes the details *the big chestnuts pawed the ground . . . doorstep* (lines 45–47) mainly for the purpose of

    (F)   adding to the visual appeal of the story.

    (G)   emphasizing Mr. Gryce's impatience.

    (H)   providing details about the omnibus.

    (J)   illustrating Lily and Mr. Gryce's common love of nature.

11. From the last paragraph, it is reasonable to infer that Lily does not attend church on this morning because

    (A)   her interest in Mr. Gryce is quickly pushed aside by her interest in Lawrence Selden.

    (B)   she comes to feel that Mr. Gryce is too materialistic and not a person whose spiritual values she shares.

    (C)   she finds it repugnant to attend church with hypocrites such as Mrs. Wetherall and Lady Cressida Raith.

    (D)   Mr. Trenor has not woken Lily on time.

12. From the description of the Wetheralls in lines 53–56, *They belonged to . . . puppets,* the author would most likely agree with which of the following statements?

    (F)   People who attend church frequently do so to foster their sense of belonging to a community.

    (G)   Acting on religious principles encourages people to behave like automatons.

    (H)   Religious belief encourages the view that the subjugation of others is acceptable.

    (J)   Many people model their behaviors after those of the people around them.

ANSWERS AND EXPLANATIONS

Suggested Passage Map Notes

Paragraph 1: Omnibus to take people at Bellomont to church

Paragraph 2: Trenor's don't often go to church; conversation between Lily and Mr. Gryce

Paragraph 3: Mr. Gryce mostly likes Bellomont; Lily a bit out of place there; Mr. Gryce approving of Lily

Paragraph 4: Mr. Gryce waits for Lily to come out for church

Paragraph 5: Wetheralls and others (the Trenor sisters and Lady Cressida) come for church

Paragraph 6: Lily has sudden change of heart and doesn't follow through on her plan for church; she's curious about Selden

1. B
2. H
3. B
4. J
5. D
6. G
7. D
8. G
9. C
10. G
11. A
12. J

1. **The best answer is B.** For Vocabulary-in-Context questions, start by going back to the sentence where the word is used and make a prediction. If you need to, read a little before and after this sentence. Despite Lily's *self-possession,* she isn't quite comfortable in the _____ _____ *atmosphere.* Here, *ambiguous* means something that would cause discomfort. For more detail, check the two previous sentences. Mr. Gryce likes the *ease and glitter* of life and Bellomont. The word *however* signals a contrast. Here, the contrast is that Mr. Gryce finds the people at Bellomont to be *materialistic.* Thus, your prediction should relate to contrast. A good prediction would be something like *contrasting* or *contradictory.* Option A is wrong because nothing in the context relates to it. Option C is a misused detail. Option D is a common meaning of *ambiguous* but not the meaning used here.

2. **The best answer is H.** For this Generalization question, you have to take into account the whole paragraph and make a prediction that's consistent with it. Still, certain phrases are the key. Here, the phrase *he was glad to find … that Miss Bart … was not at home* indicates Mr. Gryce's approval of Lily. In addition, he appreciates that she plans to go to church even though most people at Bellomont do not. Predict something along the lines of *he appreciates that she is different from the hosts and other guests at Bellomont* or *he admires her for planning to attend church.* Option H is the best match. Option F is a distortion. Though Mr. Gryce enjoys the *ease and luster,* the passage never suggests that Lily embodies it. Option G combines the distortion and out-of-scope traps. The word *ambiguous* is used, but not to describe Lily, and her intellect is not described at all. Option J is a contradiction.

3. **The best answer is B.** Use your passage notes to help you find the appropriate spots in the passage to refer to. Mrs. Trenor is discussed in paragraphs 1 and 2; Mr. Trenor is discussed in paragraph 2. At the end of paragraph 1, we read that Mrs. Trenor appears to like feeling that she *had somehow vicariously made use of* the omnibus that takes people to church. We can infer from this that Mrs. Trenor likes the idea, though not the actuality, of going to church. It pleases her that her family and guests go to church and makes her feel that she has had some part in the process. In paragraph 2, we read that Mr. Trenor goes to church only occasionally (*in a spasmodic burst of virtue,* lines 13–14), usually after a particularly wild party (*when the house had been too uproarious over night,* line 14). Taken together, it seems that the Trenors view church attendance not as a regular habit but as something they like their guests and family to do to for the sake of appearances.

This matches option B. Option A is out-of-scope. The Trenors do appear to be hospitable, but the passage doesn't say they are *widely known* for hospitality. Option C is a distortion. Mrs. Trenor does appreciate the fact that some of her guests might go to church, but she isn't *overly concerned.* Option D is a contradiction. If anything, the Trenors are seen to have relatively little control over their daughters; Mr. Trenor doesn't even always manage to get them to go to church when he wants them to.

4. **The best answer is J.** For a function question, look back to the context to make your prediction. Here, *Mrs. Trenor's theory* is something she can't prove. The governess attends a different church (*a rival fane*), and Mrs. Trenor herself stays in her room until lunch, so neither of them can confirm that the Trenor daughters go to church. Consider also the previous paragraph, which mentions that Mrs. Trenor likes to feel that she's attended church *vicariously* through other members of her household. Put the information from these two paragraphs together and it seems that Mrs. Trenor would like to believe that her daughters go to church, even though she can't prove it. Options F and G are contradictions. Option H is out-of-scope. Nothing in the passage supports this.

5. **The best answer is D.** For a function question asking about the use of a phrase, read the immediately surrounding context carefully. Notice the phrases *Now and then* (line 13) and *when the house had been…* (line 14). From this context, predict that *spasmodic burst* refers to something that happens only occasionally, under certain circumstances. Option D nicely matches this prediction. Option A is a distortion. Though Mr. Trenor is described as heavy (*his genial bulk,* line 15), the passage doesn't refer specifically to his health. Option B is a misused detail. While it's true that the Trenors regularly provide transportation to church, the fact has nothing to do with the phrase *spasmodic burst.* Option C is a distortion. The word *uproarious* is used (line 14), but the passage doesn't indicate that the Trenors are known for uproarious parties.

6. **The best answer is G.** As with all function questions, context is crucial here. Use your passage map notes. Paragraph 3 describes Mr. Gryce's attraction to Lily. The phrase *this tallied with the assurance…that she had been 'dragged into it'* (lines 23–25) gives part of the reason for Mr. Gryce's approval of Lily. Mr. Gryce appreciates *the assurance* that Lily had not willingly involved herself in the bridge game and that she is not an experienced gambler. Therefore, predict that the fact that Lily loses money inspires Mr. Gryce's admiration. This prediction fits with option G. Option F is out-of-scope. Lily's financial status as compared with that of her hosts isn't mentioned in the passage. Option H is a misused detail. The contrast between Lily and Mr. Gryce is present in the passage, but it doesn't address this particular question. Option J is a distortion. Although the passage states that the Trenor sisters *dragged [Lily] into* the bridge game, the passage never says that the Trenors have a tendency to manipulate Lily.

7. **The best answer is D.** For a Roman-numeral question, address each point one by one. Remember that you may be able to eliminate certain answer choices even before you have considered all the statements. Statement I is true (line 53). Thus you can eliminate options B and C. In considering statement II, pay attention to lines 57–58: *Mr. and Mrs. Wetherall's circle was so large that God was included in their visiting list.* From this sentence, it can be inferred that the Wetheralls view church as more of a social experience than a moral obligation. Statement II is false, which is another justification for eliminating option B. For statement III, refer to lines 53–56: *They belonged to the vast group of human automata… surrounding puppets.* This sentence supports statement III. By process of elimination, the correct answer has to be option D.

8. **The best answer is G.**   For a Generalization question, consider the specified portion of the passage, and look for particular details that justify your answer. Here, pay careful attention to lines 74–78: *She [Lily] had an idea that the sight of her in a grey gown of devotional cut . . . would put the finishing touch to Mr. Gryce's subjugation.* The word *subjugation* suggests that Lily wants to use her charms to ensure Mr. Gryce's attraction to her. This prediction best matches option G. Option F is a contradiction. Option H combines the contradiction and out-of-scope traps. Lily is described in this paragraph as being prone to sudden change, the opposite of inflexibility. The passage doesn't directly refer to any social problems Lily may have. Option J is a distortion of lines 81–82, *Lily, for all the hard glaze of her exterior, was inwardly as malleable as wax.* Option J reverses the details stated here: Lily is actually resolute on the outside but malleable on the inside. Note that *belies* in option J means *contradicts.*

9. **The best answer is C.**   For this Generalization question, consider the relative emphasis the writer gives to the different characters. In the passage Lily and Mr. Gryce are discussed more than the Trenors and the Wetheralls, so predict that the answer centers on Lily and Mr. Gryce. Only option C comes anywhere close. Option A is a misused detail. We can infer that the writer portrays the Trenors and their guests as behaving hypocritically, but this is just part of the passage, not the main focus. Option B is a misused detail. The interaction between Mrs. Wetherall and Lady Cressida is described, but it is minor. Option D is out-of-scope. It is too general to apply to this passage.

10. **The best answer is G.**   This is a function question asking about a detail, so pay attention to the immediate context. The paragraph describes Mr. Gryce waiting for Lily to appear. He hopes that he will get some time alone with her (*He found himself nourishing the hope that Miss Bart might be unaccompanied,* lines 43–44.) He is portrayed as being eager and impatient (*The precious minutes were flying,* lines 44–45.) Thus, when the writer describes even the chestnut trees as appearing to behave impatiently, the detail emphasizes Mr. Gryce's impatience. Similarly, he feels that Lily's taking so long is making time pass unrealistically slowly. The detail in the question stem, the coachman and groom *petrifying* (that is, turning to stone) is meant to convey Mr. Gryce's impatience. Option G is the best match. Option F isn't specific or relevant to the passage; it doesn't take into account the main purpose of the paragraph in the way that option G does. Option H is a misused detail. While the detail in the question stem does include a reference to the omnibus's driver, describing the omnibus itself is not the main purpose of the paragraph. Option J is out-of-scope. The passage never suggests that Lily and Mr. Gryce share a love of nature.

11. **The best answer is A.**   For a generalization question, consider the purpose of the whole paragraph and look for details that support the inference you arrive at. The paragraph states that Lily had intended to go to church: *Her intentions . . . had never been more definite,* (lines 80–81). However, she is also described as being *as malleable as wax* and as easily affected by her mood as a water plant is affected by changing tides. The name *Lawrence Selden* (line 84) seems to come out of nowhere. We can infer from the last lines of the passage that Selden is a guest who has recently arrived at Bellomont and that Lily thinks he may have come to see her. Taken together, the details in this paragraph suggest that Lily has been distracted from her intention to attend church with Mr. Gryce because she is curious about Selden. This works well as a prediction and leads us to option A. Option B includes a misused detail. The word *materialistic* is used in line 30 to describe what Mr. Gryce thinks of other guests at Bellomont, not to describe Lily's opinion of Mr. Gryce. Option C is out-of-scope. Nothing in the passage suggests that Lily doesn't want to attend church with

Mrs. Wetherall and Lady Cressida Raith, nor does the passage indicate that Lily finds them to be hypocritical. Option D is a distortion. The passage states that Mr. Trenor sometimes doesn't wake up in time to get his daughters (Muriel and Hilda) to church, but the passage doesn't indicate that Lily had been expecting Mr. Trenor to wake her up for church.

12. **The best answer is J.**   For any Writer's View question, you must infer from the words and context of the passage what the author thinks. For this question, go back to the lines cited in the question stem and pay attention to the context to make your prediction. *They* refers to the Wetheralls, who *always went to church* (line 53). The cited lines describe the Wetheralls as *automata.* Though this word may be unfamiliar to you, use your inference skills to deduce that it means something like automatons, or people who act more because they are copying the behaviors of others than because they are thinking for themselves. According to the passage, *Automata . . . perform . . . the gestures executed by the surrounding puppets.* Predict that the author uses the quotation in the question stem to describe people who copy others instead of acting on their own ideas. This prediction best matches option J. Option F is out-of-scope; there is nothing in the passage to this. Option G is a distortion that carries the inference too far. The author never suggests that people behave like *automata* because they have religious beliefs. Option H is a distortion. The word *subjugation* is used in line 78 to describe the effect Lily hopes to have on Mr. Gryce, not in the context of a statement about religious belief.

Chapter Twelve: **Reading Practice Set II—Prose Fiction**

Directions: This test contains a passage, followed by several questions. After reading the passage, select the best answer to each question. You are allowed to refer to the passage while answering the questions.

PROSE FICTION

This passage is adapted from the novel The Woman in White *by Wilkie Collins. It was first published in serial form in 1859 and 1860. The narrator, Walter, is a teacher of drawing. His friend, Pesca, is a native of Italy who teaches Italian in England.*

Pesca's face and manner, on the evening when we confronted each other at my mother's gate, were more than sufficient to inform me that something extraordinary had happened. It was
Line   quite useless, however, to ask him for an immediate explanation. I
(5)   could only conjecture, while he was dragging me in by both hands, that, knowing my habits, he had come to the cottage to make sure of meeting me that night and that he had some news to tell of an unusually agreeable kind.

We both bounced into the parlor in a highly abrupt and undig-
(10)   nified manner. My mother sat by the open window laughing and fanning herself. Pesca was one of her especial favorites, and his wildest eccentricities were always pardonable in her eyes. From the first moment she found out that the little Professor was deeply and gratefully attached to her son, she opened her heart to him unre-
(15)   servedly and took all his puzzling foreign peculiarities for granted, without so much as attempting to understand any one of them.

My sister Sarah, with all the advantages of youth, was, strangely enough, less pliable. She did full justice to Pesca's excellent quali-ties of heart, but she could not accept him implicitly, as my mother
(20)   accepted him, for my sake. Her insular notions of propriety rose in perpetual revolt against Pesca's constitutional contempt for appear-ances, and she was always more or less undisguisedly astonished at her mother's familiarity with the eccentric little foreigner. I have

(25) observed, not only in my sister's case, but in the instances of others, that we of the young generation are nowhere near as hearty and
impulsive as some of our elders. I constantly see old people flushed
and excited by the prospect of some anticipated pleasure which
altogether fails to ruffle the tranquility of their serene grandchil-
(30) dren. Are we, I wonder, quite such genuine boys and girls now as
our seniors were in their time? Has the great advance in education
taken rather too long a stride, and are we in these modern days just
the least trifle in the world too well brought up?

Without attempting to answer those questions decisively, I may
at least record that I never saw my mother and my sister together
(35) in Pesca's society without finding my mother much the younger
woman of the two. On this occasion, for example, while the old
lady was laughing heartily over the boyish manner in which we
tumbled into the parlor, Sarah was perturbedly picking up the
broken pieces of a teacup, which the Professor had knocked off the
(40) table in his precipitate advance to meet me at the door.

"I don't know what would have happened, Walter," said my
mother, "if you had delayed much longer. Pesca has been half mad
with impatience, and I have been half mad with curiosity. The
Professor has brought some wonderful news with him, in which he
(45) says you are concerned, and he has cruelly refused to give us the
smallest hint of it till his friend Walter appeared."

"Very provoking: it spoils the set," murmured Sarah to herself,
mournfully absorbed over the ruins of the broken cup.

While these words were being spoken, Pesca, happily and fussily
(50) unconscious of the irreparable wrong which the crockery had suffered at his hands, was dragging a large arm-chair to the opposite
end of the room, so as to command us all three, in the character of
a public speaker addressing an audience. Having turned the chair
with its back towards us, he jumped into it on his knees and excitedly
(55) addressed his small congregation of three from an impromptu pulpit.

"Now, my good dears," began Pesca, "listen to me. The time has
come—I recite my good news—I speak at last."

"Hear, hear," said my mother, humoring the joke.

"The next thing he will break, Mamma," whispered Sarah, "will
(60) be the back of the best arm-chair."

"Among the fine London Houses where I teach the language of my
native country," said Pesca, "is one, mighty fine, in the big place called
Portland. The golden Papa there, the mighty merchant, says, "I have
got a letter from my friend, the Mister, and he wants a recommend
(65) from me, of a drawing-master, to go down to his house in the country. Perhaps you know of a drawing master that I can recommend?"

I address myself to the mighty merchant, and I say, "Dear sir, I
have the man! The first and foremost drawing-master of the world!"

1. It can be inferred from the first paragraph that

    (A) Pesca frequently visits the narrator's mother.
    (B) the narrator does not believe that Pesca shows good judgment.
    (C) the narrator fears a hostile confrontation with Pesca.
    (D) Pesca visits the cottage fully expecting to meet up with narrator there.

2. As used in line 40, the word *precipitate* MOST nearly means

    (F) quick.
    (G) rude.
    (H) faithful.
    (J) eccentric.

3. It can be inferred from the passage that all of the following are true of Professor Pesca
    EXCEPT

    (A) he is familiar with the narrator's daily routine.
    (B) he is well-trained in public speaking.
    (C) the narrator's mother approves of him.
    (D) he has not completely mastered the subtleties of the English language.

4. A difference between older people and younger people that the narrator finds
    remarkable is

    (F) younger people are impulsive, while older people are more deliberate.
    (G) older people tend to be more curious than younger people are.
    (H) older people fail to display appropriate gratitude toward the young.
    (J) older people are more likely than younger people are to anticipate pleasures
         enthusiastically.

5. According to the passage, the narrator's mother has a high opinion of Professor Pesca
    because

    (A) she values intellectual pursuits.
    (B) Professor Pesca has been instrumental in advancing her son's career.
    (C) Professor Pesca feels a grateful attachment toward her son.
    (D) she is the sort of person who can easily overlook the faults of others.

6. It can be inferred from the passage that Professor Pesca waits until the narrator's
    arrival to tell his good news because

    (F) he is afraid that the narrator's mother would spoil the news if she heard it first.
    (G) he is uncomfortable around Sarah and is not willing to talk to her unless her
         brother is not present.
    (H) his news has nothing to do with the narrator's mother.
    (J) he wants to deliver the good news in an impressively dramatic way.

7. The passage implies that Sarah

    (A)   fails to see any good qualities in Professor Pesca.

    (B)   feels extremely protective toward her brother.

    (C)   has a strong concern for taking care of material things.

    (D)   is guilty of neglecting her elderly mother's basic needs.

8. The writer uses the phrase *while he was dragging me in by both hands* (line 5) in order to convey that the narrator

    (F)   believes Pesca's actions are characterized by rudeness.

    (G)   is reluctant to enter his mother's house in the presence of Pesca.

    (H)   is aware of Pesca's impatience.

    (J)   is frequently caught off guard by Pesca's eccentric behaviors.

9. When the narrator uses the phrase *strangely enough* (lines 17–18), he suggests that

    (A)   he is surprised that Sarah has any respect at all for Pesca.

    (B)   he would expect her to be more lenient in her judgments than she is.

    (C)   Sarah reacts in a way that is inconsistent with the advantages she has been given.

    (D)   he has never known Sarah to admit that Pesca has any good qualities.

10. The narrator's questions at the end of the third paragraph suggest that

    (F)   the narrator admires the unreserved way that members of the older generation express their feelings.

    (G)   the narrator believes that Pesca is overly concerned with appearances.

    (H)   Sarah disapproves of her mother's attitude toward Pesca.

    (J)   the narrator judges his own generation to be more genuine than his parents' generation.

11. According to the passage, in what order do the following events take place?

I. Pesca breaks the teacup.

II. Pesca arrives at the cottage.

III. The narrator's mother laughs at the behavior of Pesca and her son.

IV. The narrator enters the cottage.

    (A)   II, IV, I, III

    (B)   II, I, IV, III

    (C)   IV, II, I, III

    (D)   IV, III, II, I

12. According to the passage, the narrator wonders

 (F) whether advances in education have gone too far.

 (G) if Pesca is entirely trustworthy.

 (H) why his mother dislikes Pesca.

 (J) why Sarah's attitude is one of perpetual revolt.

ANSWERS AND EXPLANATIONS

Suggested Passage Map Notes

Paragraph 1: Pesca has good news for narrator

Paragraph 2: Narrator's mom likes Pesca

Paragraph 3: Sarah not fond of Pesca; young\old differences

Paragraph 4: Sarah seems older than mom; broken teacup

Paragraph 5: Mom eager for Pesca's good news

Paragraph 6: Sarah's annoyance

Paragraph 7: Pesca sets stage like preacher

Paragraphs 8–10: Responses to Pesca

Paragraph 11: Pesca knows rich man who needs drawing teacher

Paragraph 12: Pesca excited to know drawing teacher

 1. D
 2. F
 3. B
 4. J
 5. C
 6. J
 7. C
 8. H
 9. B
10. F
11. B
12. F

1. **The best answer is D.** For a Generalization question about a paragraph, make sure your answer is consistent with everything in the paragraph. It may be tough to predict, but you should at least refer to your passage map note and skim the paragraph before reading the answer choices. Option A is a misused detail from the second paragraph. Option B is out-of-scope. The narrator never questions Pesca's judgment. Option C is out-of-scope. Nothing in the paragraph suggests that a confrontation is likely. Option D is the best answer. The phrase *knowing my habits* (line 6) suggests that Pesca knows he will find the narrator at his mother's house.

2. **The best answer is F.** For a Vocabulary-in-Context question, go back to the sentence and check for context clues that help you predict. The sentence states the Pesca had knocked the teacup off the table while moving to greet the narrator at the door. Paragraph 1 indicates that Pesca is very eager and excited, so predict that he moved *quickly* toward the door. This prediction matches option F. Option G is a distortion. The passage states that Sarah is *perturbed* by the broken cup, but the narrator doesn't ascribe rudeness to Pesca. Option H is out-of-scope. Nothing in the sentence or passage indicates that *precipitate* could mean *faithful.* Option J is a distortion. Although Pesca is described as *eccentric* in this passage, his *advance toward the door* is not necessarily eccentric.

3. **The best answer is B.** For a broad Inference question, quickly review your passage map notes before considering the answer choices. In this case, you must eliminate choices that *are* supported by the passage. Eliminate option A because line 6 (P1) states that Pesca knows the narrator's habits. Option B is not supported by the passage and is the best answer. Although Pesca consciously uses a dramatic manner to deliver his good news, appearing to act like a preacher addressing his congregation, he does so a bit awkwardly. Nothing in the passage indicates that he is "well-trained" as a public speaker. Eliminate option C because lines 14–15 states that the narrator's mother "unreservedly" opens her heart to Pesca. Eliminate option D because Pesca's statements in the passage do not always show strong command of English. For example, in lines 64–65, Pesca says, *he wants a **recommend** from me* instead of *a **recommendation***.

4. **The best answer is J.** For a Generalization question about a contrast, review your passage map notes and skim the passage if necessary to find where in the passage to go for your prediction. In this case, your passage map notes may direct you to paragraphs 3 and 4. Predict that *the young generation [is not as] impulsive as some of our elders* (lines 25–26) and that *old people [are] excited by the prospect of some anticipated pleasure* (lines 26–27). This prediction fits well with option J. Option F is a distortion; the descriptions of young and old are reversed in this answer choice. Option G is out-of-scope. Nothing in the passage suggests that older people are more curious. Option H is out-of-scope. Older people are not described as ungrateful.

5. **The best answer is C.** For a Detail question, check your passage notes or skim the passage to find the words used in the question stem. Here, your passage map notes should direct you to paragraph 2, where lines 12–14 states that the narrator's mother has favored Pesca since *the first moment she found out that the little Professor was deeply and gratefully attached to her son.* Option A is out-of-scope. The passage says nothing about the narrator's mother valuing intellectual pursuits. Option B is a distortion. While the passage does concern Pesca's recommending the narrator for a job, the narrator's mother doesn't yet know about this when the passage opens. Option D is a distortion. The passage states the narrator's mother overlooks Pesca's faults, but it doesn't suggest that she applies this lenient attitude toward everyone.

6. **The best answer is J.** For an Inference question, read the appropriate part of the passage and draw a conclusion that doesn't stray too far from what is stated. In this case, use your passage notes to direct you to paragraphs 7–10. Pesca is described as wanting to *command us all three, in the character of a public speaker addressing an audience* (lines 57–53). Pesca's words *The time has come—I recite my good news—I speak at last* (lines 56–57), show that he wants to build a sense of anticipation and drama around what he has to say. This prediction supports option J. Option F is out-of-scope because the passage doesn't indicate Pesca

is afraid the narrator's mother would spoil his secret. As the prediction describes, it is primarily his desire to be dramatic that makes him delay. Option G is a distortion. Although Sarah displays some discomfort around Pesca (her annoyance at his breaking the teacup), Pesca is not described as feeling at all uncomfortable around Sarah. Option H is a contradiction. If anything, Pesca seems confident that the narrator's mother will be delighted by his news.

7. **The best answer is C.** For a Generalization question about a character, start with your passage map notes. In this case, they should lead you to paragraphs 3 and 4. Quickly look at these paragraphs to get a feel for how Sarah is portrayed. In addition, skim through the passage for the word *Sarah* to see if any other references will help you with this question. Then read through the answer choices and eliminate. Option A is an extreme. The passage says that Sarah *did full justice to Pesca's excellent qualities of heart, but she could not accept him implicitly* (lines 18–19). This means that Sarah acknowledges that Pesca at least has a good heart, even if she doesn't like everything about him. Option B is out-of-scope because Sarah is not described as being protective of her brother. Option C, the best answer, is justified by line 48, where Sarah is described as *mournfully absorbed over the ruins of the broken cup*. Additional support for this choice is found in lines 59–60, where Sarah is concerned that Pesca will break *the best arm-chair*. Option D is out-of-scope. The passage says nothing about the basic needs of the narrator's mother not being met.

8. **The best answer is H.** For a function question about a phrase, read around the immediate context to make your prediction. Because the narrator suspects that Pesca has come with good news, the narrator probably realizes that Pesca is eager to get him into the house. This prediction fits well with option H. Option F is out-of-scope. There is no evidence suggesting that the narrator finds Pesca to be rude. Option G is out-of-scope. Nothing suggests that the narrator wants to resist Pesca or avoid his company. Option J is a distortion. While the passage does describe Pesca as *an eccentric little foreigner* (line 23), the narrator never says he is caught off guard by Pesca's eccentricities.

9. **The best answer is B.** For a function question about a phrase, check the context of the sentence to predict. This sentence contains a comparison, *less pliable* (line 18). Briefly refer back to the previous paragraph to determine that the comparison is between Sarah and her mother. Sarah is described as having *all the advantages of youth.* Given the contrast between mother and daughter, the narrator seems to think that a younger person would be more flexible. This prediction lines up with option B. Option A is a distortion that doesn't take the contrast between youth and age into account. Option C is a distortion. The *advantages* in this context are the *advantages of youth,* not particular advantages that have been given to Sarah. Option D is an opposite. The narrator states that Sarah can see Pesca's excellent qualities of heart (lines 18–19).

10. **The best answer is F.** For a Generalization question about a paragraph, use your passage map notes and quickly review the paragraph to see if you can predict. There's a lot in this paragraph. Sarah isn't very comfortable with Pesca; the mother seems more excited to hear Pesca's good news; the narrator compares old and young, wondering if the young are a little too serious. Don't worry which is more important, but be ready to use the information to judge the answer choices. Option F is the best answer. It embraces the differences between old and young and the narrator's surprise at Sarah's attitude toward Pesca. Option G is a distortion. The passage states that Sarah disapproves of Pesca's *lack* of regard for appearances (lines 21–22). Option H is a distortion. Though lines 19–20 indicate that Sarah doesn't

share her mother's opinion of Pesca (*she could not accept him implicitly, as my mother did*), Sarah doesn't express disapproval of her mother's attitude. Option J is a distortion. The narrator asks himself if members of his own generation are *quite such genuine boys and girls now as our seniors were in their time* (lines 29–30), but he doesn't make an explicit statement that his generation is the more *genuine*.

11. **The best answer is B.**   For a Roman-numeral question about sequence, try to determine which event happened first and use that knowledge to eliminate wrong answer choices. In this case, event I comes first. This is justified by lines 6–7: . . . *knowing my habits, he [Pesca] had come to the cottage to make sure of meeting me.* Thus, eliminate options C and D. Now all that remains is to determine whether event IV preceded event I. This information lets you choose between options A and B. Lines 39–40 indicate that Pesca had been inside the cottage and broken the teacup *before* the narrator came inside: *The Professor had knocked [the teacup] off the table in his precipitate advance to meet me at the door.* Therefore option B is the correct answer.

12. **The best answer is F.**   For a broadly worded Detail question, your passage map notes and quick skimming may not be much help in directing you to the best part of the passage to refer to. If this is the case, don't spend too much time looking around. Check the answer choices and see if a quick reference to the passage can help you choose the best one. Here, option F is the best answer, but that may not be immediately apparent. Eliminate option G because the narrator never questions Pesca's trustworthiness, making this choice out-of-scope. Eliminate option H because it's a contradiction. The author states that his mother has a high opinion of Pesca. Option J is a distortion. The phrase *perpetual revolt* describes Sarah's opinion of Pesca's *contempt for appearances* (lines 21–22), but it isn't something the narrator wonders about. Working by elimination is effective for this question. Notice, however, that the lines 30–31 *has the great advance in education taken rather too long a stride?* does directly support option F.

Chapter Thirteen: **Reading Practice Set III– Social Studies**

Directions: This test contains a passage, followed by several questions. After reading the passage, select the best answer to each question. You are allowed to refer to the passage while answering the questions.

SOCIAL STUDIES

This passage is adapted from "Assessing the Values of Cultural Heritage," a report published in 2002 by the Advisory Council on Historic Preservation. This selection, written by Marta de la Torre and Randall Mason, examines the challenges involved in determining the cultural significance of historic sites to various groups, including conservation experts and ordinary citizens.

In recent decades, the concept of what is heritage has evolved and expanded, and new groups have joined specialists in its identification. These groups of citizens, of professionals from other fields,
Line and of representatives of special interests arrive in the heritage field
(5) with their own criteria, opinions, and values—which often differ from our own as heritage specialists.

This democratization is a positive development in our field and bears witness to the importance of heritage in today's society. Nonetheless, this aperture has brought new considerations to the
(10) discussions and has made them much more complex. Today the opinions of experts are often a few among many, in an arena where it is recognized that heritage is multivalent and that values are not immutable. In this changed environment, the articulation and understanding of values have acquired greater importance when
(15) heritage decisions are being made about what to conserve, how to conserve it, where to set priorities, and how to handle conflicting interests.

As conservation professionals, we are comfortable with the assessment methods used by traditional heritage experts. However,
(20) to identify and measure "social" values, we must venture into new areas. The stakeholders of social values are usually members of the public who have not traditionally participated in our work or had

their opinions taken into consideration. Today, as we recognize the importance of including all stakeholders in the process, we must
(25) turn to other disciplines to bring these new groups into the discussions.

Anthropologist Setha M. Low has introduced ethnographic research as a way of bringing new groups of stakeholders into the values identification process. The field of environmental conserva-
(30) tion has a relatively long tradition of consultation with a broad spectrum of stakeholders. Approaches from the environmental field are often held up as examples to be emulated in the heritage field. Theresa Satterfield's work in this area has been a model for assessment tools and methods that might be productively applied in our
(35) own field. Economists seem to have the most developed and widely accepted value assessment tools. However, these tools might not be as accurate in measuring cultural values as has been accepted in the past. A number of economists are now searching for ways of honing their tools to make them more useful in the heritage field. The
(40) work of researchers in all three of these areas points us toward collaboration with other disciplines.

A discussion of values, of how social contexts shape heritage and conservation, and of the imperative of public participation provides examples of issues that challenge conventional notions of conserva-
(45) tion professionals' responsibilities. How to champion conservation principles (traditional ones, centered on the sanctity and inherent meaningfulness of material heritage) while managing an open democratic process that may conclude by underselling conservation in favor of other social goals? This issue gets to the essential nature of
(50) the field and of conservation as a profession: Are we advocates? Are we neutral professionals and experts?

Conservation professionals are faced with two particular challenges arising out of these social and political contexts: power sharing and collaboration. Broader participation poses a challenge to
(55) the roles and responsibilities of conservation professionals: some suggest that bringing conservation policies and decisions in line with democratic values would undermine the authority of conservation professionals and would even amount to an abdication of professional responsibility. In other words, democratization of con-
(60) servation decision making could contradict the professional devotion to conservation—what happens when the democracy of voices decides that a heritage site can be destroyed? Do we as conservation professionals have a right, or even a responsibility, to speak against the democratic will?
(65) The probability is not that actual decision making power will be democratized but, rather, that the process of value elicitation will be included. Democratization of the processes of consultation and assessment of heritage values is not likely to be a threat to the sovereignty of the field, but it still requires a change of attitude and

(70)   training. The inevitability of trade-offs and compromises and the
respectful and meaningful gathering of different modes of valuing
have to be recognized.

      Using new methods from different fields means collaborating
with more and different professionals, anthropologists and econo-

(75)   mists, for instance. Such collaboration raises questions about who
is in charge of which part of the process. What are the relative
roles and contributions and responsibilities of this different cast of
characters? Does the conservation professional's role become that
of an orchestrator of specialists or of one specialist among others?

(80)   It seems that the conservation professional has moved to play the
dual role of specialist and orchestrator. The tasks associated with
the latter function call for new ways of thinking as well as for new
skills. The challenge ahead is to continue searching for the means to
serve the public good by preserving material remains of the past.

1.   What is the fundamental question addressed by the passage as a whole?

    (A)   What is the role of the ordinary citizen in determining what conservation pro-
fessionals should preserve?

    (B)   What are the best methods to use to ensure reliable conservation of culturally
significant sites?

    (C)   In what ways can anthropologists contribute to the field of conservation?

    (D)   How is the role of the conservation professional changing in light of social and
political concerns about the democratization of conversation activities?

2.   This passage is written from the point of view of

    (F)   a politician whose main concern is balancing the needs of various interest
groups.

    (G)   an anthropologist who is eager to see her methodology applied in the field of
conservation.

    (H)   a specialist in the field of conservation who believes that conservation profes-
sionals have much to contribute.

    (J)   an economist who is pushing for the value assessment tools used in economics
as the basis for conservation decisions.

3.   The phrase "democracy of voices" in line 61 most likely refers to

    (A)   the opinion of a large number of ordinary citizens.

    (B)   a government run by the people.

    (C)   the viewpoint of a citizen who is politically active.

    (D)   a traditional influence on decisions about heritage conservation.

4. A possible drawback of power sharing and collaboration in the conservation field that the passage refers to is that

   (F) the authority of the specialist would be undermined.

   (G) the ordinary citizen lacks knowledge relating to historic sites.

   (H) the general public does not express much interest in historic conservation.

   (J) most conservation specialists lack the skills needed to lead group collaboration.

5. In the context of the passage as a whole, the questions at the end of the sixth paragraph serve to

   (A) address a concern that the writer will later resolve.

   (B) reflect uncertainty about future goals.

   (C) expose a flaw in a current theory.

   (D) point the way to a clearly defined solution to a problem.

6. The sentence *A discussion of values…responsibilities* (lines 42–45) suggests that

   (F) championing traditional conservation principles must be made a priority.

   (G) conservation professionals' traditional view of their responsibilities did not demand that they take social contexts into account.

   (H) the field of conservation has been mired in convention for too long.

   (J) ethnographic research should be used to inform the values identification process.

7. The writer believes that the effect of democratization in the conservation field will

   (A) be a threat to the sovereignty of the field.

   (B) mean that different ways of assessing value will have to be recognized.

   (C) ultimately lead to conservation decisions being made by the people.

   (D) serve the public good by completely reforming the practices of conservation specialists.

8. As used in the passage, the word *orchestrator* (line 79) most nearly means

   (F) manager.

   (G) creator.

   (H) person with particular expertise.

   (J) musical director.

9. The writer's view of the outlook for the conservation field is

   (A) grounded in cynicism.

   (B) cautiously optimistic.

   (C) tinged with reservations.

   (D) fairly pessimistic.

10. According to the passage, the notion of what heritage is has evolved

    (F) to reflect a multitude of social changes in recent years.

    (G) because heritage specialists have been considered too old-fashioned in their values.

    (H) by recognizing the values of those who aren't professionals in the field.

    (J) to reflect a growing trend toward democratization in many academic specialties.

11. The phrase *underselling conservation in favor of other social goals* (lines 48–49) is used to describe

    (A) the way in which the values of conservation are being neglected because of economic concerns.

    (B) the priority that has been given to social goals over economic considerations.

    (C) the fear that inviting a democratic process may dilute the traditional goals of conservation.

    (D) the challenges that currently face conservation professionals.

12. Setha M. Low and Theresa Satterfield are mentioned in the passage as

    (F) conservation professionals who are fighting the democratization of their field.

    (G) economists who point to the need for heritage professionals to take economic values into account.

    (H) citizens who are fighting to have their voices heard in decisions that are made about which historic sites are preserved.

    (J) experts in other fields who have contributions to make to the direction that conservation should move it.

ANSWERS AND EXPLANATIONS

Suggested Passage Map Notes

Paragraph 1: New groups affecting heritage field

Paragraph 2: Democratization positive but complex

Paragraph 3: Importance of determining social "values"

Paragraph 4: Other fields help bring new groups into values ID process

Paragraph 5: Tension between conservation principles and democratization

Paragraph 6: Resulting challenges

Paragraph 7: Democratization requires changes for professionals

Paragraph 8: Collaboration w/experts outside conservation field

1. D
2. H
3. A
4. F
5. A
6. G
7. B
8. F
9. D
10. H
11. C
12. J

1. **The best answer is D.** For a broad Generalization question, keep the overall purpose of the passage in mind. Incorrect answer choices may refer to too small a part of the passage. Predict that the purpose of the passage is to address challenges faced by conservation professionals. Option D best captures this purpose. Option A is a distortion. It uses several words from the passage, but it puts the emphasis in the wrong place by focusing on citizens instead of professionals. Option B is out-of-scope. The passage doesn't address particular methods of conservation. Option C is a misused detail. Paragraph 4 discusses contributions from anthropologists, but the focus of the whole passage is much broader.

2. **The best answer is H.** For a Writer's View question, take the whole passage into account and don't put excessive emphasis on a particular detail. Lines 18 and 62 both use the word *we* with the phrase *as conservation professionals,* making it clear that the writer identifies with this group. Option H is the only choice supported by this prediction. Option F is a distortion. The passage mentions *political contexts* but does not refer at all to politicians. Option G is a distortion. The passage mentions Low, an anthropologist, but doesn't describe her as being eager to see her methodology used by conservation professionals. Option J is a distortion. Although the passage mentions economists, they are not described as pushing to have an influence in the field of conservation.

3. **The best answer is A.** For an Inference question that asks about the meaning of a phrase, pay close attention to the context of the paragraph. Here, the paragraph refers to *power sharing* (lines 53–54) that might *undermine the authority of conservation professionals* (lines 57–58). There is a tension here between allowing the opinions of new groups into the discussion and maintaining the traditional role of the conservation professionals, because it's possible that the new groups would contradict the professionals. This prediction leads to option A. Option B is out-of-scope. There is nothing in the passage to indicate that *government* works in this context. Option C is out-of-scope. *Politically active* citizens aren't mentioned in the passage. Option D is an opposite. The phrase in question refers to those who might oppose the *traditional influence.*

4. **The best answer is F.** To predict for a Detail question, refer to your passage map notes to direct you to the right spot in the passage. If the notes don't suggest a particular paragraph to research in, skim the passage for the words used in the question stem or words with a similar meaning. Here, *power sharing and collaboration* appear in paragraph 6 in the context

of *challenges* that are presented by allowing more groups into the discussion. The writer states that *some suggest [that allowing more groups in] would undermine the authority of the conservation professional* (lines 57–58). This prediction leads directly to option F. Option G is out-of-scope. The ordinary citizen's knowledge of historic sites is not mentioned in the passage. Option H is out-of-scope. The passage never states that the general public lacks interest in historic sites. Option J is out-of-scope. The passage doesn't question the leadership skills of *most conservation professionals.*

5. **The best answer is A.** For a Function question, pay close attention to the context. Read a little above and a little below the cited lines to make your prediction. Here, context of the lines below puts the answers to the questions in a balanced perspective: *The probability is not that actual decision making power will be democratized, but, rather, that the process of value elicitation will be included* (lines 65–67). Predict from this that the questions at the end of paragraph 6 can be answered in ways that are not alarming. This prediction lines up with option A. Option B is a distortion that doesn't take information from paragraph 7 into account. Although the questions point to *uncertainty,* the writer immediately addresses the issue with a firm expectation that is not uncertain. Option C is out-of-scope. The passage examines questions and processes but does not mention a theory. Option D is a distortion. Paragraph 7 does begin to suggest a solution to the problem of how to allow more voices in the discussion of conversation values, but the last sentence of the paragraph, *The inevitability…to be recognized* (lines 70–72), indicates the solution has a tentative, not a *clearly defined,* quality.

6. **The best answer is G.** To predict for an Inference question, carefully read the cited lines and, if necessary, their immediate context, to draw a conclusion that doesn't stray too far from what is stated. Here, the word *challenge* indicates a tension: the possible conflict between *the imperative of public participation* (lines 43–44) and *conventional notions of conservation professionals' responsibilities.* Predict that the conventional notions did not previously take into account the necessity of public participation. This prediction matches well with option G. Option F is a contradiction. The whole point of the passage is about finding ways to accept input from outside the realm of *traditional conservation principles.* Option H is a distortion of the word *conventional* as it's used in the passage. Option J is a misused detail. This comes from paragraph 5 and doesn't relate to the line that this question stem refers to.

7. **The best answer is B.** A Writer's View question demands that you keep the overall purpose of the passage in mind. To predict, look for where *democratization* is mentioned in the passage. Your passage map notes should lead you to paragraphs 5 and 7. Read in paragraph 7 to predict that democratization is part of a process of assessing values and will lead to changes for professionals. This prediction supports option B, which is also consistent with the passage overall. Option A is a contradiction of lines 67–69, *Democratization…is not likely to be a threat…the field.* Option C is a distortion. While the people will take a greater role, the writer states that it will be in *consultation and assessment* (lines 67–68) rather than in the ultimate decision making. Option D is an extreme. While the writer does suggest changes in process and attitude, there is nothing in the passage to suggest that the field will be *completely reformed.*

8. **The best answer is F.** For a Vocabulary-in-Context question, read the sentence carefully, and, if necessary, the preceding and following sentences, to search for clues to predict the meaning. In this case, the sentence itself presents a contrast. There are two different possibilities for the role of the conservation professional, first, *an orchestrator of specialists* and,

second, *one specialist among others.* This contrast suggests that the *orchestrator* somehow places above the other specialists, so predict that it means something like *leader* or *one who takes priority over.* This prediction fits well with option F. Option G is a distortion that might be tempting if you're thinking of a musical orchestra instead of paying attention to the context. Option H is a distortion that gives too much emphasis to the word *specialist* in the sentence and misses the idea of the orchestra having a role above and beyond that of *specialist.* Option J is out-of-scope. It draws on a completely different meaning of the word that is not relevant to this passage.

9. **The best answer is D.**   For a Writer's View question, keep in mind the tone of the passage as a whole. For this question, also research in the passage for the area that discusses *the outlook for the conservation field.* To predict, carefully read the last paragraph. It brings up questions about the role of the conservation specialist, but it also poses an answer: *It seems that…orchestrator* (lines 80–81). It mentions changes that will be necessary to meet *the challenge ahead,* but does not suggest that these challenges will be insurmountable. Therefore, predict something like *concerned but hopeful.* This prediction leads directly to option D. Option A expresses a bleaker view than the passage justifies. The word *tinged* has a negative connotation that makes it sound as though the *reservations* are the primary factor in the writer's outlook. Option B is also too negative. The writer mentions the challenges in a hopeful rather than a pessimistic tone. Option C is out-of-scope. While the author attempts to take a balanced view, looking at both challenges and ways to address them, there is nothing cynical in the tone or approach.

10. **The best answer is H.**   To predict for a Detail question, use your passage map notes or skim the passage for key words in the question stem. In this case, your passage map notes may lead you to paragraph 1. From the first sentence, predict that the concept of heritage has broadened as new groups have influenced its meaning. The next sentence identifies these others as citizens, experts in other fields, and special-interest groups. This prediction matches well with option H. Option F is a distortion. The passage indicates that the notion of heritage is changing as a result of new social contexts, but it doesn't refer to anything like *a multitude of social changes.* Option G is out-of-scope. Heritage specialists are clearly attempting to redefine their role, but the passage doesn't state that they have become *too old-fashioned.* Option J is a distortion. The passage does mention *democratization* but only as it relates to the conservation field, not to any other *academic specialties.*

11. **The best answer is C.**   For a Function question about a phrase, pay close attention to the surrounding sentences. The phrase is used here in the context of asking how to support traditional conservation goals in the face of needing to accept *an open democratic process* (lines 47–48). This is a contrast that leads to the prediction that traditional goals and the *other social goals* are potentially conflicting. Predict that *underselling* indicates fears that the other goals might take precedence over the traditional goals. This prediction matches with option C. Option A is a distortion. The passage mentions economists in a discussion of determining values but doesn't discuss conservation values as being in conflict with economic values. Option B is also a distortion. It reverses the terms used in option A, but both options address a tension that isn't present in the passage. Option D is a misused detail. Although the purpose of the passage is to discuss current challenges, this detail doesn't answer the question posed in the question stem.

12. **The best answer is J.**   For a Function question about a detail, pay close attention to the context in which the detail is mentioned. Passage map notes for the paragraph are usually helpful. In this case, your note may indicate that the paragraph discusses experts in other fields who have done work that might be helpful to conservation specialists. This makes a great prediction that lines up with option J. Option F is a distortion of two details that are present in the passage: *conservation professionals* and *democratization.* Option G is a mis-used detail. *Economists* are mentioned in the passage, but the passage clearly indicates that Low and Satterfield are associated with other fields. Option H is out-of-scope. The passage doesn't specifically mention any groups who are *fighting to have their voices heard.*

Chapter Fourteen: **Reading Practice Set IV— Humanities**

Directions: This test contains a passage, followed by several questions. After reading the passage, select the best answer to each question. You are allowed to refer to the passage while answering the questions.

HUMANITIES

This passage is taken from a collection of essays about 20th-century British novelists.

British novelist Barbara Pym has been described as a novelist of manners, a twentieth-century Jane Austen. Despite this
comparison with such a famous literary figure, Pym, for most of
Line   her own life, was relatively unknown. She came to the attention
(5)   of the public only three years before her death when the *Times
Literary Supplement* asked for opinions about the "most underrated novelist" of the twentieth century. Barbara Pym was the only
novelist to be named by two of the respondents, the novelist and
poet Philip Larkin and the literary scholar Lord David Cecil. This
(10)   recognition led finally to a surge in her popularity, and Pym lived to
see the publication of most of the novels she had written previously.
        Pym, born in 1913, began writing novels at the age of 16. Her
first effort was titled "Young Men in Fancy Dress." In 1931, she
entered St. Hilda's College at Oxford, where she read English lit-
(15)   erature. Following her graduation, she began working on the novel
Some Tame Gazelle, centered on the daily lives of two women in
their fifties. Pym based this story on the way she imagined her life
and the lives of her sister and their friends from Oxford as it might
be thirty years into the future. Pym completed this novel in 1935
(20)   but had no luck in finding a publisher for it. She kept writing, however, producing several novels and short stories by crafting some of
her own life experiences into literary form.
        During World War II, Pym worked first at the Censorship
Office in Bristol, England and later with the Women's Royal Naval
(25)   Service in Naples, Italy. On her return to England, she worked

KAPLAN

at the International Africa Institute in London. Her job as assistant editor for the journal *Africa* put her in contact with the world of anthropological scholarship. Her stories include characters who work in academics and are presented in a mostly appreciative and
(30) humorous way.

Pym's artistic perseverance paid off when her revision of *Some Tame Gazelle* was finally accepted by Jonathan Cape, who published the novel in 1950. Contemporary critics reviewed this work favorably, so Pym was finally established as a writer. For the next
(35) decade, Pym enjoyed some success, seeing the publication of several more novels. *Excellent Women* was published in 1952, and *Jane and Prudence* came out the following year. Every three years until 1961, Pym published a new novel. Scholars see these first six novels as an important body of work marking Pym as a significant author with
(40) a unique voice. She wrote about ordinary people living quiet lives, often in provincial locations and small towns in England. The novels include detailed descriptions of characters, clothing, meals, local gossip, and activities of Anglican clergy and church members.

Pym's consistent publishing success throughout the 1950s even-
(45) tually came to an end. In 1963, when she presented her next novel, *An Unsuitable Attachment,* to her publisher, it was considered out of date and was rejected. Pym, though disappointed, did not give up. She submitted the novel to several other publishers. After receiving several rejections, she revised and resubmitted it. All told,
(50) twenty publishers rejected this novel during the 1960s. Over the next fifteen years, Pym fought against losing hope that her writing would ever again be appreciated. She worked on yet another book, *The Sweet Dove Died.* This novel, darker than her earlier ones, about an older woman attracted to a much younger man, was again
(55) rooted in Pym's personal experience. Like her previous novel, *The Sweet Dove Died* was not accepted by any publisher.

Even though Pym's rejections were compounded by health crises, including a cancer diagnosis in 1971 and a stroke in 1974, she continued to write. After retiring from her job at the Africa
(60) Institute, she wrote *Quartet in Autumn,* her darkest novel yet, about four office workers facing their own upcoming retirement. When Pym submitted this work to publishers in 1976, it was again rejected by all.

Pym's citation by Philip Larkin in the *Times Literary Supplement*
(65) pulled her out of obscurity. Macmillan published *Quartet in Autumn* in 1977 and *The Sweet Dove Died* the following year. *Quartet* was nominated for the Booker Prize, Britain's prestigious literary award. When these last two novels attracted critical attention in England, Macmillan reprinted all of Pym's earlier novels.
(70) When American audiences discovered Pym's work, Dutton published all of her novels in the United States. Her work was published in translation, bringing her even wider readership. Despite

declining health, Pym worked to finish her last novel, *A Few Green Leaves,* before she died in 1980. Following Pym's death,
(75) *An Unsuitable Attachment,* the novel earlier rejected, was published, along with two other novels, *Crampton Hodnet* and *Civil to Strangers.* Pym has continued to generate interest among scholars for her philosophical outlook and distinctive voice.

1. The writer of this passage adopts a tone that can best be described as

   (A) detached but mildly appreciative.
   (B) zealously enthusiastic.
   (C) overtly biased.
   (D) impatient and critical.

2. According to the passage, *The Sweet Dove Died* was published in

   (F) 1952.
   (G) 1961.
   (H) 1977.
   (J) 1978.

3. The writer uses the phrase *throughout the 1950s* (line 44) to emphasize that

   (A) the 1950s was a stable time for British society.
   (B) Pym's reputation was not consistent throughout her lifetime.
   (C) Pym's publishing house saw remarkable success during the 1950s.
   (D) *Excellent Women* was one of the novels published during the 1950s.

4. Regarding her life experience, the passage implies that

   (F) Pym's ultimate rejection by Jonathan Cape hurled her into a depression.
   (G) Pym's interest in the culinary arts led her to see descriptions of food as being as important as character development in a novel.
   (H) Pym was relieved to be named the most underrated novelist of the twentieth century.
   (J) Pym did not view her life as something that should be kept entirely separate from her novels.

5. The passage states that all of the following novels were eventually published during Pym's lifetime *EXCEPT*

   (A) *Some Tame Gazelle.*
   (B) *Quartet in Autumn.*
   (C) *The Sweet Dove Died.*
   (D) *Crampton Hodnet.*

6. The second paragraph functions in the passage primarily as

   (F)   a detailed description of the sources of *Some Tame Gazelle.*

   (G)   an argument that *Some Tame Gazelle* should not have been rejected by Jonathan Cape.

   (H)   a chronology of significant dates in the first part of Pym's life.

   (J)   a summary of Pym's literary career.

7. It may be inferred from the last paragraph that

   (A)   Pym did not let her declining health interfere with her artistic goals.

   (B)   Philip Larkin was single-handedly responsible for salvaging Pym's literary reputation.

   (C)   *Quartet in Autumn* was written after Pym retired from her job at the Africa Institute.

   (D)   Pym has the most distinctive voice of any 20th-century novelist.

8. The writer suggests in the first paragraph that

   (F)   the article in the *Times Literary Supplement* generated renewed interest in Pym's earlier novels.

   (G)   the *Times Literary Supplement* rejected several of Pym's short stories.

   (H)   Pym suffered a stroke in 1974.

   (J)   Pym enjoyed a long friendship with Philip Larkin and Lord David Cecil.

9. According to the passage, Pym was employed at various times by which of the following?

   I. The *Times Literary Supplement*
   II. St. Hilda's College of Oxford
   III. The Women's Royal Naval Service
   IV. The journal *Africa*

   (A)   I, II, III, and IV

   (B)   I, III, and IV

   (C)   I and III only

   (D)   III and IV only

10. Which of the following novels is *NOT* mentioned in the passage as being associated in some way with Pym's own life?

   (F)   *Some Tame Gazelle*

   (G)   *Civil to Strangers*

   (H)   *The Sweet Dove Died*

   (J)   *Quartet in Autumn*

11. The writer uses the phrase *artistic perseverance* (line 31) to show that

    (A)   Pym did not give up when her publishers first rejected her work.

    (B)   Pym worked harder on *Some Tame Gazelle* than she had on "Young Men in Fancy Dress."

    (C)   rejection at some point is inevitable for all writers.

    (D)   Pym's subtle artistry was appreciated by contemporary critics.

12. According to the author, Barbara Pym's literary work may compared to that of

    (F)   Philip Larkin.

    (G)   Lord David Cecil.

    (H)   Jane Austen.

    (J)   Jonathan Cape.

ANSWERS AND EXPLANATIONS

Suggested Passage Map Notes

Paragraph 1: Pym's work popular late in her life

Paragraph 2: Early efforts at writing

Paragraph 3: Work history

Paragraph 4: Novels finally published

Paragraph 5: Later novels rejected

Paragraph 6: Continued working

Paragraph 7: Eventual acclaim

  1. A

  2. J

  3. B

  4. J

  5. D

  6. H

  7. A

  8. F

  9. D

10. G

11. A

12. H

KAPLAN

1. **The best answer is A.** For a Writer's View question, keep the big picture in mind and pay attention to words that indicate the writer's opinion. Here, the overall tone is detached and analytical. The writer appears to admire Pym's persistence, as evidenced by phrases such as *she kept writing, however* (line 20), *Pym's artistic perseverance paid off* (line 31), and *Even though Pym's rejections were compounded . . . she continued to write* (lines 57–59). Therefore, predict that the tone is primarily detached but colored with admiration. This prediction matches option A. Option B is out-of-scope. Nothing about the tone of the passage suggests zealousness. Option C is a distortion. The mild admiration implied by the author is not the same as an overt bias. Option D is a contradiction. *Impatient and critical* is the opposite of detached and admiring.

2. **The best answer is J.** For a Detail question, make sure you refer to the appropriate portion of the passage to make your prediction. You may have to read especially carefully when dates are involved to avoid misused detail traps. Quickly scan the passage for *The Sweet Dove Died.* It appears in line 53 and in line 66. The relevant reference here is line TK (P7). Predict that the novel was published in the year *following* 1977, making option G the correct answer. Options F, G, and H are all misused details. These dates are all mentioned in the passage but do not correctly answer the question posed by this question stem.

3. **The best answer is B.** For a Function question asking about a phrase, read the sentence carefully to make your prediction. Here, notice that the sentence describes a contrast: *continued success . . . came to an end.* Predict that the phrase *throughout the 1950s* is used to develop and emphasize this contrast. This prediction matches well with option B. Option A is out-of-scope. The passage focuses on Pym and makes no general statements about *British society.* Option C is a distortion of the word *success* as it's used in the passage. The *success* mentioned in this sentence is Pym's, not that of her publisher. Option D is a misused detail. It makes a statement that is consistent with the passage, but it doesn't relate to the question posed by the question stem.

4. **The best answer is J.** For a Generalization question, remember to keep the big picture in mind. If it's tough to predict, work through the answer choices one by one and eliminate those that don't fit. Eliminate option F because it's out-of-scope. Be careful not to read too much into the passage. It doesn't suggest anywhere that the rejection *hurled Pym into a depression.* Eliminate option G because it's a distortion. Although the passage does say that descriptions of meals are included in Pym's novels, it doesn't suggest that they are *as important as character development.* Eliminate option H because it's an extreme. The passage states that Pym was named as *one* of the most underrated writers, but it would be reading too much in to infer that she is *the* most underrated writer. The process of elimination leaves option J, which is the best answer. It is justified in several places in the passage, including Lines 21–22, *by crafting some of her own life experiences into literary form.*

5. **The best answer is D.** For a Detail question phrased with the word EXCEPT, check in the passage to see which choice is *not* supported by the passage. Option D is the best answer because lines 74–76 indicate that *Crampton Hodnet* was published following Pym's death. Options A, B, and C are mentioned in the passage as having been published while Pym was still living.

6. **The best answer is H.** For a Function question that asks about a paragraph, use your passage map notes and think about how the paragraph works in the passage as a whole. The passage describes Pym's literary career, and the second paragraph discusses her early work as a writer. Use this as a prediction and work through the answer choices. Option H is the

best choice, even though the prediction is not worded in exactly the same way as this answer choice. The second paragraph does include dates, making *chronology* appropriate here. In addition, the prediction *early work* matches well with the wording *first part of Pym's life* in option H. Option F is a misused detail. The paragraph does mention *Some Tame Gazelle*, briefly noting its connection to Pym's personal life, but it doesn't give a *detailed* description of the novel's sources. Option G is out-of-scope. The writer makes no attempt to argue the wisdom of the publisher's decision. Option J is out-of-scope. The answer choice is much too broad to describe the second paragraph.

7. **The best answer is A.** For a Generalization question based on a paragraph, try using your passage map notes or reading the paragraph. There's a lot in this last paragraph, so it may be difficult to predict. Work through the answer choices, being careful not to fall for traps. Option A is the best answer. It's a reasonable inference to make from lines 72–73, *Despite declining health, Pym worked to finish her last novel.* Eliminate option B because it's an extreme. Though you can certainly infer that Larkin had a strong influence on Pym's reputation, the passage doesn't justify the notion that he was *single-handedly* influential. Eliminate option C because it's a misused detail. It contains a true statement that's mentioned in paragraph 6, but this question stem asks for an inference based on paragraph 7. Eliminate option D because it's an extreme. Paragraph 7 does mention Pym's *distinctive voice* but doesn't suggest that it is *the most distinctive voice.*

8. **The best answer is F.** For a Generalization question about a paragraph, review your notes and the whole paragraph, if necessary. Predict if possible, and if not, work through the answer choices. For the first paragraph, your passage note may refer to Pym's achieving literary success later in life. This is not an exact match but is consistent with option F, the best answer. Eliminate option G because it's a distortion. The passage doesn't suggest that it was the *Times Literary Supplement* that rejected Pym's stories. Eliminate option H because it's a misused detail. This answer choice is indeed a true statement from the passage, but it doesn't address the question in this particular question stem. Eliminate option J because it's a distortion. The passage mentions both Philip Larkin and Lord David Cecil, but only in the context of the *Times Literary Supplement.* There is nothing in the passage to suggest that either of them was a friend of Pym.

9. **The best answer is D.** For a Detail question that uses Roman numerals, check each detail one by one, referring to the passage. Look for ways to use logic to save you time. For example, in this case, detail I is not consistent with the passage: Pym is not described as having been employed by the *Times Literary Supplement.* Because each answer choice except option D includes detail I, you can eliminate options A, B, and C. Note, however, that option D is also supported by lines 24–25, which states that Pym worked for the Women's Royal Naval Service, and line 27, which states that she worked for the journal *Africa.*

10. **The best answer is G.** For a Detail question phrased with NOT, refer back to the passage to check each answer choice one by one. Eliminate option F because lines 17–18 states that *Some Tame Gazelle* is based *on the way she imagined her life . . . as it might be.* Eliminate option H because line 55 states that *The Sweet Dove Died* was *again rooted in Pym's personal experience.* Eliminate option J because *Quartet in Autumn* is described as a novel about retirement that Pym started work on after her own retirement.

11. **The best answer is A.** For a Function question about a phrase, examine the immediate context to make your prediction. The sentence includes the word *finally* (line 32), which indicates that Pym's success was not immediate. Predict that her *artistic perseverance* is

used to show that she kept on writing novels even while working at the Africa Institute. This prediction is a good match for option A. Option B is a distortion. Both the novel *Some Tame Gazelle* and the unpublished first novel, "Young Men in Fancy Dress," are mentioned, but the passage doesn't compare how hard Pym worked on one relative to the other. Option C is an extreme. It uses the word *all* and makes a general statement that is much broader than anything expressed in the passage. Option D is a distortion. The context here does mention *contemporary critics* (line 33), but the answer choice inappropriately twists the passage's phrasing *reviewed favorably* (lines 33–34) to appreciating *subtle artistry*.

12. **The best answer is H.** A Detail question like this is hard to predict for. There are no words in the question stem that you can scan the passage for, and passage notes likely guide you to both the first and last paragraphs. The best thing to do in this case is to look at the answer choices and skim the passage for each, eliminating if necessary. Eliminate option F because, although Larkin is mentioned in both the first and last paragraphs, Pym's work is not compared to his. Eliminate option G for the same reason. Option H is the correct answer and is supported by the first sentence of the passage. Eliminate option J because Jonathan Cape is mentioned as a publisher, not as a writer.

Chapter Fifteen: **Reading Practice Set V— Humanities**

Directions: This test contains a passage, followed by several questions. After reading the passage, select the best answer to each question. You are allowed to refer to the passage while answering the questions.

HUMANITIES

This passage focuses on garden design.

A garden is a living work of art that blends elements of space and mass, light and shade, the natural and the manmade, along with color, scent, texture, and climate. As with any other art, the
Line evolution of garden design may be seen as reflecting the interests
(5) and values of groups of people living in a particular time and place. It is not surprising, then, that the history of the garden illustrates in various ways the principles of both continuity with and reaction against earlier trends in design. An especially notable example of a reaction against an existing style is the *jardin anglais,* or the English
(10) garden, that became popular in France and other parts of Europe during the mid-18th century.

In the early 18th century, French cultural influence dominated Europe, leading to the popularity of the highly formal garden, sometimes known as the French garden. This garden style is
(15) characterized by rigidly formulated geometric patterns in which precision, regularity, and proportion are dominant. The garden at Versailles, one of the largest and best known formal gardens, is the epitome of the style that was emulated on a smaller scale at other locations. Typical of the style it represents, the colossal garden at
(20) Versailles is based on designs that are strongly geometrical, including areas separated by long straight lines and circular pools dividing symmetrical areas. Canals, fountains, and statuary are used to emphasize the balanced forms.

Versailles, like many formal gardens, made use of the bosquet,
(25) a precisely planted grove in which trees are planted so as to be
perfectly aligned according to a pattern. Another feature of the
formal garden used extensively at Versailles is the *parterre,* a sort
of garden-within-a-garden. Several types of *parterres* were used,
including the *parterre de broderie,* or embroidered *parterre,* in which
(30) neatly trimmed boxwood shrubs were planted in designs suggestive
of botanical shapes. In the embroidered *parterre,* the box plantings
were set against turf or colored earth. Other types of *parterres* used
different kinds of flowers and other plants, but the use a formal
pattern was common to all types of *parterres.*

(35) It was in the context of such highly stylized and classical designs
that the English landscape garden came into being. Reaction against
formality came in part from the British poet and literary critic
Alexander Pope, who in 1713 published an essay on gardening in
The Guardian. Eschewing the balance, formality, and rigid symme-
(40) try popular in gardens of the time, Pope called instead for the cre-
ation of gardens that reflect the "amiable simplicity of unadorned
nature." Pope argued that the design of a garden should take its
cues from local topography rather than starting from a precon-
ceived plan that is artificially imposed on the landscape.

(45) In England, two of the most famous designers of landscape
style gardens were William Kent and Lancelot (better known as
"Capability") Brown. Kent, a friend of Alexander Pope, drew inspiration from the ideas of the literary critic. Kent, who had studied
art in Italy, was highly receptive to Pope's notion that "all garden-
(50) ing is landscape painting." One of the best examples of Kent's work
is found in the garden at Rousham House in Oxfordshire. This garden, started in 1738, typifies the landscape principle of making the
surrounding countryside an integral part of the experience of the
garden. Kent used outlying buildings in a picturesque Gothic style
(55) to call attention to the larger surrounding area and the garden's
place within it.

Following Kent and achieving even greater fame, Capability
Brown was the next great English landscape gardener. Fittingly,
Brown earned his nickname from his tendency to talk to his cli-
(60) ents about the "capabilities" of their land. Among Brown's most
famous works is the landscaping on the grounds of Blenheim Palace
in Oxfordshire. Here he created a free-flowing expanse marked by
large grassy areas, irregularly shaped bodies of water, and seemingly
random plantings of trees, both isolated and in clustered groupings.
(65) The naturalistic designs that Brown perfected may be seen as the
polar opposite of the highly stylized and artificial designs in the
garden at Versailles. Admirers of the more formal gardens such as
the one at Versailles have criticized Brown for destroying some of
the best examples of formal gardens in England, while those who
(70) appreciate the naturalistic style celebrate Brown's achievement.

Capability Brown influenced Humphrey Repton, who continued
to create designs that were largely similar to those of his predeces-
sor. In addition, Repton had some literary talent and in the late
18th and early 19th centuries produced several books document-
(75)   ing the landscape styles that were popular at the time. Though the
landscape or "English" style garden eventually saw a decline in
popularity in its country of origin, it enjoyed further longevity in
continental Europe, particularly in France.

1. The writer's tone in this passage is

    (A)   critical and judgmental.

    (B)   scholarly and detached.

    (C)   overly involved.

    (D)   decidedly persuasive.

2. According to the passage, all of the following were known for their garden designs
    EXCEPT

    (F)   Alexander Pope.

    (G)   Humphrey Repton.

    (H)   Capability Brown.

    (J)   William Kent.

3. The primary contrast in this passage revolves around

    (A)   the relative importance of nature and artificiality in garden design.

    (B)   the comparative significance of Alexander Pope's and William Kent's
          garden designs.

    (C)   two artists working in the same era but producing distinctive though
          related work.

    (D)   the dominance of the French culture over the English culture during the
          18th century.

4. One inference that may be drawn from the fourth paragraph is that

    (F)   British poets in the early 18th century rebelled against formality.

    (G)   a desire to rebel against formality was a crucial element of Alexander Pope's
          poetry.

    (H)   creative pursuits in diverse areas did not always exist in isolation from each
          other.

    (J)   knowledge of European painting influenced William Kent's garden designs.

5. Based on information in the passage, which statements are true about the garden at Versailles?

    I. It made use of geometric designs that mimicked botanical forms.

    II. The surrounding landscape was considered a crucial part of the garden's design.

    III. It was featured in a book of garden designs published by Humphrey Repton.

    IV. Bosquets and *parterres* were among the patterns designs featured.

    (A)   I, II, III, IV

    (B)   II, III, IV

    (C)   I and IV

    (D)   IV only

6. As used in line 18, the word *epitome* most nearly means

    (F)   best example.

    (G)   balanced plan.

    (H)   artistic creation.

    (J)   inevitable result.

7. According to the passage, the work of Capability Brown

    (A)   was strongly influenced by the designs of Humphrey Repton.

    (B)   was a source of inspiration for Alexander Pope's poetry.

    (C)   is a subject of some disagreement among critics.

    (D)   exemplifies the use of geometrical forms in garden design.

8. Based on information provided in the passage, which of the following would be *LEAST* likely to be found in a "French garden"?

    (F)   Two rows of trees planted in precisely parallel lines

    (G)   Low trimmed bushes planted in a circular maze design

    (H)   Four similar statues each placed in the corners of a square *parterre*

    (J)   A randomly curved stone path surrounding a large grassy area

9. The writer mentions *Rousham House* (line 51) for the purpose of

    (A)   describing gardens that contrast with those found at Blenheim Palace.

    (B)   providing an example of a famous estate in Oxfordshire.

    (C)   explaining how the principles of French garden design were adapted to the British landscape.

    (D)   illustrating an important aspect of William Kent's work.

10. In the passage as a whole, paragraph 2 functions as

    (F) a detailed description of the gardens at Versailles.

    (G) an explanation of a concept necessary to differentiate between different gardens.

    (H) a criticism of the balanced geometrical designs used in the French style garden.

    (J) an argument that statuary and lakes are an essential feature of a formal garden.

11. The writer mentions *Blenheim Palace* (line 61) in order to

    (A) provide an example of one of Capability Brown's most well-known projects.

    (B) suggest that it plays a transitional role in the development of European garden styles.

    (C) criticize its designer for destroying a valuable example of the formal French garden.

    (D) prove that Oxfordshire was home to more landscape-style gardens than any other county in England.

12. The primary purpose of this passage is to

    (F) present a detailed description of some of the most famous gardens of the 19th century.

    (G) argue that a palatial residence cannot be considered complete unless it includes an extensive garden.

    (H) support the view that the French and English gardens in the mid-1800s had some significant features in common.

    (J) discuss two contrasting styles that are important in the history of garden design.

ANSWERS AND EXPLANATIONS

Suggested Passage Map Notes

Paragraph 1: Background on garden design; English garden a reaction

Paragraph 2: French garden style; Versailles—geometrical, symmetrical

Paragraph 3: Versailles cont'd—*parterres*

Paragraph 4: Pope started reaction against earlier style, urged focus on nature

Paragraph 5: Kent's work in landscape style

Paragraph 6: Brown; Blenheim Palace—criticized by some

Paragraph 7: Repton; landscape garden style outside of England

1. B
2. F
3. A
4. H
5. C
6. F
7. C
8. J
9. D
10. G
11. A
12. J

1. **The best answer is B.**   For a Writer's View question, consider the passage as a whole. The tone of this passage is descriptive and analytical. It mentions a controversy (the opinions of Capability Brown's work in paragraph 6) in passing but doesn't take a side. Predict that the tone is descriptive and detached. Option B is the best match. Option A is a contradiction because the writer is not judgmental. Option C is a contradiction because the writer doesn't take sides. Option D is a contradiction because the writer is merely explaining, not attempting to persuade.

2. **The best answer is F.**   A detail question that uses *EXCEPT* is one of the few question types that you shouldn't spend time predicting for. Instead, go straight to the answer choices and research the passage for each one. Remember that for an *EXCEPT* question, the correct answer is the one that you do NOT find supported in the passage. Option F is the best answer because, although Pope is mentioned in the passage, he is described as a *poet and literary critic* (line 37), not as a garden designer. Eliminate option G because Repton is mentioned in line 71. Eliminate option H because Brown is described as a landscape designer in lines 46–47. Eliminate option J because Kent is also referred to as a landscape designer.

3. **The best answer is A.**   For a generalization question, your answer must be based on the passage as a whole. Use your passage notes to help here. Predict that the primary contrast is between the garden at Versailles and the landscape style garden. The garden at Versailles is described in lines 15–16 as being *characterized by rigidly formulated geometric patterns in which precision, regularity, and proportion are dominant*. Paragraph 4 describes the landscape garden as being a *reaction against formality* (lines 36–37). Predict that the answer has something to do with the difference between a highly formal style and a more natural style. This prediction matches best with option A. Option B is a distortion. Although Kent is mentioned in the passage as a designer of gardens, Pope is not. Option C is a distortion. Although three garden designers are mentioned (Kent, Brown, and Repton), their work is described as largely continuous, not *distinctive*. Option D is a misused detail. The dominance of French culture is cited, but in passing, not as a major element of the passage.

4. **The best answer is H.**   For a Generalization question about a paragraph, use your passage notes. Paragraph 4 discusses a poet's influence on the field of garden design. The best answer will be consistent with this idea, and option H matches well. Option F combines the out-of-scope and distortion answer traps. It's out-of-scope because the passage focuses on

landscape design, not poetry. The phrase *rebel against formality* in option F is a distortion of the phrase *reaction against formality,* (lines 36–37), which is used in the passage in relation to garden design, not poetry. Option J is a misused detail. The reference to Kent's study of art in Italy comes in paragraph 5, but this question stem asks about an inference based on paragraph 4.

5. **The best answer is C.** For a Roman-numeral question, consider each statement separately and eliminate answer choices when you find a statement isn't true. Statement I is true. Lines 30–31, *neatly trimmed boxwood shrubs were planted in designs suggestive of botanical shapes,* justify this statement. Knowing that statement I is true, we can eliminate option B. We still have to consider statements II and III. Statement II is not true of the garden at Versailles. The surrounding landscape is mentioned in the passage as being important in Kent's landscape style garden (lines 52–53). Statement III is not true. Though that passage states that Repton *produced several books documenting the landscape styles that were popular at the time* (lines 74–75), Versailles is not described as having a landscape style garden. Knowing that statements II and III aren't true, you can eliminate option A. Because you've already eliminated options A and B and you know that statement I is true, you can eliminate option D without even considering statement IV. (Note, however, that statement IV is indeed justified by the description of the Versailles garden in lines 24–28.)

6. **The best answer is F.** For a Vocabulary-in-Context question, pay attention to clues in the sentence that tell you what the word means. In this case, reading the previous sentence is also helpful. The previous sentence describes the style of garden known as the French garden, suggesting that the garden at Versailles is presented as an example of this style. This leads to a prediction of *example,* and option F matches nicely. Option G is a misused detail. While the garden at Versailles exhibits a *balanced plan,* that is not the meaning of the word *epitome.* Option H is a misused detail. Though *artistic style* is relevant to the passage, it doesn't fit in this context. Option J is out-of-scope. There's no cause-and-effect relationship indicated here, so *result* doesn't work in this context.

7. **The best answer is C.** For a Detail question, your passage map notes can help you know where to look to make your prediction. For this question, look back to paragraph 6. The question is broadly worded, so it's hard to make a precise prediction. Skim the paragraph so that you're familiar with what it says: The grounds at Blenheim Palace are a famous example of Brown's work, and they reflect the naturalistic style; Brown has been criticized for destroying great examples of formal gardens. Read through the answer choices and eliminate as you go. Option A is a contradiction. Repton followed Brown, so Brown could not have been influenced by him. Option B combines the distortion and out-of-scope answer traps. Although Pope is mentioned in the passage, Brown is not discussed as a source of inspiration for Pope's poetry. Option C fits with your general prediction, particularly taking into account lines 67–70, *Admirers of the more formal gardens…Brown's achievement.* Option D is a contradiction. The passage states that Brown, instead of using geometrical forms, created *a free-flowing expanse, marked by…irregularly shaped bodies of water and seemingly random plantings* (lines 62–64).

8. **The best answer is J.** For a Generalization question such as this one, determine what information you need to take from the passage. Your prediction should involve referring to the passage to make sure you're clear about how a *French garden* is described. Your passage map notes direct you to paragraph 2, where the French garden is described as featuring *precision, regularity, and proportion* (line 16). With this in mind, consider each answer choice and eliminate choices that don't match. Option F is a contradiction because *precisely*

planted parallel lines might easily have appeared in a French garden. Option G is also a contradiction. *A circular maze design* features the geometry that is characteristic of a French garden. Option H is a contradiction because the statues placed in the four corners of a square exemplify the geometrical form and symmetry found in a French garden. Option J is the best answer. The *random* curve and *large grassy area* do not fit in the highly stylized plan of a French garden as it's described in the passage.

9. **The best answer is D.**　For a Function question, pay attention to context and think about the writer's purpose. Your passage map notes should tell you that the purpose of paragraph 5 is to discuss William Kent's work. The immediate context states that Rousham House is *one of the best examples of Kent's work* (line 50). This makes a great prediction, which nicely fits with option D. Option A is a misused detail. Blenheim Palace is not discussed in connection with Kent's work. Option B is a distortion. While Rousham House is indeed described as an example of something, it is not presented as *an example of a famous estate.* Option C is both a misused detail and a contradiction. French design principles have nothing to do with Rousham House, and the passage never says that French design principles were adapted to the English landscape.

10. **The best answer is G.**　For a Generalization question that asks how a paragraph functions, use your passage map notes, and consider the passage as a whole. Predict that paragraph 2 discusses the French garden, with the garden at Versailles as an illustration, and that it's used to show the contrasts between the French style and the landscape style used in England. This prediction lines up nicely with option G. Option H is a distortion. While paragraph 2 does describe the garden at Versailles, the description is brief, and this option says nothing about how the paragraph fits into the passage as a whole. Option H is a contradiction. Nothing in paragraph 2 indicates criticism of the French garden style. Option J is a distortion. It's true that *statuary* is mentioned in paragraph 2, but the author never argues that statues are essential to the style.

11. **The best answer is A.**　For a Generalization question that asks about a detail, consider the context of the sentences surrounding it. The context states that Blenheim Palace is *among Brown's most famous work* (line 61). Predict that Blenheim Palace is used to illustrate Brown's work. This prediction matches option A. Option B is a distortion. The passage does treat the development of garden styles, but the focus is on the French style that came *before* the landscape style Brown worked in. If the writer were suggesting that Brown's style is *transitional,* he would have to state what style followed it, and the passage doesn't do this. Option C is a misused detail. It's true that the paragraph indicates some have criticized Brown for destroying examples of formal gardens, but the writer doesn't say that Brown destroyed a formal garden in carrying out his work at Blenheim. Option D combines the out-of-scope and extreme traps. The writer never even states, much less attempts to prove, that Oxfordshire has more landscape gardens than anyplace else. The phrasing *more...than any other* in this answer choice should alert you that it may be an extreme trap.

12. **The best answer is J.**　For a Generalization question about the purpose of the whole passage, use your passage map notes to predict, and avoid tempting wrong answers that address only part of the passage. Here, your prediction should include something about the difference between the two styles of garden design discussed in the passage. Option J is a great match. Option F is out-of-scope. Its description *some of the most famous gardens of the 19th century* is too broad. Option G is out-of-scope. *Palatial residences* are not mentioned as such and are not the focus of the passage. Option H is a distortion. Though both garden types are discussed, the author focuses on their differences, not their similarities.

Chapter Sixteen: **Reading Practice Set VI— Natural Science**

Directions: This test contains a passage, followed by several questions. After reading the passage, select the best answer to each question. You are allowed to refer to the passage while answering the questions.

NATURAL SCIENCE

This passage is adapted from a document describing research done by the United States Geological Survey. The selection below concerns the effects of wind power developments on migrating birds.

Interest in developing wind power as an alternative renewable energy source has increased in recent years. In the eastern
United States, exposed summits or ridge crests in the Appalachian
Line Mountains have high wind power potential, and numerous wind
(5) power projects are being proposed. While generally supportive
of energy development from renewable sources, the U.S. Fish &
Wildlife Service, state wildlife agencies, nongovernmental organizations, and the public are concerned about potential impacts of wind
power development on wildlife.
(10) During their seasonal migrations, large numbers of birds and
bats cross or follow the mountainous landforms used for wind
power. Wind power development could potentially impact populations of several species. Baseline information on nocturnally
migrating birds and bats has been collected at some wind power
(15) development sites in the Appalachians, generally within a single
season. However, a stronger scientific basis is critically needed to
assess and mitigate risks at a regional scale.
The United States Geological Survey (USGS) is studying the
distribution and flight patterns of birds and bats that migrate at
(20) night. Researchers are analyzing weather surveillance radar data
(NEXRAD) to allow for a broad view of spring and fall migration through the Appalachians and to assess the response of
migrant birds to mountain ridges and other prominent landforms.

Although NEXRAD data provide information on the broad-scale
(25)   spatial and temporal patterns of nocturnal migration through
the region, the devices generally do not detect bird or bat targets
within the altitudinal zone potentially occupied by wind turbines.
Therefore, researchers are using two complementary ground-based
techniques, acoustic detection and portable radar sampling, to
(30)   obtain site-specific information on the abundance and flight characteristics of nocturnal migrants in lower airspace.

USGS is conducting acoustic monitoring at 31 sites scattered
throughout the central Appalachians. Researchers are recording the
calls made by migrating birds in flight to index the migrants' abun-
(35)   dance and species composition at different locations. Data is being
collected in the spring and fall. During the most recent season,
there has been minimal disturbance from animals to the recording devices, so data from this season are expected to provide more
complete coverage.

(40)   Researchers are working diligently to process and analyze the
sound recordings. Because the recording units operate continu-
ously, 24 hours a day, the first step in the analysis is the identification and separation of the night-time segments from the recordings. These night-time recordings are then scanned for flight calls
(45)   using sound analysis software called XBAT, developed by Harold
Figueroa and Matt Robbins. An XBAT extension, developed by
Kathy Cortopassi, searches for and flags sounds of a user-specified range of durations with a user-specified range of frequen-
cies. Spectrograms of these sounds are then reviewed to eliminate
(50)   sounds that are not bird calls. Sound files can also be scrolled
through manually, with flight call spectrograms selected and out-
put. Calls are identified by species, when possible, by matching
them to a reference set. For each hour of sampling at each site,
recorded calls are tallied to index migrant abundance within and
(55)   among nights.

Researchers are continuing to process these recordings.
Preliminary analysis, however, indicates that more flight calls have
been recorded at the sites during the fall migrations than during
the spring. In addition, during both spring and fall, there is con-
(60)   siderable variation among nights, both within and among sites.
Researchers have been able to match some of the calls to particular
species, but most calls can be placed only in species groups (for
example, warblers, sparrows, thrushes) because their spectrograms
are not clear. Researchers speculate that this lack of clarity occurs
(65)   because many of the calls are made by birds flying at the outer limits of the recording. The microphones can record calls up to about
300 meters above ground level.

The acoustic monitoring is supplemented with portable radar
sampling at three sites to provide additional data on the passage of
(70)   migrants, including their flight altitudes and directions. The data

from these radar samplings will be used to model the effects of
topography, weather, and other variables on migrant abundance
and flight to assess where and when migrants might be at risk from
wind power development.

(75)   The data from all these sampling techniques will collectively
allow researchers to understand migrant flight dynamics and
behavior and conditions that influence them. Predicted migrant
densities and flight characteristics will be mapped region-wide
as a function of topographic characteristics, and densities will be

(80)   summed across dates within seasons to identify locations over
which large numbers of migrants pass, or pass at altitudes within
the sweep reach of wind turbine rotors, either consistently or occasionally. This information will be used to develop a summary map
of areas where the risk of migrant interactions with potential wind

(85)   power projects is expected to be low, moderate, or high.

1.   Based on the passage as a whole, it can be inferred that the development of wind
power in the Appalachians could potentially affect

    (A)   warblers, sparrows, and thrushes.

    (B)   multiple species of birds and bats.

    (C)   all kinds of wildlife.

    (D)   several species of deer as well as migrating birds and bats.

2.   According to the author, which of the following are concerned about the effect that
wind power developments could have on birds?

I. State wildlife agencies

II. Harold Figueroa and Matt Robbins

III. The U.S. Fish and Wildlife Service

IV. The general public

    (F)   I and II only

    (G)   I, II, and III

    (H)   II, III, and IV

    (J)   I, III, and IV

3.   According to the passage, the USGS is currently studying the habits of migrating birds

    (A)   all across the country.

    (B)   on a year-round basis.

    (C)   during the spring and fall.

    (D)   by using XBAT to analyze NEXRAD data.

4. It can be inferred from lines 36–39, *During the most recent . . . coverage,* that

   (F) promising results can be obtained only when more complete coverage becomes available.

   (G) there have been some disturbances to the recording devices in previous seasons.

   (H) researchers are devising data collection techniques that minimize potential interference from wildlife.

   (J) further research will be needed to assess and mitigate the risks wind power developments pose for wildlife.

5. It can be inferred from the passage as a whole that

   (A) the turbines used in generating wind power create well-defined risks for migrating bats.

   (B) weather surveillance radar data may be used independently to assess risks to wildlife.

   (C) computer technology is an essential part of investigations about the risks of wind power to wildlife.

   (D) acoustic monitoring is the best currently available data collection technique for assessing wind power's potential threats to migrating bats.

6. The primary purpose of the passage is to

   (F) discuss ongoing research about the habits of migrating birds and bats to determine how wind power developments will affect them.

   (G) persuade the public that the well-being of birds and bats will be threatened by any new wind power developments in the Appalachians.

   (H) examine the process of analyzing data collected by acoustic monitoring devices.

   (J) argue that XBAT software is essential in investigating the habits of migrating species.

7. The seventh paragraph functions as

   (A) an explanation of how portable radar sampling works.

   (B) evidence about the flight altitudes of migrating animals.

   (C) a description of how spectrograms are used in acoustic monitoring.

   (D) a brief mention of a kind of data collection that is used in conjunction with acoustic monitoring.

8. It can be inferred from the second paragraph that

   (F) the migration path of some animals is along mountain ranges.

   (G) more bird migrations occur in the Appalachians than elsewhere in the country.

   (H) there have been animal disturbances to the acoustic monitoring equipment used during bird migrations.

   (J) birds and bats have numerous similarities in addition to their migrating habits.

9. The writer uses the phrase *lack of clarity occurs . . . at the out limits* (lines 64–66) in order to describe

    (A) an error in the researchers' technique.

    (B) a condition that is inevitable.

    (C) a possible explanation for a situation.

    (D) an argument that this more sensitive equipment is essential.

10. The goal of the research described in this passage is to

    (F) provide evidence that wind power developments are detrimental to migrating birds and bats.

    (G) make use of some sophisticated data collection and analysis techniques, including NEXRAD and XBAT.

    (H) determine which areas in the Appalachians could be used as sites for wind power developments while posing minimal threats to migrants.

    (J) assess the concerns of various groups, including the U.S. Fish & Wildlife Service, state wildlife agencies, and nongovernmental organizations, regarding wind power projects.

11. As used in line 23, the word *prominent* most nearly means

    (A) famous.

    (B) projecting.

    (C) advancing easily.

    (D) tree-covered.

12. As stated in the passage, the threats posed by wind power projects to migrating animals

    (F) have been well-documented.

    (G) are a source of contention between governmental agencies and the public.

    (H) should be assessed after enough data has been collected.

    (J) are a problem in all regions of the country.

ANSWERS AND EXPLANATIONS

Suggested Passage Map Notes

Paragraph 1: Groups concerned about wind power's effects on animals

Paragraph 2: More info needed to determine risks to bats and birds

Paragraph 3: U.S. studying bird and bat migration using radar and other techniques

Paragraph 4: Acoustic monitoring

Paragraph 5: Software used to analyze acoustic data

Paragraph 6: Preliminary results of acoustic monitoring

Paragraph 7: Portable radar technique

Paragraph 8: Data from all techniques to be combined in map

1. B
2. J
3. C
4. G
5. C
6. F
7. D
8. F
9. C
10. H
11. B
12. H

1. **The best answer is B.**   For a Generalization question, keep the entire passage in mind. Here you can predict that the passage describes research about bird and bat migrations. This prediction is a good match for option B. Option A is a misused detail. Option C is an extreme. The passage discusses studies about bats and birds only, not *all wildlife.* Option D is out-of-scope. The passage doesn't refer to *deer* at all.

2. **The best answer is J.**   For a Roman-numeral Detail question, check each item individually and use logic where possible to eliminate incorrect answer choices. Your passage map note should point you toward paragraph 1 to predict. Lines 6–10 mention several groups that are concerned about wind power effects: *the U.S. Fish & Wildlife Service, state wildlife agencies, nongovernmental organizations, and the public.* Thus, items I, III, and IV are justified. Only Option J includes all three of these. (Note also that item II is a misused detail from paragraph 5).

3. **The best answer is C.**   For a Detail question, use your passage map notes or skim the passage for key words in the question stem to help you find the right spot in the passage to read for your prediction. Here, either your notes or skimming should direct you to paragraphs 3 and 4. The question is worded broadly, so your prediction might cover a lot: The USGS is studying the habits of migrating birds in the Appalachians, using acoustic monitoring, in the spring and fall. The only choice that matches anything in this prediction is option C. Option A is out-of-scope. The passage doesn't mention any studies outside the Appalachian area. Option B is out-of-scope. The passage states that researchers are interested in the habits of migrating bats and birds, and migration doesn't occur all year long. Option D is a distortion. XBAT is described in the passage as a tool for analyzing the acoustic data.

4. **The best answer is G.**   For an inference question, read the quoted lines carefully and make a prediction that doesn't stray too far from the text. Here, notice that the sentence in question contains an implied contrast: *during the most recent season* is mentioned, suggesting that there's a difference between this season and previous seasons. Predict that the answer has something to do with this contrast, something like *in previous seasons there has been significant interference on the recording devices from animals.* Option G is a great match for this prediction. Option F is an extreme. Nothing in the passage justifies the use of the word *only.* Option H is out-of-scope. This choice goes too far beyond what's stated in the passage. Option J is a contradiction. The meaning of the quoted sentence is that this season's data are expected to be much more useful, not that *further research* is needed.

5. **The best answer is C.** For a Generalization question, keep the purpose of the whole passage in mind and work through the answer choices, eliminating incorrect ones. The purpose of the passage is to discuss research being done to assess the risks of wind power projects on migrating bats and birds. Option A is a contradiction. According to the passage, the risks are not yet *well-defined.* The research is being done to get a better handle on what those risks are. Option B is an extreme because it uses the word *independently.* Weather surveillance radar data are being used, but the passage also mentions two other monitoring techniques that are being used: acoustic monitoring and portable radar sampling. Option D is an extreme. Acoustic monitoring is certainly important, but the passage doesn't state or imply that it's *the best currently available* technique.

6. **The best answer is F.** For a Generalization question that asks about the purpose of the whole passage, use your passage map notes and remember not to focus too heavily on a particular detail. Here, predict that the purpose of the passage is to discuss methods of monitoring the habits of migrating birds and bats in order to determine what threats wind power development may pose to them. Option F is a great match for your prediction. Option G is a contradiction because the passage does not attempt to persuade the reader, only to inform. Option H is a misused detail. It's true that the passage contains information about acoustic monitoring, but that is only one of the research techniques discussed in the passage. Option J is a contradiction based on a misused detail. The passage makes no argument about XBAT being essential and, in any case, XBAT is only a small part of the passage and doesn't address the purpose of the passage as a whole.

7. **The best answer is D.** For a Function question about a paragraph, use your passage map notes and consider the context of the previous and following paragraphs. Here, paragraph 7 discusses one technique, portable radar, giving this technique much less attention than acoustic monitoring got in paragraphs 4–6. Paragraph 8 discusses all of the research techniques as a whole. Predict that the purpose of paragraph 7 is to briefly introduce a research technique. This prediction matches well with option D. Option A is a distortion. While the paragraph does discuss portable radar sampling, it doesn't explain how the technique works. Option B is a distortion. Paragraph 7 mentions *flight altitudes* as something portable data sampling is used to investigate, but the paragraph doesn't present any evidence about *flight altitudes.* Option C is a misused detail. Acoustic monitoring and spectrograms are discussed in paragraphs 5 and 6, not paragraph 7.

8. **The best answer is F.** For a Generalization question about a paragraph, read the paragraph carefully and draw a conclusion that doesn't go too far beyond what is stated. Use elimination if necessary to work through the answer choices. In this case, elimination is helpful. Option F is the right answer because it sticks closely to what the passage states. It restates the first sentence of the paragraph, using *some animals* where the passage says *birds and bats.* Remember that the correct answer to an Inference question does not necessarily say anything new. Sometimes, as here, just reading the passage and stating the obvious will get you to the correct answer. Option G is out-of-scope. The passage focuses on migrations in the Appalachians and doesn't say anything specific about migrations in other parts of the country. Option H is a misused detail from paragraph 4. Option J is out-of-scope. The only similarities between bats and birds that the passage is concerned with are their migratory behaviors.

9. **The best answer is C.** For a Function question about a phrase, read carefully in the context, paying attention to the lines before and after the quoted phrase. Here, the phrase appears in a sentence that begins *Researchers speculate.* Predict that the phrase is used to

describe the researchers' theories about information in the previous line, why some *spectrograms are not clear* (lines 63–64). This prediction matches well with option C. Option A is out-of-scope. The paragraph doesn't mention any error in carrying out the research. Option B is out-of-scope. The paragraph simply mentions a problem and a possible explanation; it doesn't state that the problem is unavoidable. Option D is out-of-scope. While the problem described could probably be remedied by *more sensitive equipment,* the paragraph does not state that better equipment *is essential.*

10. **The best answer is H.**   For a broad Generalization question, keep the purpose of the passage as a whole in mind. Predict that the passage examines research about bird and bat migration in the Appalachians to assess the potential risks of wind power development on these animals. Option H closely matches this prediction. Option F is a distortion. The goal of the research is to determine how detrimental wind power projects could be, not to argue that they *are* detrimental. Option H is a distortion. NEXRAD and XBAT are mentioned in the passage, but the research has a more specific purpose than simply making use of these methods. Option J is a distortion. All of the groups in option J are mentioned in the passage, but the research discussed is research about bats and birds, not about the concerns of the various people.

11. **The best answer is B.**   For a Vocabulary-in-Context question, read carefully in the immediate context looking for clues that help you predict. Here, the context is *other prominent landforms* (line 23). Just before this phrase, the sentence mentions *mountain ridges.* Thus, you know that *prominent* could also be used to describe mountain ridges. Use this knowledge to predict that *prominent* in this context means *elevated.* This prediction matches well with option B. Option A is out-of-scope. It gives a common meaning of *prominent* that is not justified at all in the context of the passage. Option C is out-of-scope. There is nothing in the context to suggest that *advancing* is relevant here. Option D is a distortion. *Tree-covered* might make sense if you think only of mountains, birds, and bats, but it doesn't take into account the clues that relate the word *prominent* to *other . . . landforms* like *mountain ridges.*

12. **The best answer is H.**   For a Detail question, consider your passage map notes to help you know where to read to predict. Here, your notes should guide you to paragraph 1. Paragraph 1 states that researchers are studying the effects of wind power development on migrating animals. You may need to use this prediction in combination with your understanding of the passage as a whole to eliminate wrong answer traps. Option F is a distortion. The passage mentions risks, but it discusses methods of assessing risk and does not conclude that risks have been well-documented. Option G is a distortion. The passage mentions both government agencies and the public but does not state that the two groups are in conflict. Option J is out-of-scope. The passage doesn't refer to all regions of the country, only to research being done in the Appalachians.

Chapter Seventeen: **Reading Practice Set VII—Natural Science**

Directions: This test contains a passage, followed by several questions. After reading the passage, select the best answer to each question. You are allowed to refer to the passage while answering the questions.

NATURAL SCIENCE

This passage is adapted from the paper "Indigenous Uses, Management, and Restoration of Oaks of the Far Western United States." It was issued by the U.S. Department of Agriculture Natural Resources Conservation Service in 2007.

Today, oaks are plagued with problems. There is lack of regeneration in populations of certain species. Pests such as the acorn weevil and the filbert worm eat away at acorns and prevent germi-

Line   nation. By undermining the root systems of seedlings and saplings,
(5)   ground squirrels, gophers, and other small mammals often prevent these young plants from reaching tree size. Severe diseases, such as sudden oak death, kill many adult oaks. Many mature oaks are having a tough time with fire suppression. In the past, with light surface fires, the oaks had been able to maintain a stronghold where
(10)   other plants were not able to compete and died out. Now oaks are being toppled by trees that have a higher tolerance for shade and are not fire resistant; earlier such trees would have been killed when Native Americans set fires.

Given all of these challenges, the "old-growth" oaks—the large
(15)   old valley oaks, Garry oaks, coast live oaks, and canyon live oaks that have huge girth and large canopies—may become a thing of the past. These oaks in particular are important because there are often more terrestrial vertebrates living in mature oak stands than in seedling and sapling areas. This prevalence of animals occurs
(20)   because the large crowns of such oaks provide cover and feeding sites for a large variety of wildlife.

The University of California has embarked on an ambitious and necessary research program called the Integrated Hardwood Range

(25) Management Program to explore the significant causes of oak decline and offer varied solutions. These include investigating the use of grassing regimes that are compatible with oak seedling establishment, revegetating sites with native grasses to facilitate better germination of oak seedlings, documenting insects and pathogens that attack oaks, and exploring the ways that native people man-
(30) aged oaks in the past. Scientists at the Pacific Northwest Research Station in Olympia, Washington and at Redwood National Park in northern California are reintroducing the burning practices of Native Americans. When used in Garry oak ecosystems, fires keep Douglas firs from encroaching on the oaks and promote the growth
(35) of wildflowers that are important food plants. Further investigations about these fire practices may be essential in figuring out how to maintain oaks in the western landscape today, given that the fires address many of the factors that are now causing oak decline— from how to eliminate insect pests of acorns to how to maintain an
(40) open structure in oak groves.

Ecological restoration, the traditional approach to woodland maintenance, referred to humans intervening on a very limited time scale to bring back plants and animals known to have existed in an area historically. However, the decline of oaks, one of the
(45) most significant plants to Native Americans, shows us that humans may play an integral part in the restoration of oak areas. While animals such as jays have been recognized as crucial partners in oak well-being, human actions through the eons may also have been key to the oaks' flourishing.

(50) Sudden oak death, for example, although of exotic origin, may be curtailed locally by thinning around coastal oaks and tan oaks and setting light surface fires, simulating ancient fire management practices of Native Americans. Indigenous shrubs and trees that grow in association with oaks are hosts to the sudden oak death
(55) pathogen. By limiting the growth of these shrubs, burning that mimics earlier Native American ways may reduce opportunities for disease agents to jump from other plants to oak trees. With a more open environment, it may be harder for sudden oak death to spread.

(60) The oak landscapes that we inherited, which still bear the marks of former Native American interactions, demand a new kind of restoration that complements other forms of ecological restoration. This new kind of restoration could be called *ethnobotanical restoration,* defined as reestablishing the historic plant communities of a
(65) given area and restoring indigenous harvesting, vegetation management, and cultivation practices (seedbeating, burning, pruning, sowing, tilling, and weeding) necessary to maintain these communities in the long term.

Thus, this kind of restoration is not only about restoring
(70) plants, but also about restoring the human place within nature.

Ethnobotancial restoration is viewed not as a process that can be completed, but rather as a continuous interaction between people and plants as both their fates are intertwined in a region. Uniting oaks and people once again through harvesting acorns, making
(75) products from all parts of the tree, knocking the trees, and setting light fires may offer us ways to coexist, receive products from, and benefit the long-term health and well-being of the remarkable oak.

1. All of the following challenges to the health of the oak population are mentioned in the passage *EXCEPT*

    (A) small mammals attacking the root systems of young trees.

    (B) sudden oak death caused by a pathogen.

    (C) grazing deer removing bark from the tree trunks.

    (D) competition from other plants such as shade tolerant trees.

2. As described in the passage, traditional ecological restoration differs from ethnobotanical restoration in that

    (F) ethnobotanical restoration takes place over a longer period of time than ecological restoration.

    (G) ecological restoration involves introducing particular plants and management practices, whereas ethnobotanical restoration involves only the introduction of plants.

    (H) only ecological restoration follows historically proven ecological principles.

    (J) ecological restoration is meant to be used in conjunction with other restorative practices, whereas ethnobotanical restoration is meant to be used in isolation.

3. An important assumption underlying this passage is that

    (A) the decline of the oak population is due primarily to root damage caused by ground squirrels, gophers, and other small mammals.

    (B) reinstituting indigenous cultivation practices is likely to be sufficient to restore the health of the oak population.

    (C) damage to many species of oak started centuries ago when Native Americans selectively set fires in many areas.

    (D) the practices of Native Americans offer lessons to modern researchers about how to promote a healthy oak population.

4. According to the passage, one way to reduce the incidence of sudden oak death is to

    (F) reduce the population of animals that destroy the root systems of the oaks.

    (G) control the number of certain shrubs that grow in the vicinity of oak trees.

    (H) regulate the importation of the exotic plants that introduced the sudden oak death pathogen to the United States.

    (J) plant several varieties of oaks, particularly tan oaks and coastal oaks, to strengthen the oak population in general.

5. The author refers to the *huge girth and large canopies* (line 16) of the old-growth oaks in order to

    (A) provide a description of what the various old-growth oak trees look like.

    (B) argue that the old-growth trees are too large to be sustained in a modern ecosystem.

    (C) support the explanation of why more vertebrates live in mature oak stands.

    (D) indicate that Native Americans valued these trees for their ability to produce shade.

6. The primary purpose of the first paragraph is to

    (F) discuss how oak trees provide a habitat for various animals.

    (G) suggest ways in which the declining oak population can be restored.

    (H) support the argument that sudden oak death is not as common as rampant forest fires.

    (J) describe current challenges to the health of the oak population.

7. Based on the passage as a whole, it is likely that

    (A) human intervention will be crucial in restoring the native oak population.

    (B) despite much historical study, it will be impossible to recreate the cultivation practices of early Native Americans.

    (C) documentation of the insects and pathogens that attack oak trees is the best way to begin the restoration process.

    (D) native shrubs and trees that grow near oaks have served as kindling for many fires that damaged the oak population.

8. The author mentions *trees that have a higher tolerance for shade* (line 11) as an example of

    (F) one type of vegetation that is desirable to plant near oaks.

    (G) a currently existing problem that presents a new kind of threat to the oak population.

    (H) one of the drawbacks associated with several of the old-growth oak species.

    (J) the types of plants Native Americans cultivated.

9. It can be inferred from the third paragraph that

    (A) the oak population in Redwood National Park has faced greater threats than oak populations elsewhere.

    (B) native grasses have been shown to deprive oak seedlings of nutrients.

    (C) the sudden oak death pathogen has been the primary cause of oak decline.

    (D) researchers are interested in finding multiple avenues to restoring the health of the oaks.

10. As stated in the passage, the effect of light surface fires on oaks is to

   (F) promote the health of oaks by limiting vegetation that would compete with them.

   (G) reduce the number of oak trees by destroying the acorns before they can seed.

   (H) create scars in the bark that allow for the entrance of the sudden oak death pathogen.

   (J) harm the oaks by destroying the nests of jays.

11. From the last paragraph, it is reasonable to infer that the author would agree with all of the following statements *EXCEPT*

   (A) The well-being of people is related to the well-being of plant populations.

   (B) It is advisable to complete the restoration of the oaks before turning to other types of ethnobotanical restoration.

   (C) Human intervention is not always harmful to the health of the natural world.

   (D) Harvesting parts of the oak tree to make products for human use need not harm the oak population as a whole.

12. The word *curtailed* as used in line 51 most nearly means

   (F) eliminated.

   (G) ended.

   (H) explored.

   (J) limited.

ANSWERS AND EXPLANATIONS

Suggested Passage Map Notes

   Paragraph 1: Problems facing oak populations

   Paragraph 2: Importance of "old-growth" oaks

   Paragraph 3: Research being done to learn about problems and solutions

   Paragraph 4: Ecological restoration

   Paragraph 5: Sudden oak death

   Paragraph 6: Def. of ethnobotanical restoration

   Paragraph 7: Importance of people in ethnobotanical restoration

KAPLAN

1. C
2. F
3. D
4. G
5. C
6. J
7. A
8. G
9. D
10. F
11. B
12. J

1. **The best answer is C.**   For a Detail question that uses EXCEPT, go straight to the answer choices and check the passage for each one. Eliminate option A because it's cited in lines 4–6. Eliminate option B because *sudden oak death* is mentioned in line 7, and the *pathogen* that causes it is mentioned in line 55. Eliminate option D because it's mentioned in line 11. Option C is the correct answer because the passage says nothing about grazing deer.

2. **The best answer is F.**   When a Detail question asks you to describe a contrast, make sure you read enough to determine what the passage says about both things contrasted. Here, research in paragraph 6 to predict that ethnobotanical restoration is a new approach that involves introducing plants and practices that were used in the past and working on long-term maintenance (lines 63–68). Research in paragraph 4 to predict that ecological restoration is used in a limited time frame and refers only to introducing plants and animals that were historically present (lines 42–44). Option F matches perfectly with the time frame the prediction points to. Option G is a distortion because ecological restoration isn't described as involving *management practices.* Option H is a contradiction because both types of restoration are described as being historically based. Option J is a distortion. The descriptions of the two kinds of restoration are reversed in the wording of this answer choice.

3. **The best answer is D.**   A Generalization question about an underlying assumption may be tough to make a prediction for. Still, try making a quick prediction that at least addresses the purpose of the passage, and then check through the answer choices. In this case, your prediction might be something along the lines of *restoring the health of the oak populations is an important endeavor.* None of the answer choices matches this prediction exactly, but option D comes very close, and it is true that the writer values the practices of Native Americans. Thus, option D is the best answer. Option A is a misused detail. Damage done to oaks by small mammals is mentioned, but it is not described as being the primary cause of the oaks' decline. Option B is a distortion; you should pay special attention to the word *sufficient* in this choice. While ethnobotanical restoration does include bringing in Native American practices, the passage describes ethnobotanical restoration as something that *complements other forms of ecological restoration* (line 62). Option C is a contradiction. Lines 13 refer to fires set by Native Americans as protecting oaks by limiting the growth of other trees that competed with oaks.

4. **The best answer is G.** For a Detail question, use passage map notes to guide you to the right part of the passage. Paragraph 5 discusses sudden oak death. It states that a way to reduce the spread of sudden oak death is to limit the growth of shrubs that harbor the sudden oak death pathogen. Option G matches this prediction. Option F is a misused detail. Animals that destroy the root systems of oaks are described as a problem, but addressing this problem is not mentioned as a way to reduce sudden oak death. Option H combines the misused detail and out-of-scope traps. Sudden oak death is described as having an *exotic origin* (line 50), but there is nothing in the passage about regulating imports. Option J combines the misused detail and out-of-scope traps. There is nothing in the passage suggesting that planting tan oaks and coastal oaks will strengthen the oak population in general.

5. **The best answer is C.** When a Function question asks about a phrase, consider the sentence it appears in and the sentences before or after, if necessary. Here, predict that the phrase *huge girth and large canopies* describes trees in *mature oak stands* (line 18), which the passage states are home to more small animals (the *terrestrial vertebrates* in line 18) than younger trees are. This prediction fits with option C. Option A is a misused detail. It's true that the phrase describes the appearance of the trees, but that doesn't address the author's purpose for describing this appearance. Option B is out-of-scope. The passage never says that the trees are too large for a modern ecosystem. Option D is a misused detail. Both *Native Americans* and *shade* are mentioned in the passage, but not in the context of the oaks' *huge girth and large canopies.*

6. **The best answer is J.** When a Function question asks about the purpose of a paragraph, keep in mind how its topic relates to the passage as a whole. Here, predict that paragraph 1 introduces the topic by discussing problems facing oak trees. Option J is a great match for this prediction. Option F is a misused detail. The animals that live in oaks are mentioned in paragraph 2, not paragraph 1. Option G is a misused detail. This statement is true of the passage as a whole but doesn't relate to the first paragraph. Option H is a distortion. The passage mentions both fires and sudden oak death but doesn't compare their effects.

7. **The best answer is A.** For a broad Generalization question, keep the entire passage in mind. Predict that the passage concerns problems facing oaks and proposed solutions. Option A goes just a little beyond this prediction but is consistent with the passage because solutions to the problems involve human intervention. Thus, option A is the best answer. Option B is a contradiction. Lines 65–66, discuss *restoring indigenous . . . cultivation practices* as though it's reasonable to expect that such things can be accomplished. Option C is an extreme. Though the passage mentions the pathogen and *pests* (line 39), it doesn't say that dealing with them is the *best* way to start the restoration process. Option D is a distortion. The fires that are mentioned in the passage (e.g., line 9) are described as protecting the oak population, not damaging it.

8. **The best answer is G.** For a Function question about a particular detail, focus on the immediate context to make your prediction. Here, pay attention to the first part of the sentence: now *oaks are being toppled by trees that have a higher tolerance for shade* (line 10–11). Predict that the shade-tolerant trees are overpowering the oaks. This prediction works well with option G. Option F is an opposite: because shade-tolerant trees are *toppling* the oaks, it would not be good to plant them near the oaks. Option H is a distortion. The passage mentions *old-growth oaks* but doesn't describe them as being at all shade-tolerant. Option J is a distortion. The passage mentions *Native Americans* but doesn't say that they planted the highly shade-tolerant trees.

9. **The best answer is D.**   For a Generalization question about a paragraph, use your passage map notes and keep the purpose of the paragraph in mind. Here, predict that the best answer will have something to do with finding ways to improve the declining strength of the oak population. Option D fits perfectly with this prediction. Option A is a misused detail. Redwood National Park is mentioned in the paragraph, but nothing in the paragraph suggests that oaks there are in worse shape than they are elsewhere. Option B is a contradiction. The paragraph states that native grasses can *facilitate better germination of oak seedlings.* Option C is a misused detail. Although sudden oak death is mentioned in the passage, nothing is said about it in paragraph 3. (This answer choice also uses the extreme language *primary cause,* which should put you on alert.)

10. **The best answer is F.**   If your passage map notes do not direct you to a particular place in the passage to answer a Detail question, skim the passage quickly for a phrase from the question stem or another phrase that means something similar. Here, the exact phrase *light surface fires* appears in lines 8–9. Read the sentence and predict that *they,* here referring to the oaks, *were able to maintain a stronghold* (line 9) because the fires kept in check plants that competed with the oaks. Option G is a distortion. The passage does mention acorns, but not in connection with fires. Option H is out-of-scope. The passage does not say anything about scars forming on the bark of oak trees. Option J is a distortion. *Jays* are mentioned in the passage, but not in relation to fires.

11. **The best answer is B.**   Remember that for an *EXCEPT* question, three of the four choices will be supported by the passage. Work through each choice and eliminate as you go. Option A is justified by line 73 as *both their fates* [i.e., plants' and people's] *are intertwined.* Option B is not justified by the passage and so is the correct answer here. Option C is supported particularly in lines 73–76, *uniting oaks and people . . . offering us ways to coexist.* Option D is justified by the suggestion that people should *make products from all parts of the tree* (lines 74–75).

12. **The best answer is J.**   For a Vocabulary-in-Context question, go back to the passage and look for clues in the sentence that allow you to predict what the word means. In this case, information in the rest of the paragraph can also help you eliminate choices. The subject of the sentence where the word appears is *sudden oak death.* Because the passage identifies this disease as a problem facing oaks, and the passage addresses solutions, predict that *curtailed* means something like *minimized* or *reduced.* This prediction matches well with option J, which is the best answer. Options F and G are both extremes. Nothing in the rest of the paragraph suggests that sudden oak death can be completely eradicated. Option H is a distortion that might result from putting too much emphasis on the phrase *exotic origin* used in the sentence.

Chapter Eighteen: Reading Practice Set VIII— Social Science

Directions: This test contains a passage, followed by several questions. After reading the passage, select the best answer to each question. You are allowed to refer to the passage while answering the questions.

SOCIAL SCIENCE

This passage is adapted from New Discoveries at Jamestown: Site of the First Successful English Settlement in America *by John L. Cotter and J. Paul Hudson published in 1957.*

Archeological explorations at Jamestown, Virginia, have brought to light thousands of colonial period artifacts that were used by the Virginia settlers from 1607 until 1699. A study of these objects,
Line   which were buried under the soil at Jamestown for decades, reveals
(5)   in many ways how the English colonists lived on a small wilderness island over 300 years ago. Artifacts unearthed include building materials and handwrought hardware, kitchen utensils and fireplace accessories, furniture hardware, and many items relating to household and town industries.
(10)   These artifacts provide valuable information concerning the everyday life and manners of the first Virginia settlers. Excavated artifacts reveal that the Jamestown colonists built their houses in the same style as those they knew in England, insofar as local materials permitted. There were differences, however, for the set-
(15)   tlers were in a land replete with vast forests and untapped natural resources close at hand that they used to their advantage.
The Virginia known to the first settlers was a carpenter's paradise, and consequently the early buildings were the work of artisans in wood. The first rude shelter, the split-wood fencing, the clap-
(20)   board roof, puncheon floors, cupboards, benches, stools, and wood plows are all examples of skilled working with wood.
Timber at Jamestown was plentiful, so many houses, especially in the early years, were of frame construction. During the first decade or two, house construction reflected a primitive use of

(25)   materials found ready at hand, such as saplings for a sort of fram-
         ing, and use of branches, leafage, bark, and animal skins. During
         these early years, when the settlers were having such a difficult time
         staying alive, mud walls, wattle-and-daub, and coarse marsh-grass
         thatch were used. Out of these years of improvising, construction

(30)   with squatted posts, and later with studs, came into practice. There
         was probably little thought of plastering walls during the first two
         decades. When plastering was adopted, clay, either by itself or
         mixed with oyster-shell lime, was first used. The early floors were of
         clay, and such floors continued to be used in the humbler dwellings

(35)   throughout the 1600s. It can be assumed that most of the dwellings,
         or shelters, of the early Jamestown settlers had a rough and primi-
         tive appearance.

         After Jamestown had attained some degree of permanency,
         many houses were built of brick. It is quite clear from documen-

(40)   tary records and archeological remains that the colonists not only
         made their own brick but also that the process, as well as the fin-
         ished products, followed closely the English method. Four brick
         kilns were discovered on Jamestown Island during archeological
         explorations.

(45)   While some of the handwrought hardware found at Jamestown
         was made in the colony, most of it was imported from England.
         Types of building hardware unearthed include an excellent assort-
         ment of nails, spikes, stapes, locks, keys, hinges, pintles, shutter fas-
         teners, bolts, hasps, latches, door knockers, door pulls, bootscrapes,

(50)   gutter supports, wall anchors, and ornamental hardware. In many
         instances, each type is represented by several varieties. It is believed
         that wooden hardware was used on many of the early houses.

         A few glass window panes may have been made in the
         Jamestown glass factory, which was built in 1608. Most of the win-

(55)   dow glass used in the colony, however, was shipped from England.
         Many of the early panes used were diamond-shaped pieces known
         as "quarrels" and were held in place by means of slotted lead
         strips known as "cames." The window frames used in a few of the
         Jamestown houses were handwrought iron casements. Most of the

(60)   humbler dwellings had no glass panes in the windows. The window
         openings were closed by batten shutters, operated by hinges of
         wood and fitted with wooden fastening devices.

         Busy conquering a stubborn wilderness, the first Jamestown
         settlers had only a few things to make their houses cozy and cheer-

(65)   ful. In most cases, their worldly goods consisted of a few cooking
         utensils, a change of clothing, a weapon or two, and a few pieces of
         handmade furniture. After the early years of hardship had passed,
         the colonists began to acquire possessions for more pleasant living;
         by 1650 the better houses were equipped with most of the neces-

(70)   sities of life of those times, as well as a few luxuries of comfortable
         living.

1. According to the author, artifacts discovered in Jamestown are worthy of study because they

    (A)   are made of valuable materials.

    (B)   offer information about the daily lives of settlers.

    (C)   indicate that life in Jamestown was not as difficult as had been previously thought.

    (D)   display a remarkable degree of artistic ingenuity.

2. All of the following are given as examples of skilled woodworking *EXCEPT*

    (F)   puncheon floors.

    (G)   benches.

    (H)   kitchen utensils.

    (J)   stools.

3. The primary purpose of the passage is to

    (A)   discuss artifacts found at the Jamestown settlement.

    (B)   argue that life in Jamestown was harder for the settlers than life in England had been.

    (C)   persuade the reader to visit Jamestown.

    (D)   describe the ways in which colonists rejected English traditions when they came to Jamestown.

4. As used in line 23, the word *frame* most nearly means

    (F)   outline.

    (G)   wood.

    (H)   picture-like.

    (J)   brick.

5. It can be inferred that *wattle-and-daub* in line 28 refers to

    (A)   a type of food consumed by the Jamestown settlers.

    (B)   decorative hardware used on colonial furniture.

    (C)   tools the archeologist used in the process of studying the Jamestown settlement.

    (D)   natural materials used in the construction of houses in Jamestown.

6. According to the author, which of the following examples of hardware were found at the Jamestown settlement?

   I. Nails

   II. Door knockers

   III. Curtain rods

   IV. Bootscrapes

   (F)   I and II

   (G)   I, II, IV

   (H)   II, III, IV

   (J)   III and IV

7. It can be inferred from lines 38–39, *After Jamestown...brick,* that one reason the earliest houses built by the settlers were made of wood was that

   (A)   Jamestown lacked facilities for manufacturing brick.

   (B)   it was initially unclear how long the settlers would remain in Jamestown.

   (C)   climate conditions in Virginia made it impossible to produce the kind of brick the settlers had been familiar with in England.

   (D)   the settlers had not brought any building materials with them from England.

8. It can be inferred from the last paragraph that concern with domestic comforts was a priority for the settlers

   (F)   because most of them had lived relatively luxurious lives before leaving England.

   (G)   only after the necessities of basic survival had been addressed.

   (H)   by the time the Jamestown settlement had been in existence for two years.

   (J)   because they needed relief from the harshness of the wilderness.

9. According the passage, clay was used for floors

   (A)   because the supply of timber was scarce.

   (B)   exclusively during the early years of Jamestown's existence.

   (C)   in all types of buildings at the settlement.

   (D)   for many years in the settlement's more modest houses.

10. As used in the passage, the phrase *replete with* in line 15 most nearly means

    (F)   finished by.

    (G)   lacking in.

    (H)   filled by.

    (J)   constrained by.

11. As stated by the author, a glass factory was built in Jamestown:

    (A)   in 1699.

    (B)   over 300 years ago.

    (C)   sometime before 1650.

    (D)   in 1608.

12. It can be inferred from that *there was probably little thought of plastering walls during the first two decades* (lines 30–32) because

    (F)   the materials necessary to make plaster were difficult to obtain.

    (G)   plastered walls were not a requirement of survival.

    (H)   the studs used at the time were too primitive to hold plaster.

    (J)   the rough and primitive appearance of unplastered walls was desirable to most settlers.

ANSWERS AND EXPLANATIONS

Suggested Passage Map Notes

Paragraph 1: Artifacts at Jamestown

Paragraph 2: Houses—similarities/differences w/England's

Paragraph 3: Woodworking

Paragraph 4: House construction details—initially wood

Paragraph 5: Brick used for houses—later

Paragraph 6: Hardware imported

Paragraph 7: Windows

Paragraph 8: More comforts by 1650

1. B
2. H
3. A
4. G
5. D
6. G
7. B
8. G
9. D
10. H
11. D
12. G

1. **The best answer is B.** For a Detail question, start by using your passage map notes to direct you to the right part of the passage to make your prediction. Here, paragraph 1 states that studying the objects found at Jamestown shows *how the English colonists lived* (line 5), and paragraph 2 specifically refers to *the everyday life* (line 11) of the settlers. These ideas form a good prediction, which matches perfectly with option B. Option A is out-of-scope because the artifacts aren't described as being made from expensive material. Option C is a distortion. While the passage does refer to the difficulty of the settlers' lives, it doesn't link this difficulty to the artifacts described. Option D is out-of-scope. The artistic qualities of the objects found at Jamestown are not addressed in the passage

2. **The best answer is H.** For a Detail question that uses *EXCEPT*, find support for three answer choices in the passage and eliminate them. The choice that is *not* supported in the passage is the correct answer here. Use passage map notes to refer you to paragraph 3. Here you find that puncheon floors, benches, and stools are all listed as *examples of skilled working with wood* (line 21). Kitchen utensils are mentioned, but later in the passage (lines 65–66) and not as examples of hardware. Option H is the best answer.

3. **The best answer is A.** For a Generalization question about the purpose of the passage, keep the big picture in mind. If you need help predicting, check your passage map notes. Also keep the tone of the passage in mind. This passage discusses the artifacts turned up by archeological explorations in Jamestown and what those artifacts indicate about the settlers' lives. The tone is detached and explanatory. Option A is a good match for this prediction. Option B is a distortion. The passage does mention some challenges faced by the settlers, but it doesn't discuss the relative difficulty of their lives in England and Jamestown. Option C is out-of-scope. The passage is meant only to describe the settlement, not to persuade the reader to visit it. Option D is a contradiction. England is mentioned in regard to housing styles; the passage states that the settlers built their houses in the same style as those they knew in England, insofar as local materials permitted.

4. **The best answer is G.** For a Vocabulary-in-Context question, read the sentence the word appears in and look for clues to help you predict. In this sentence, the words *timber* and *so* are important to focus on. The sentence states that *timber . . . was plentiful.* It makes sense, especially given the use of the word *so,* that if wood is abundant in the area then it would be used to build houses. Predict that *frame* as used here means *made of wood.* This prediction matches option G. Option F is out-of-scope. *Outline* is a common meaning of *frame* but is not justified in this context. Option H is out-of-scope. It may be tempting to associate *frame* with the word *picture,* but the meaning doesn't fit here. Option J is a misused detail. Brick is mentioned elsewhere in the passage but not in this context.

5. **The best answer is D.** For an Inference question, read a little bit before and after the words referred to in the question stem. Make a prediction by drawing a conclusion that doesn't go too far beyond what is stated. Here, the phrase *wattle-and-daub* appears in a list of materials that were used for building. Because the other items mentioned, *mud* and *marsh-grass thatch,* are natural resources, predict that *wattle-and-daub* describes other natural materials used in building. This prediction matches option D. Option A is out-of-scope. The passage never mentions food. Option B is a misused detail. Hardware is mentioned elsewhere in the passage but isn't related to this question stem. Option C is a distortion. The passage concerns archeological topics, but the tools used by archeologists are never mentioned.

6. **The best answer is G.** For a Roman-numeral Detail question, check each item one by one to see if it's mentioned in the passage. The long list of hardware discovered at Jamestown,

Types of building hardware . . . ornamental hardware (lines 47–50) includes items I, II, and IV. The passage never mentions *curtain rods.* Note that logic can also help with a question like this. If you recognize immediately that item III is not justified by the passage, you can eliminate options H and J. Then, to choose between options F and G, you need only determine whether item IV is mentioned.

7. **The best answer is B.** For an Inference question, read the sentence containing the lines in the question stem, and be ready to read a little before and after that if necessary. Here, the first part of the sentence, *After Jamestown had attained some degree of permanency,* suggests that Jamestown was at first possibly only a temporary settlement. The phrase *of the early Jamestown settlers* (line 36) in the previous sentence supports this idea. The prediction matches well with option B. Option A is contradicted by the passage in lines 39–41. Option C is a contradiction because the passage states that brick made in Jamestown was similar to brick made in England. Option D is out-of-scope. The passage doesn't say the settlers didn't bring materials, and option B follows more directly from the passage.

8. **The best answer is G.** For an Inference question, read the appropriate part of the passage and draw a conclusion that doesn't stray too far. The first part of the sentence referred to in the question stem describes the settlers as *busy conquering a stubborn wilderness,* (line 63). A few lines later you read that *the colonists began to acquire possessions for more pleasant living* (line 68) *after the early years of hardship had passed.* Therefore, predict that during the early years, settlers at Jamestown had to focus on basic survival needs more than comfort. This prediction fits well with option G. Option F is out-of-scope. The passage says nothing about luxuries in England. Option H is a distortion. This choice gets it right that comfort wasn't a priority for the earliest settlers, but the passage doesn't say that it took the settlers only two years before they could focus on domestic comforts. Option J is a distortion. Although the passage does mention the *stubborn wilderness,* it is mentioned as something that *prevented* the settlers from thinking about comforts, not as something that *caused* them to do so.

9. **The best answer is D.** For a Detail question, start by using your passage map notes to determine where to go back and read to make your prediction. Here, your notes should direct you to paragraph 4. The passage says that clay was used for *early floors* (lines 33–34) and *in humbler dwellings throughout the 1600s.* This prediction leads to option D. Option A is a contradiction. Line 22 says that timber was *plentiful.* Option B is an extreme. The word *exclusively* is a red flag. This answer choice can't work unless this extreme language is justified by the passage. Option C is also an extreme because of the word *all.*

10. **The best answer is H.** Treat a Vocabulary-in-Context question that asks about a phrase just as you would any other Vocabulary-in-Context question: Go back to the sentence and look for clues to help you predict. Here the words *vast* forest and *untapped* resources suggest abundance. This prediction lines up nicely with option H. Option F is out-of-scope. Nothing in the context suggests an ending. Option G is an opposite. Option J is out-of-scope. There is nothing to indicate constraint or limitation in connection with forests or natural resources.

11. **The best answer is D.** Use your passage map notes to determine where to look to make your prediction for a Detail question. In this case, your notes should lead you directly to paragraph 7. The first sentence states that the Jamestown glass factory was built in 1608. This prediction leads to option D. Options A, B, and C are all misused details. They use dates that are indeed mentioned in the passage, but not in connection with the glass factory.

12. **The best answer is G.**   For an Inference question, be prepared to read a little before and after the lines cited in the question stem. In this case, your prediction should come from several sentences earlier. If *the settlers were having a difficult time staying alive* (lines 27–28), it makes sense that survival concerns would prevent them from worrying about whether the walls were plastered. This prediction leads to option G. Option F is a distortion. The passage describes the materials but doesn't imply that they are hard to get. Option H is a distortion. Studs are mentioned in the passage but are not described as being weak. Option J is a distortion. The word *primitive* is used in the passage but not as a desirable stylistic feature.

Chapter Nineteen: Introduction to ACT Writing

A strong ACT essay has three characteristics. First, it persuades effectively. Though you can't know in advance exactly what question you'll see in your ACT booklet on Test Day, you do know that the question will relate to a specific issue and that you'll be required to formulate an answer to the question and persuade the reader that your viewpoint is valid. A second characteristic of a superior ACT essay is that it presents the question in a larger context. To do this, don't just jump in and start answering. Rather, give a little background about the topic to show that you've thought about why the question is important and why your answer matters. At some point in the essay, you should also discuss a possible objection to your viewpoint and respond to that objection. The third characteristic of a high-scoring ACT essay is, not surprisingly, that it uses language clearly and correctly. This chapter looks in detail at how you can practice incorporating all of these features in your ACT essay. First, we'll review the Kaplan method and look at how ACT essay graders evaluate your writing.

REVIEW OF THE KAPLAN METHOD FOR THE ACT ESSAY

Take a few minutes to see if you can remember the four steps of the Kaplan method we discussed in the chapter on strategies. (Hint: they all begin with the letter *P*.)

Kaplan Method for ACT Essay Writing:

1. _____

2. _____

3. _____

4. _____

The four *P's* here are *prompt, plan, produce,* and *proofread.* As you read here about the characteristics of a strong essay, pay special attention to suggestions about when, in working through the method, you should think about each characteristic.

THE SCORING RUBRIC FOR THE ESSAY

The ACT essay is scored *holistically*, which means that the grader assigns a score based on his or her overall impression. The test maker provides a rubric, or checklist, of aspects to assess, but there are no specific point values assigned to each aspect. Let's look at the rubric.

ACT Writing Section Rubric

The ACT essay graders read your essay with the following questions in mind:

1. How well did the writer **understand the prompt?**
2. Did the writer display an **understanding of the complexity of the issue?**
3. How effectively did the writer **develop ideas?**
4. Did the writer stay **focused on the topic** in the prompt?
5. Is the essay **organized** in a logical way?
6. Did the writer make **effective use of transition words and phrases?**
7. How effective are the **introductory** and **concluding sentences?**
8. How well does the writer exhibit competent **language skills?**
9. Does the essay contain few, if any, **errors** that distract from its readability?

A STRONG ESSAY PERSUADES EFFECTIVELY

As you know, being persuasive means trying to convince someone to see and even agree with your viewpoint. In writing a persuasive essay, you're creating an argument. The first thing you must do is generate a *thesis statement,* that is, a clear and unambiguous statement of the position you will argue. Following the Kaplan method, you formulate your thesis statement during the prompt and plan steps.

The Thesis Statement

Before you can create a thesis, you need to understand the issue. Start with step 1 and read the prompt. To help you focus on the topic, it's a good idea to underline key words in the prompt as you read. Key words are the nouns and verbs that form the backbone of the prompt. These are words that you'll need to use in your essay to help you stay focused on your topic.

After reading the prompt, you move to step 2, making your plan. You should create a brief written plan before you start writing your essay, but you don't need to do this immediately after reading the prompt. Take a minute to think about the question posed in the prompt. Do you have an immediate and strong reaction to it? Sometimes, you'll know right away how you feel about the question, and ideas and examples will pop into your head even as you're reading the prompt. At other times, though, you might be a little less certain. Perhaps both sides of the issue seem equally valid to you, and you can think of reasons to support both. In this case, don't spend too long deliberating. Remember, the questions posed in ACT prompts are chosen precisely because two reasonable people might have very legitimate reasons for supporting opposite views. Your essay score is not affected by which viewpoint you choose to defend.

Therefore, don't spend too much time deliberating over which side of the issue to support. Choose one viewpoint and jot down a list of evidence you can use to support that viewpoint. If you feel the opposite argument has validity, that's great, because you'll find it easy to think of a counterargument. (You can read more about that in the sections that follow.) Once you've chosen a viewpoint, you need to formulate a good *thesis sentence*. A thesis sentence is a clear, simple statement that describes the position you will support in your essay. Let's consider what a good thesis sentence should look like. A strong thesis sentence

- answers the question in the prompt;
- leaves no doubt about where you stand on the issue; and
- doesn't necessarily contain reasons but does set the stage for your presentation of evidence that will follow.

WRITING EXERCISE 1

Suppose your essay prompt asks whether or not administrators should abolish the honor roll at your school. Consider each of the following sentences and put an asterisk next to the ones you think would make a good thesis sentence:

1. _____ I've always felt bad because I don't usually make the honor roll.
2. _____ The honor roll serves several educational purposes.
3. _____ Our school should continue to publish an honor roll.
4. _____ The honor roll actually distracts students from learning well.
5. _____ The honor roll unfairly rewards students with natural academic ability.
6. _____ We should maintain the honor roll because it continues to serve a useful purpose.
7. _____ While I do think students should be recognized for their academic successes, I think the honor roll as we know it should be discontinued.
8. _____ Teachers tend to give better grades to students they know have already been on the honor roll.

Sentences 3, 6, and 7 are the most appropriate thesis sentences. Sentences 1, 2, 4, 5, and 8 all discuss the honor roll, but they don't state a position relating to the question in the prompt. These sentences might be appropriate as part of your argument in the essay, but they can't take the place of a thesis sentence.

Examples and Evidence

Now that you know what an appropriate thesis sentence is, let's consider what your evidence should look like. The most important thing to remember in selecting evidence is that it should be specific and relevant to your topic. You should identify your examples and reasons in brief written notes in the plan step, but you'll actually flesh out your evidence in the produce step. That's when it's important to focus on developing your evidence specifically. A problem many unprepared students have with the ACT essay is not making evidence specific. Working under time pressure, many students don't plan evidence well, and they wind up talking in generalities instead of presenting specific evidence that supports a thesis. With practice, you can avoid this common flaw. Try the following exercise to work on generating specific evidence.

WRITING EXERCISE 2:

Suppose you want to support the viewpoint that students' cell phones should be turned off during school hours. Consider each of these sentences, and indicate whether it provides evidence that specifically supports your viewpoint:

1. _____ These days everybody has a cell phone.
2. _____ Ringing cell phones cause distractions in the classroom.
3. _____ The school makes too many rules that are unfair to students.
4. _____ Students who are texting in class are not learning the material the teacher is presenting.
5. _____ Pretty much everyone would agree with me that it's impossible to live without a cell phone.
6. _____ Teachers decide what we study, assign homework, and determine grades, but it's obvious that they should not tell us to turn off our phones during school time.
7. _____ Focused attention is necessary for learning, and having cell phones turned on compromises students' ability to focus.
8. _____ It's amazing how many things I can do with my tiny cell phone.
9. _____ The use of cell phones in the classroom, even for silent functions, can be annoying and distracting to other students.
10. _____ Using cell phones in the classroom takes students' attention away from the lesson and is therefore rude to teachers.

Did you notice that not every sentence that contains the words *cell phone* necessarily provides evidence supporting the argument? Only sentences 2, 4, 7, 9, and 10 present specific reasons supporting the argument that cell phones should be turned off in school. Notice that a couple of others use broad generalizations that aren't specific and relevant to the position. Be wary of using words such as *everybody* (sentence 1) and *everyone would agree with me* (sentence 5). You should also avoid a phrase like *it's obvious that* (sentence 6) because such wording assumes the reader sees your point. Your task in this essay is not to take the reader's agreement for granted but rather to use evidence that inspires agreement.

Because your ACT essay is an argument, you should take time during the planning step to reflect on the best way to organize your material. An essay that has a clear organization will be easy to follow and more likely to persuade the reader that you know what you're talking about and have good reasons for taking your position. The few minutes you spend in planning are crucial to organization. While you don't have to preplan every word you write, you should plan the key elements of your argument. If you know the topic of each paragraph, you're off to a good start.

Organization

A simple description of a well-organized essay is that it has a clearly thought out beginning, middle, and end, and stays focused on the topic at hand. The work you do in step 2, the planning stage, is crucial to writing an essay that reflects strong organization. Planning doesn't have to be intimidating if you think of this step as running through the following series of questions:

Questions to Consider in Step 2—Plan

- What is my thesis statement?
- How can I set this argument in a broader context, explaining why the question is an important one? What are the implications of my argument: What would be the results of implementing my viewpoint?
- What specific examples will I use as evidence? What reasoning will I present?
- What is one counterargument I can address and respond to?

The written notes you make in the planning step don't have to be extensive, but you should at least write down a couple of examples you'll discuss. The important thing is that you take a few minutes before you start writing to formulate what you're going to say. If you plan ahead, you can choose the best order to present your examples and evidence. Because of the time constraints on the ACT, you can't just write whatever pops into your head. Writing your ACT essay is different from writing a paper for school. On Test Day, you'll be working with pencil and paper, and you won't have the flexibility of rearranging your words easily like you may be accustomed to if you usually write papers on the computer. Before you leave the planning step and move on to producing your essay, you should know what viewpoint you intend to support and the examples or evidence you'll use to support it.

A STRONG ESSAY PLACES THE QUESTION IN A BROAD CONTEXT

One thing an ACT essay grader expects to find in a top-scoring essay is an indication that the writer understands the complexity of the question in the prompt. The strongest ACT essays not only effectively argue a position but also illustrate an understanding of the ramifications of that position. Two excellent ways to give your essay a broad context are to use the introduction to discuss the background of the question and to include a counterargument and response to it later in the essay.

The Introductory Paragraph

Many students feel that they have to start their essay with the thesis sentence, but this isn't necessarily the case. While you definitely need to include a thesis statement, it's perfectly fine to discuss the question before you state your answer to it. Your introductory paragraph should set the question in a broader context than the prompt offers. Think about what the prompt does: It brings up a question and offers two points of view. Brief reasons are given to support each side. The prompt doesn't usually explain *why* the question is an important one or indicate *what* the consequences of implementing a particular plan will be. If you discuss these factors at the beginning of your essay, even before you present your own thesis, you'll show that you've thought carefully about the issue and understand its complexity.

Here's a suggestion to give your introductory paragraph a smooth and sophisticated touch: Try to frame your essay in such a way that it will make sense to someone who doesn't have the prompt available to refer to. Of course, your essay *must* reflect that you have read and thought carefully about the question in the prompt. To do this, however, you don't need to refer explicitly to the prompt. Consider this sentence, for example: *As stated in the prompt, some people consider the honor roll to be valuable.* Think about it. You don't really need the phrase, *as stated in the prompt.* Try to make your essay understandable on its own. That is, the reader shouldn't need the prompt to refer to. You should use words that appear in the prompt to help you keep your focus on the topic, but references to the prompt itself don't serve any purpose in advancing your argument.

Introducing and Responding to a Counterargument

Including a counterargument in your essay is another good way to illustrate your understanding of the complexity of the issue. A counterargument is an objection that someone might bring up about your argument. While you need to support your own position strongly, describing an objection that someone might make to it illustrates that you have the capacity to see both sides of the issue. Strongly supporting your own argument doesn't preclude acknowledging that someone on the other side may disagree with you for a particular reason. Discussing a counterargument, acknowledging its validity, and then proceeding to give your response to it actually strengthens your own argument. You can bring up a counterargument in either the middle or closer to the end of your essay. Effectively responding to an objection can be a part of your concluding paragraph.

A STRONG ESSAY DISPLAYS CLEAR AND CORRECT USE OF LANGUAGE

In your practice for the English section of the ACT, you're learning rules and principles to help you make the best choices about wording in the English passages. It's important that you keep these rules and principles in mind for the ACT Writing section as well. Remember that the last step of the Kaplan method for the ACT essay is to proofread. If you spend an adequate amount of time on the prompt, plan, and produce steps, you'll have only about five minutes to proofread. Let's give some attention to the best ways to use this time effectively.

Be Careful with Pronouns!

When you're writing under pressure, as you are on the ACT, it's easy to make some grammatical mistakes that affect the logic of your essay. The use of pronouns is an area that many students have trouble with. If you train yourself to pay attention to pronouns and think about what's involved in using them correctly, it will be easier to catch pronoun problems and correct them even when you're proofreading quickly. Everything you know about pronouns that you apply to the English section also holds true for the Writing section. Refresh yourself on the guidelines described here.

Pronoun Reference Rule

A pronoun refers to a noun or another pronoun. Do not use a pronoun if the sentence it's in or the sentence before it doesn't contain a word for the pronoun to refer logically to.

Pronoun Number Rule

A pronoun must agree in number with the noun or pronoun it refers to. Do not use a plural pronoun to refer to a singular noun.

Pronoun Shift Rule

Do not switch between the words *one* and *you* in a given context.

For most people, it's easier to spot mistakes in something written by someone else. It can be tough to identify errors in your own writing, but pronouns are an area you can easily work on. Try the following pronoun exercise.

WRITING EXERCISE 3

In the following essay excerpts, watch for errors in the use of pronouns. Circle the mistakes and write down the corrections.

1. _____ When one works hard on academics all semester, you expect to get some kind of recognition.

2. _____ School authorities shouldn't try to control the lives of students completely. If a student doesn't want to perform community service, they shouldn't have to.

3. _____ The school administration has given a lot of thought to the value of the honor roll. They feel that by doing away with the honor roll, students will lose motivation to work hard.

4. _____ Our school administration is debating whether or not to allow the use of films in the classroom. They say that movies are effective at capturing the interest of students.

5. _____ A girl who has attended a single-sex school is likely to report that they feel teachers take their opinions seriously.

6. _____ Student council exists to serve the student body. Therefore, they should have the responsibility of electing the representatives.

7. _____ A bilingual classroom doesn't help a non-native English speaker learn English quickly. They should get tutoring and extra help, but they should attend classes in English.

8. _____ I've read the newspaper every day for the past five months, and they say that education is one of the most pressing issues in the upcoming election.

9. _____ Every student deserves the right to wear what they want to, within reasonable boundaries of course.

10. _____ Educators, because they have more experience, know what's best for students. They should be the ones who decide about new course offerings.

This exercise should have increased your awareness of sloppy pronoun usage. Question 1 is wrong because it shifts between *one* and *you*. Many of the others are wrong because the pronoun *they*, which is plural, appears without a plural noun that it can logically refer to. Here are some corrections you could have made. Note that you might have come up with different revisions that effectively correct the pronoun errors.

1. When one works hard on academics all semester, **one expects** [*not* you expect] to get some kind of recognition.

2. School authorities shouldn't try to control the lives of students completely. If a student doesn't want to perform community service, **he or she** [*not* they] shouldn't have to.

3. The school administration has given a lot of thought to the value of the honor roll. **Administrators** [*not* They] feel that by doing away with the honor roll, students will lose motivation to work hard.

4. Our school **administrators are** [*not* administration is] debating whether or not to allow the use of films in the classroom. They say that movies are effective at capturing the interest of students.

5. A girl who has attended a single-sex school is likely to report that **she feels** [*not* they feel] teachers take **her** [*not* their] opinions seriously.

6. Student council exists to serve the student body. Therefore, **students** [*not* they] should have the responsibility of electing the representatives.

7. A bilingual classroom doesn't help **non-native English speakers** [*not* a non-native English speaker] learn English quickly. They should get tutoring and extra help, but they should attend classes in English.

8. I've read the newspaper every day for the past five months, and **many reporters and columnists** [*not* they] say that education is one of the most pressing issues in the upcoming election.

9. **All students deserve** [*not* Every student deserves] the right to wear what they want to, within reasonable boundaries of course.

10. **Educators, because they have more experience, know what's best for students and should be the ones who decide about new course offerings.** [The problem is that "they" in the original sentence could logically refer to either "students" or

"educators." You could also correct the problem by simply changing "they" to "educators" instead of rewriting the whole sentence.]

Avoid Slang and Clichés

Although some slang words and expressions are acceptable in ordinary conversation, you should avoid slang in your ACT essay. The purpose of the essay is to present a logical argument based on reasoning and evidence, and the language you choose should reflect the seriousness of the task. As you practice, become sensitive to the tone of various expressions. If you think something is slang or too informal, ask yourself if there's a more appropriate phrasing.

Like slang, clichéd language is best avoided in your ACT essay. A cliché is a worn-out, overused expression. Your essay should show that you're taking a fresh and thoughtful approach to the question posed, and the overuse of clichés undercuts the serious and thoughtful attention you bring to your argument.

WRITING EXERCISE 4

In the following sentences, circle slang and clichéd expressions. Write an alternative in the space provided.

1. _____ Most kids don't have time to hold jobs during the school year.

2. _____ The idea of making math teachers give writing assignments to students is just crazy.

3. _____ Politicians say they have everyone's best interests in mind, but those guys don't really see the big picture.

4. _____ It's true that some kids do act like jerks, but the entire student body shouldn't have to pay for the misbehavior of a few bad apples.

5. _____ If this change is implemented, all students will have the chance to get the best ever education.

6. _____ It's been shown over and over again that everyone needs encouragement.

Answers to Writing Exercise 4

1. *Kids* is slang. Change to *teens, teenagers, high school students,* or *adolescents.*

2. *Just crazy* is slang. Change to *unrealistic, unworkable,* or *impractical.*

3. *Those guys* is slang. Change to *they* or *most of them.*

4. *Kids* and *jerks* are slang, and *a few bad apples* is a cliché. Rewrite the sentence as something like, *It's true that some students do act inappropriately, but the entire student body shouldn't have to pay for the mistakes of a few.*

5. *The best ever* is a cliché. Change to *a sound* or *an excellent*.

6. *Over and over again* is a cliché (and it's wordy). Change to *repeatedly*.

Use Correct and Varied Sentence Structure

Sentence structure is tested directly in the ACT English section, but it's also very important for the essay you produce in the Writing section. To apply the principles of correct sentence structure in your essay, think about how you combine groups of words into sentences. You can avoid sentence fragments by making sure that each sentence includes a subject and a verb and expresses a complete thought. You can avoid run-ons by making sure that ideas are joined with proper punctuation and connections (transitions) words. The following exercise is designed to help you review what you learned about sentence structure in the English section.

ESSAY EXERCISE 5

Following is a run-on sentence. Write out three acceptable ways to correct it.

Teenagers value driving as a privilege, most work hard to be safe drivers.

1. _____

2. _____

3. _____

Here are our answers, each followed by a general guideline.

1. Because teenagers value driving as a privilege, most work hard to be safe drivers. [Use a connections word to introduce the first clause.]

2. Teenagers value driving as a privilege, so most work hard to be safe drivers. [Use a comma followed by a FANBOYS word to combine the two clauses.]

3. Teenagers value driving as a privilege; therefore, most work hard to be safe drivers. [Use a semicolon and a non-FANBOYS connections word to combine the two clauses.]

"Varied" sentence structure means sentences of different lengths. Your essay shouldn't use all short, choppy sentences, but you should use some shorter sentences to provide variety among longer, complicated sentences. During the proofread step, you're likely to find spots in your essay where you can make a few quick adjustments, say, inserting a word or changing the punctuation, to help you improve your sentence structure. If you follow the guidelines above for properly combining clauses into sentences, your essay's sentence structure should be in good shape.

Avoid Unnecessary Repetition

When you're writing an essay under very tight time constraints, as you must on the ACT, it's easy to find yourself using the same words and phrases frequently. Such repetition can detract from the effectiveness of your essay. You need to stay focused on the topic, that's true. However, if you use the same words and phrases repeatedly, it's a sign that you may not be developing your ideas thoroughly. Thus, the first remedy for needless repetition comes in the planning stage: Make sure you've reflected carefully about your viewpoint. To earn a high score, you must go beyond the ideas offered in the prompt; you must expand upon your own position with reasoning and evidence. Thinking through your plan and writing brief notes in the test booklet helps to ensure that you'll develop your ideas adequately during the production step. It can also help if you think of some synonyms for key words and phrases that are important to the topic.

WRITING EXERCISE 6

Imagine that the topic of your essay question somehow relates to academic success. Take a few minutes to write down some words and phrases that might be relevant in the space provided:

_____

_____

_____

_____

There are no right or wrong answers here, and, of course, the ones you choose to use in your essay will depend upon the focus of the particular question and the angle from which you approach it. Some phrases that relate to "academic success" are *academic achievement, excellence, scholarship, academic arena, intellectual development, effective learning strategies, motivation, diligence.*

Though thinking carefully during the planning step can help you minimize repetition in your essay, repetition is still something you should watch for when you're proofreading. Making a slight change in a word or phrasing is quick to do and can introduce greater variety and effectiveness in your choice of vocabulary.

WRITING EXERCISE 6

The following examples all include unnecessary repetition. Some could be made more concise. In each example, underline the repeated words and phrases, and then rewrite the examples to be less wordy and more varied in word choice.

1. Funding arts programs is important to student achievement. Studies show that musical training leads to increased student achievement.

_____

_____

2. Bilingual education is an important topic in education today. Bilingual education is necessary for students whose first language is not English.

    _____

    _____

3. My school allocates too much money to sports programs. I know many students who don't participate in sports. Money allocated for sports programs doesn't benefit them. The school could achieve a better balance by allocating more money to programs that promote social activities and creative pursuits.

    _____

    _____

    _____

4. School newspapers serve several important functions. One of them is to let students decide what is worthy of publication and what is not. This function of a school newspaper would be completely taken away if a panel of teachers were to take over the decisions about what is worthy of publication.

    _____

    _____

    _____

For many students, proofreading is the most difficult part of writing. Remember, the ACT essay graders don't expect your essay to be flawless. However, you can improve your writing even by making only a few small corrections during the proofreading step. Don't worry if you didn't make the same corrections that we did. However, do work on identifying repetition and wordiness in your own writing. Here are some possible ways of correcting the examples. We've reprinted them and highlighted repetition and wordiness in boldface type.

1. Funding arts programs is important to **student achievement**. Studies show that musical training leads to increased **student achievement**.

    Funding arts programs is important because studies show that musical training leads to increased student achievement [or "academic performance"].

2. **Bilingual education** is an important topic in **education** today. **Bilingual education** is necessary for students whose first language is not English.

    Bilingual education is an important topic today because public schools serve many students whose first language is not English.

3. My school **allocates** too much **money** to **sports programs**. I know many students who don't participate in **sports**. Money allocated for **sports programs** doesn't benefit them. The school could achieve a better balance by **allocating** more **money** to **programs** that promote social activities and creative pursuits.

    My school allocates too much money to sports programs. This funding doesn't benefit the many students I know who are not athletically inclined. The school could achieve a better balance by directing more resources to social activities and creative pursuits.

4. **School newspapers** serve several important **functions.** One of them is to let students decide **what is worthy of publication and what is not.** This **function** of a **school newspaper** would be completely taken away if a panel of teachers were to take over the decisions about **what is worthy of publication.**

   School newspapers serve several important functions, one of which is giving students the opportunity to decide what is appropriate for publication. This function would be removed if the determination about what is worthy of publication were made by a panel of teachers instead of students.

Chapter Twenty: **Writing Prompt I**

Directions: This section will test your writing ability. You will have 30 minutes to compose an essay in English. Prior to planning your essay, pay close attention to the essay prompt so that you understand exactly what you are supposed to do. Your essay's grade will be based on how well it expresses an opinion on the question in the prompt, as well as its logical construction, supporting evidence, and clarity of expression based on the standards of written English.

PROMPT

Some high schools have implemented a program of team-taught courses as part of the required curriculum. These courses focus on multidisciplinary topics and are taught by two teachers from different disciplines. Supporters of this multidisciplinary program believe that team-taught courses promote critical thinking by encouraging students to view a topic from more than one perspective. Others, however, believe that requiring these courses is detrimental for students, because a multidisciplinary approach dilutes the subject matter expertise that a single teacher brings to a class in his or her own field. In your opinion, should high schools require each student to take at least two multidisciplinary classes as part of the graduation requirement?

In your essay, take a position on this question. You may write about either one of the two points of view given, or you may present a different point of view on this question. Use specific reasons and examples to support your position.

Before you read the sample responses, practice writing your own essay on this topic. Work in a place with no distractions when you have a full 30 minutes to write. Set a timer or alarm. Remember to pay attention to timing throughout the whole 30 minutes and allot time for each step of the Kaplan method. The time you spend considering the prompt, making a written plan, and proofreading are just as important to your score as the time you spend in the production stage.

Good luck! After the timer goes off, take a short break. Come back to your essay a little later and evaluate your work.

_____

_____

_____

_____

_____

_____

_____

_____

_____

_____

_____

_____

_____

_____

_____

_____

_____

_____

_____

_____

_____

_____

Welcome back! Now that you've written your essay and taken a break to grab a drink, shoot some hoops, or do some yoga, it's time to take a look at your work.

Keeping in mind the ACT essay grader's criteria, ask yourself the following questions:

- How well did I **understand the prompt?**
  - Where was my thesis statement?
  - Did I express my viewpoint confidently and unambiguously?
- Did I display an **understanding of the complexity of the issue?**
  - If so, how? If not, how could I have fit in an acknowledgement of complexity?
  - Should I have presented more background information about the topic before stating my thesis?
  - Could I have addressed a counterargument?
- How effectively did I **develop my ideas?**
  - What did I present for evidence and examples?
  - Did I explain how each example relates to my thesis?
- Did I stay **focused on the topic** in the prompt? If not, where did I veer off to irrelevant statements?
- Is the essay **organized** in a logical way?
  - Did I write a clear introduction?
  - Does each paragraph address only one major topic?
  - Did I write a strong conclusion?
- Did I make **effective use of transition words and phrases?** If not, where in my essay could have I used logic?
  - Are there any areas where I could have added a cause-and-effect transition such as *as a result, therefore, so,* or *because*?
  - Are there any areas where I could have added a contrast transition such as *while, despite,* or *on the other hand*?
  - Have I used transitions between paragraphs or made it clear that each new paragraph is adding a new element to my argument?
- How effective are my **introductory and concluding sentences?**
  - Is the first sentence focused clearly, even if broadly, on the topic in the prompt?
  - Is the last sentence strong and decisive?
  - Could I have improved my introductory or concluding sentences by giving them a little more attention during the proofreading step?
- How well did I apply strong **language skills?**
  - Is my essay free of run-ons and fragments?
  - Did I pay attention to pronouns, making sure that each pronoun correctly and logically refers to another word close to it in the essay?
  - Did I use verb tenses consistently and logically?

— Is my word choice precise and concrete, or are there any vague or awkward phrasings that I should have revised?

• Did I correct any **errors** such as misspellings or omitted words that would detract from the reader's understanding?

It can be tough to evaluate your own writing. However, this checklist will help you reflect on different aspects of your essay as they relate to the ACT essay grader's standards. Do not skip this self-assessment. Reflect carefully and identify the strengths and weaknesses you find. Note them in the space provided:

Strengths to maintain: _____

_____

_____

Weaknesses to improve: _____

_____

_____

SAMPLE RESPONSE 1

Planning Notes
• Team taught multidisc. classes NOT good for students
• Better to get good grounding in particular subject area
• H.S. lays groundwork, time later for multidisc.

I consider that the main purpose of my high school education is to give me a good grounding in the basic subjects of history, literature, science, math, and language. Because I value learning the specific knowledge that's part of each of these courses, I would not want to participate in multidisciplinary classes in high school. Therefore, I don't think such classes should be part of the required curriculum. They would only dilute the foundational content knowledge that high school students should be learning. In addition, I'm aware of the huge bureaucracy involved in administering my large public high school. Requiring all students to take at least two multidisciplinary classes before graduation would seriously increase teachers' workloads and the administrative red tape. I favor eliminating extra bureaucratic issues and letting **each** teacher concentrate on what **they** know best. For this reason, I am opposed to having our school add a requirement for each student to take at least two multidisciplinary team-taught courses as a graduation requirement.

My opinion is based on the idea that high school is not meant to provide a complete education for students but rather should give us a solid foundation on which to further our learning, either in college or through our own reading and activities. It's not that I wouldn't value or enjoy a team-taught course that offers the perspective of two teachers from different subject areas. In fact, I think such courses could often be interesting and enlightening. It's just that I don't think they belong in high schools. High school is the last opportunity many students have to get a strong grounding in all subject areas. High school administrators and teachers should see to it that they give each student an excellent foundation in the basics.

Here's an example of why basics are important. I remember hearing my sister, who's in college, talking about reading the novel *Cold Mountain* as part of an American Studies class. She was very excited about it; she said she loved how the course connected history and literature. However, she had already taken U.S. History and AP American Lit. By the time she took the American Studies course, she already knew something about how to understand a novel and how the Civil War fit into the context of American history. Thus, in college, she was at an appropriate level to benefit from a multidisciplinary course. I think that, say, a freshman in high school, who is still working on building a good understanding of history, would not benefit by combining a study of history and literature. Team-taught multidisciplinary courses could overwhelm students and dilute the concentrated education that a course taught by an expert in one subject could provide. Letting teachers who are experts in their fields help students acquire basic familiarity with the subject should, I believe, take precedence over a multidisciplinary approach in high school.

Right now, I value **each** teacher's knowledge and passion in **their** own subject areas. I may not be in any courses that ask me to consciously relate what I'm learning in one subject with what I'm learning in the others, but I try to do some of this on my own when it's possible. Because I'm getting a good grounding in each individual subject now, I'll be better able to handle multidisciplinary approaches in college and later in my career. While a multidisciplinary approach is ultimately essential in college, work, and even life, the best preparation for it comes from focused classes in individual subject areas, taught by teachers who are excited about their own fields and are not so bogged down in educational bureaucracy that that don't have time to stay up to date with new developments in their fields. At the high school level, students will get the best education from knowledgeable, informed teachers who focus on the content and skills that are unique to a single discipline.

Comments on Sample Response 1

This is a strong essay because it takes a clear position on the prompt and supports that position with reasoning and examples. The writer acknowledges the complexity of the issue in this essay not by addressing a counterargument, but by discussing when and where multidisciplinary courses have value.

The organization and development of ideas are strong. The first paragraph introduces the topic and a basic assumption on which the argument rests: that high school students should learn the basic content in individual fields from teachers who are experts and have the time to stay current in their fields. The second paragraph expands on the assumption that the purpose of high school is to get a good general education. The third paragraph includes a concrete example from the writer's experience that supports the argument. Notice that the writer actually has some very positive things to say about multidisciplinary courses, but these positive aspects do not detract from the writer's focus on why high school is not the best time for students to take such courses.

The last paragraph also draws on the writer's personal experience, relating his high school experience to his hopes for the future. The writer concludes by restating the major reason for his viewpoint: that high school is a time when focused learning is more appropriate than team-taught courses that may dilute basic knowledge.

This essay displays good language skills. The writer applies the principles of correct sentence structure and uses varied sentence structure. There is some repetition of wording, but it isn't excessive. There are some pronoun agreement errors, but they aren't distracting to the reader. The same mistake occurs in paragraphs 1 and 4. The word *each* is singular, so a singular pronoun should refer to it. (*He or she* should be used instead of *they*.)

SAMPLE RESPONSE 2

Planning Notes
- Multidisc. classes beneficial
- Enable students to see how different people work together
- Encourage creativity and critical thinking by not limiting students to one discipline
- Prepare for college and work, when need to view problems from different perspectives
- Examples: assignment from two teachers
- Motivating students

The main purpose of a high school's academic program is to teach students to think critically. The specific content we learn in various subjects can be important and useful, but learning how to think is the skill that will serve us best in the future. Given this perspective, **I believe that** making two team-taught, multidisciplinary classes part of the graduation requirement is a good idea. Participating in these courses will be a strong advantage for students.

In addition to learning content and how to think, another area students need experience and advice in is working with other people. Team-taught courses serve this need well. With two teachers from different disciplines working together to structure and implement a course, students will see in action an example of how two adults can work together for a common purpose. This is a benefit of team-taught courses that is not present in traditional courses that cover a single subject area presented by one teacher.

An example from my own experience illustrates this idea nicely. Although I've never had the opportunity of participating in a semester-long team-taught course, I have worked on a research paper in which both my history and English teachers were involved. The two teachers worked together to structure the requirements of the assignment, monitor students' progress, and assign the final grades. I found this experience beneficial to my learning. By combining the advice and tips I got from both teachers during the research and writing process, I felt that I learned a lot more than I would have if only my English or my history teacher had assigned this project. Comments that my English teacher made about the organization of my first draft actually led me to go back and do a little more research. That extra research was the foundation of what my history teacher pointed out as one of my paper's greatest strengths. In my experience, the perspective of two teachers helped me learn more than I would have if I'd been working with only one teacher or the other. **I think** this kind of magnified learning would occur readily if our school were to implement full-semester team-taught courses. Making these courses a graduation requirement would ensure that all students have the opportunity to benefit from the multidisciplinary approach.

While some people might argue that teachers in each field have their own areas of expertise and should not teach "outside their fields," I think the benefits of seeing two approaches far outweigh the drawbacks. In our future jobs, we are bound to face challenges and problems in which we don't feel we are experts, but we will still have to deal with them. The example of teachers working collaboratively, stretching themselves beyond their own limited areas, would provide excellent role modeling for us.

A final point that **I think** favors team-taught courses is that teachers need to motivate students and excite them about learning. With two teachers from different fields involved in a course, there is a greater chance of captivating the interest of more students. Consider a student who just doesn't like science, but who is very motivated to recycle and protect the environment. With a biology and a chemistry teacher teaming up on an environmental science course, there will be more variety in the kinds of science content covered. A student may find it easier to get excited about one field than another. I might loathe chemistry but find biology more interesting. A course that builds on both could help my excitement about the one field carry over to the other. Thus, increasing student interest and motivation is another point in favor of mandatory multidisciplinary courses.

Comments on Sample Response 2

This essay is well-thought-out and exhibits strong organization and consistent focus on the topic. Clearly, the writer took adequate time to plan. The essay addresses the complexity of the issue, first, by giving a little background in the first paragraph about the purpose of education. These reflections set the stage for a clear thesis statement at the end of the paragraph. The writer also acknowledges complexity by introducing and responding to a counterargument in the fourth paragraph.

This essay includes good evidence and examples. The second paragraph discusses teachers modeling team work as a benefit for students. The third paragraph uses the example of a paper supervised by teachers in different fields. The fifth paragraph, which serves as the conclusion, briefly discusses an example relating to student interest and motivation.

This essay displays a competent use of language skills. Sentence structure is correct and varied. There are few grammatical and spelling errors. The writer uses transition words and phrases to help the reader easily grasp the logical flow of the argument.

One small drawback of this essay is the writer's use of phrases such as *I believe that* and *I think*. While not a terrible, flaw, the use of such phrases is unnecessary. The ACT essay expresses the writer's opinion, so there's no need to add words such as *in my opinion* or *I feel that*. These phrases are filler phrases and do not contribute to the development of your argument. Therefore, try to avoid writing them so you can make the best use of your limited time. Note, however, that it is perfectly okay to use the word *I* and discuss examples from or provide reasons based on your own experience.

Chapter Twenty-one: **Writing Prompt II**

Directions: This section will test your writing ability. You will have 30 minutes to compose an essay in English. Prior to planning your essay, pay close attention to the essay prompt so that you understand exactly what you are supposed to do. Your essay's grade will be based on how well it expresses an opinion on the question in the prompt, as well as its logical construction, supporting evidence, and clarity of expression based on the standards of written English.

PROMPT

> Some schools have instituted rules that forbid students from wearing any clothing with words other than the name of the school. Proponents of this rule argue that it prevents distractions in the classroom and allows teachers and students to focus on education. Opponents argue that such a rule violates students' freedom of expression and, therefore, should not be in place. Should schools forbid the wearing of all clothing that has words other than the name of the school?
>
> In your essay, take a position on this question. You may write about either one of the two points of view given, or you may present a different point of view on this question. Use specific reasons and examples to support your position.

Again, set your timer for 30 minutes and apply the Kaplan method to write your own essay. After you've written your essay and taken a break, refer to chapter 20 for the self-assessment checklist to help you identify strengths and weaknesses in your essay before you look at the sample responses provided. Use the space here to summarize your findings.

Strengths to maintain: _____

_____

_____

Weaknesses to improve: _____

_____

_____

SAMPLE RESPONSE 1

Planning Notes

- No—schools shouldn't forbid legible clothing
- Removes students' freedom of choice and sets up authoritarian structure
- Is impractical in today's world
- Counter—distractions are part of life, learn to deal

The significance of clothing is important to many teenagers. A lot of us enjoy choosing clothing that expresses our own style. The color, fabric, shape, and design, and even a written message printed on an article of clothing can help one express a mood or an attitude, and help a person define himself. Because clothing choices are so individual and so personal, students should be given as much leeway as possible to wear what they want to. If this includes clothing with a written slogan or message, then such items should be allowed as long as the words are not **judge** to be rude, offensive, or distasteful to members of the school community. A rule forbidding "legible" clothing in our school would send students the message that they cannot be trusted to make appropriate choices about what others might find offensive. The majority of students do deserve that trust, and, therefore, I don't think legible clothing should be forbidden.

The first reason I don't support the banning of all legible clothing is that it sets up an authoritarian structure when there is no need for it. Teenagers are faced with many rules and restrictions, but schools should not implement regulations unnecessarily. In my own school, the teachers and staff work hard to create a climate that is tolerant and respectful of everyone. Most of the students appreciate this atmosphere and attempt to behave in ways that maintain it. Most of us do wear shirts with words or messages at some point during the school year, but I don't remember ever seeing a classmate's shirt that was offensive. If the administrators can trust students to make good judgments most of the time, then we do not need a rule forbidding clothing with messages. If, on occasion, a particular student does wear legible clothing with an offensive message, such an instance could be dealt with on an individual **base.**

A second reason I oppose forbidding legible clothing is that it is simply impractical. If the no-words-on-clothing rule were in place, how far would administrators take it? Many, if not most, brands of clothing today have a label on the outside identifying the company. Would such clothing be forbidden? Where would administrators draw the line? Because of the impracticality of enforcing a rule against clothing with words, it would be better to leave clothing decisions up to the students and trust that we can make appropriate decisions.

It's understandable that some people might want to maintain a rule against legible clothing because they believe that clothing with any message at all, even if it's not an offensive message, might be distracting in school. While I can understand this concern, I would argue that distractions are a part of life, and students must learn to work around them.

Overall, the need for schools to encourage a climate of trust, tolerance, and support is a primary concern. Needless rules about what clothing students can and can't wear **diminishes** the sense of trust in a school. Respect and tolerance are important, but it's better to let students try to work out for themselves what these things mean than it is for administrators to try to prevent problems by implementing rules that may not actually be necessary.

Comments on Sample Response 1

This is a strong essay with a clear thesis statement. Notice that the thesis statement isn't articulated until the very end of the first paragraph. The writer uses most of the first paragraph to set the issue in a broader context, explaining why clothing choices matter to teenagers and indicating that trust is important to the atmosphere of a high school. The writer's viewpoint, opposing a ban on clothing with words, flows directly out of these ideas.

The essay is well organized; clearly, the writer gave some thought to how to structure the essay. Two paragraph transitions are predictable (*the first reason* and *a second reason*) but they do the job of showing that the writer has thought about logic and organization. The essay ends with a strong conclusion that's tied to the writer's primary reason: The proposed clothing rule will diminish the climate of trust in the school.

In addition to setting the question in a broader context in the first paragraph, the writer introduces a counterargument in the fourth paragraph. The response is fairly brief, but it does show that the writer has considered an alternative viewpoint. The writer also addresses the complexity of the issue in the second paragraph by acknowledging a student might on occasion wear clothing with an inappropriate message, but suggests that such an instance is better handled on an individual basis.

The essay includes a couple of errors that the writer missed during the proofreading stage (*judge* instead of *judged* in the first paragraph, *base* instead of *basis* in the second paragraph, and *rules...diminishes* instead of *rules . . . diminish* in the fifth paragraph), but these errors aren't terribly distracting to the reader.

SAMPLE RESPONSE 2

Planning Notes
- Yes—schools should forbid legible clothing
- School purpose is learning; students too focused on appearance
- Dress-down days distracting
- Bumper sticker analogy
- Admin. should send message that academics most important
- Counter—student freedom; time outside of school

The primary purpose of school is to give students **and** excellent academic experience, and any regulations should be made with this goal in mind. Appearances and self-expression are very important in our society, especially to teenagers. There is plenty of time outside of the school day for teens to express themselves through clothing. Freedom of expression in regard to clothing, however, should not be **there** primary concern during the school day. Because I consider academics to be the most important aspect of the school experience, I fully support a rule to ban clothing with written messages in school.

In my experience, the way people are dressed affects their behavior. This phenomenon is widely recognized. Many companies that used to allow their employees to vary the typical dress code during "casual Fridays" are starting to change their policy to permit only clothing that is suitable for a business environment. This makes sense, because often it's difficult for people working in sloppy clothing to take each other seriously. I have seen similar effects when my school has had "dress-down days." On these days, when students and teachers dress in a highly relaxed manner, I find that the focus on learning is distorted. Class discussions are more likely to get off topic, and teachers have a harder time maintaining attention on the day's lesson. A casual style of dress winds up being distracting and unproductive. Likewise, when students wear clothing with messages, distractions will occur.

For many teens, who are stressed and face family problems, **it's** difficult to concentrate on schoolwork in the best of circumstances. The problem is only compounded when they sit in a classroom where many people are wearing clothing with slogans, messages, and comic strip characters. Even if such clothing is completely benign and not at all offensive in what it says, the potential for distracting other students from academics makes clothing with words a bad idea.

My point about words on clothing has a parallel with bumper stickers. Freedom of speech is one of the greatest gifts our country offers its citizens. It's a huge value that we can say almost anything we want to at any time. Realistically, however, some times and places are better than others are. Bumper stickers with long messages and slogans, while good in that they reflect freedom of speech, can be extremely distracting. When I'm driving, I find my eye is drawn to bumper stickers on other cars. It's distracting. It would be easier to concentrate on road conditions if people didn't use bumper stickers. This problem with distraction is the same one that occurs when students are allowed to wear clothing with words. It's not that I oppose freedom of speech; rather, I maintain that just because we *can* express **and** opinion doesn't always mean we *should*

do so. In the school classroom, the teacher's presentation and plans for the student's academic development **is** so important that the environment should be structured to support them. More learning will take place when students focus on schoolwork, so distractions from clothing should not be allowed.

My support for this rule all comes down to the role of administrators in helping students concentrate on schoolwork as the primary focus. Students in my school need strong leadership and guidance from adults. If the school has a rule that words and messages on clothing aren't allowed and the reasons are explained, it sets the expectation that all students are in school to learn and develop their minds. The kind of freedom of expression that is important in the classroom is the ability to examine and express important ideas, not the freedom to sport messages on our clothes.

Comments on Sample Response 2

This essay uses solid reasoning and analogies to support the view that legible clothing should not be allowed. The first sentence immediately places the question in a broader context by indicating what purpose should underlie all school rules. The rest of the paragraph expands on this context, discussing teens' relation to clothing and the importance of freedom of speech before concluding the paragraph with a strong thesis statement.

The second paragraph develops the idea that clothing affects behavior by discussing a corporate environment and applying the lessons learned there to the school environment. The third paragraph explicitly discusses clothing with words as causing distractions in the classroom.

The fourth paragraph does a good job of acknowledging the complexity of the issue. It does so not by introducing a counterargument, but, rather, by discussing one important factor in the issue, the idea of freedom of speech. The writer uses the analogy of bumper stickers and legible clothing to point out that freedom of speech is a great value, but that applying it in certain situations is not necessary and can be detrimental.

The essay ends with a strong conclusion that brings in one more piece of support for the argument, the notion that school leaders have the responsibility of sending a message to students about the importance of academics. Because of this responsibility, the writer justifies the rule about clothing.

This essay contains some minor mistakes that the writer didn't catch during the proofreading stage. In the first paragraph, *and* should be *an* and *there* should be *their*. In the third paragraph, *its* should be *it's*. In the fourth paragraph, *and* should be *an* and *is* should be *are* to agree with the subject *presentation and plans*. These examples do constitute errors in language use, but they aren't excessively distracting to the reader. You should proofread carefully and do your best to correct any errors you find, but don't stress and think your essay needs to be perfect. Remember, the essay is graded holistically. If you do a competent job thinking through the issue and supporting your viewpoint, you don't need to worry about a few minor errors in spelling, grammar, or word usage.

NOTES

NOTES

NOTES

NOTES

NOTES